"In a world where generative AI is *rewriting* the rules of s
companies must rethink their approach to stay competiti
global experience make this essential reading for any or
strategic processes."

"Tim Lewko brings clarity and speed to strategy in a way few others can. *MOVE* captures the practical, no-nonsense approach I experienced working with him – now enhanced with the power of GenAI to help leaders think better and move faster."

Ricardo Alberto Cons, *CEO & Head of Business Area North America, Electrolux AB*

"The timing for a book like *MOVE* – one that focuses on the real issues facing executives and how they can utilize GenAI to make important decisions faster and better without the delay of third-party reports – is opportune. It addresses the real questions C-suite executives want answered now."

James B. Rybakoff, *President & CEO, Akin Bay Company LLC*

"I've worked with Tim for almost 20 years on the framework of decisions that have successfully guided my business along the way. Just as the world has evolved, so has the process – becoming more nimble, faster to develop, simpler to execute, and quicker to deliver results while adapting to change. Tim's approach has always focused on ownership, speed, engagement, agility, and execution. Incorporation of GenAI is the logical next step in the evolution of the process."

Steve Cassidy, *Chairman of the Board, Selig Group*

"I have never had a conversation with Tim where I have not learned something. He always gives me a sense of urgency."

Simon A. Davis, *President & CEO, DuraVent Group*

"Tim's ability to simplify strategy, then turn it into living action by helping executives maintain strategy in focus at all times, makes him one of my favorite strategy leaders – and this book sums it up marvelously."

Debby Morris, *President, AccessHope, Author,* Unbreakable Determination

"I've known Tim for over 25 years, and he's one of the sharpest strategy minds I've worked with. *MOVE* distills the practical tools and thinking frameworks that I've seen him use to help leadership teams drive growth and real results."

Roger Miller, *Vistage, Master Chair*

"You are uniquely positioned, having worked with so many leading companies, to write this book, Tim. I expect your book on the intersection of AI and strategy will be a groundbreaking addition to the field – packed with your usual practical tools to get to actionable strategy."

Andrew Warrington, *Ph.D., Chief Executive Officer, UCC Environmental (United Conveyor Corporation)*

"I've known Tim Lewko for years, and MOVE perfectly reflects his mastery in helping leaders think faster and act smarter. In a world where speed is the new competitive advantage, this book is a powerful guide to staying ahead – with AI as your thinking partner."

Paolo Moresco, *Managing Director,*
Bassano Pressing, Veneto, Italy

"The pace of business continues to increase, and AI will only accelerate it further. Incorporating the use of AI into business processes and strategic decision-making will be key to setting – or keeping – the pace. Tim's thoughtful approach will benefit any company."

Dan Starck, *(Retired) Chief Executive*
Officer, Apria Healthcare

"In more than 30 years in business education, I have worked with many exceptional students. But every so often, I encounter one whose mind is wired for something rare – a kind of sixth sense in a particular domain. For Tim Lewko, that domain was strategy and vision. While he was a strong student overall, in this area, he was extraordinary – able to see what others could not, to frame choices with uncanny precision, and to guide decisions that consistently led to results. For a long time, I believed this kind of instinct was a marvel to observe but could not be taught. But in *MOVE*, Tim has proven me wrong. He has taken what I once believed to be unteachable – the instinctive, real-time thinking behind great strategy – and made it visible, accessible, and actionable. If you are a leader who sees the need to make better decisions faster – especially in today's uncertain world – this book delivers a rare gift: a way to see around corners, to see over hilltops, with clarity and confidence. Tim Lewko has not just written a smart book. He has written an important one."

Al H. Ringleb, *J.D., Ph.D., President &*
Founder, CIMBA – The Consortium Institute of
Management and Business Analysis (University of Iowa)

MOVE

Developed by Tim Lewko, a 25-year strategy veteran, *MOVE* shows leaders how to embed artificial intelligence (AI) directly into the strategy process and validate strategic bets, pressure-test assumptions, and adapt faster than the competition – all while maintaining control over final decisions.

Traditional strategy frameworks cannot keep up with trade wars, supply chain disruptions, and shifting consumer behavior, and leaders can no longer afford to wait for annual planning cycles or lengthy strategy retreats.

MOVE responds to this rapid change by simplifying strategy into a clear, repeatable system of seven essential tools – all powered by AI to accelerate decision-making and execution. It's a practical, leadership-owned operating system that aligns strategic assumptions, project prioritization, and quarterly execution cycles.

Through examples, this book reveals how AI can power real-time data analysis, surface critical indicators that signal when a strategic bet is veering off-course, and show when emerging threats require immediate attention. In a rapidly changing world, *MOVE* is a key tool for senior executives, business leaders, board members, CEOs, Presidents, and P&L owners to regain control across the entire execution cycle.

Tim Lewko is the CEO of Thinking Dimensions Global, a strategic advisory firm specializing in decision-making frameworks that drive visible, leadership-owned execution. Over the past 25 years, he has guided executive teams across North America, Europe, and Asia, helping them generate over $2B in EBITDA through strategic advisement.

MOVE

AI-Powered Strategy for a Fast World

Tim Lewko

LONDON AND NEW YORK

Designed cover image: Saad Ali

First published 2026
by Routledge
4 Park Square, Milton Park, Abingdon, Oxon OX14 4RN

and by Routledge
605 Third Avenue, New York, NY 10158

Routledge is an imprint of the Taylor & Francis Group, an informa business

© 2026 Tim Lewko

The right of Tim Lewko to be identified as author of this work has been asserted in accordance with sections 77 and 78 of the Copyright, Designs and Patents Act 1988.

All rights reserved. No part of this book may be reprinted or reproduced or utilised in any form or by any electronic, mechanical, or other means, now known or hereafter invented, including photocopying and recording, or in any information storage or retrieval system, without permission in writing from the publishers.

For Product Safety Concerns and Information please contact our EU representative GPSR@taylorandfrancis.com. Taylor & Francis Verlag GmbH, Kaufingerstraße 24, 80331 München, Germany.

Trademark notice: Product or corporate names may be trademarks or registered trademarks, and are used only for identification and explanation without intent to infringe. MOVE Strategy System™ is a registered trademark of ThinkingStrat Holdings Inc., protected via CIPO and WIPO in CAN, USA, and UK.

British Library Cataloguing-in-Publication Data
A catalogue record for this book is available from the British Library

ISBN: 978-1-041-16045-8 (hbk)
ISBN: 978-1-041-15608-6 (pbk)
ISBN: 978-1-003-68245-5 (ebk)

DOI: 10.4324/9781003682455

Typeset in Optima
by codeMantra

To Laura (LA), Sarah, Gio, and Tom:

For your patience when I was "in the room" but not quite present, for your inspiration when strategy felt stuck, and for reminding me that the best moves happen at home.

And to Einstein the cat and Roger the bearded dragon, who kept watch during countless writing sessions and never once questioned my strategic assumptions.

To the hundreds of executives who invited me into their boardrooms:

Thank you for the privilege of working on your toughest problems. Your trust, candor, and willingness to move when it mattered taught me everything worth knowing about strategy.

This book exists because you chose action over analysis, clarity over complexity, and results over reports.

With gratitude and respect

Contents

Figures

Acknowledgments

This book exists because executives across four continents opened their strategic thinking to me over 38 years. While the companies and situations are anonymized to protect confidentiality, the insights come from real leaders facing real challenges.

From the Canadian prairies to São Paulo's boardrooms, from Stockholm's industrial giants to Shanghai's emerging enterprises, I've had the privilege of working with leaders who transformed their organizations. They've taught me that while business contexts vary – Nordic pragmatism differs from Latin American dynamism – the fundamental challenge remains universal: how to create strategic clarity that drives execution.

I'm grateful to the aviation pioneers who navigated deregulation while teaching me that strategy requires knowing your destination before you hit turbulence. To the energy sector leaders who managed boom-bust cycles while demonstrating that scenario planning beats prediction. To the retail executives who localized global giants, proving that strategic relevance is always local you can't lead with the playbook alone.

The healthcare leaders showed me that when lives are at stake, strategic clarity isn't optional. Home healthcare executives who helped patients maintain dignity while building sustainable businesses. Medical device leaders who balanced global standards with local market needs across Latin America. Claims management innovators who turned data into competitive advantage through speed and precision.

From furniture manufacturers who transformed traditional businesses into lifestyle brands, to pharmaceutical executives navigating complex regulatory landscapes, to food industry leaders who discovered that running five strategies in one company guarantees failure – each taught me something essential about making strategy real.

Special appreciation to those who led through crisis: the executives who weathered housing crashes, supply chain disruptions, and technological upheaval while maintaining strategic focus. You proved that clarity under pressure separates winners from survivors.

To the more than 100 CEOs who shared not just their successes but their struggles – from heated debates where paper balls flew to admissions that some acquisitions happened just because "everyone was doing it" – thank you for showing me strategy as it really happens, not as case studies pretend it does.

The geographic breadth enriched every insight. Working across time zones from Vancouver to Veneto, from corporate headquarters to factory floors, revealed that great strategic thinking transcends borders while respecting local truths. Whether in a German engineering firm's precision or an Italian company's adaptability, the need for visible, aligned thinking proved universal.

To my clients in industries from rope manufacturing to artificial intelligence, from family-owned businesses to global multinationals your willingness to try different approaches, to make your thinking visible, to challenge conventional wisdom made *MOVE* possible.

Finally, to every leader who's sat in the room where strategy actually happens and had the courage to ask, "What are we really betting on?" – this book is for you. May these tools help you create the clarity that turns strategic intent into operational reality.

The insights here aren't mine alone. They belong to everyone who's faced the gap between knowing and doing, and chose to bridge it.

How to Use This Book

MOVE isn't a book you need to read cover to cover – though you certainly can. It's a strategic toolkit designed to meet you where you are.

If You're New to MOVE

Start with the Introduction and Part I (Chapters 1–3) to understand why traditional strategy tools are failing and how AI changes the game. Then work through Part II (Chapters 4–9) sequentially. Each tool builds on the previous one, creating an integrated strategic system.

If You're Facing a Specific Challenge

Tuesday morning crisis? Jump to Chapter 12 (BUSTED) for rapid response frameworks.

Considering an acquisition? Go directly to Chapter 14 (BETTER) to maximize post-transaction value.

Budget season approaching? Chapter 15 (BUDGET) shows how to align resources with strategy.

New CEO or senior role? Chapter 16 (BOARD READY) maps your first 100 days.

Team stuck in safe thinking? Chapter 13 (BOLD MOVES) provides five questions to break through.

Understanding the Tools

Each MOVE tool chapter (4–9) follows the same structure:

- **The problem** it solves through a real story
- **The tool** explained with step-by-step instructions
- **Blank template** for your use
- **Completed example** from Farella Foods
- **AI prompts** to accelerate your analysis

You'll find 18 figures throughout – every tool has both a blank template and filled example. Use these as guides for your own strategic work.

Three Ways to Apply MOVE

1. **Full Implementation.** Work through all tools sequentially with your leadership team. Build your complete strategic system from Strategic Assumptions through Quarterly Business Reviews.
2. **Targeted Application.** Pick the tool that addresses your biggest current challenge. For example, if resource allocation is your issue, start with the Product-Market Matrix (Chapter 6).
3. **Crisis Response.** Use Part IV situations for immediate guidance. Apply the frameworks to generate strategic options when you need them fast.

Working with Your Team

MOVE tools work best when thinking is visible. You'll need:

- Whiteboards or flip charts
- Blocks of uninterrupted time
- The right people in the room (those who own P&Ls or understand markets)
- Willingness to surface hard truths

A Note on AI

Throughout this book, you'll find AI prompts that accelerate analysis. These are optional but powerful. Always use your company's secure AI environment for sensitive data. The prompts are designed to expand your thinking, not replace it.

Making It Stick

Strategy isn't what you plan – it's what you do. After reading, pick one tool and use it this week. Start with whatever challenge is keeping you up at night. The tools only create value when you apply them.

Remember: You don't need perfect data or conditions. You need to start. Make your thinking visible. Make choices clear. Make resources follow strategy.

Then move.

Introduction

Why MOVE Matters Now

Tuesday morning. 9:47 AM.

Your biggest competitor just announced an AI-powered service that makes your core offering look obsolete. Your stock drops 12% before lunch. The board wants answers by Thursday.

What's your move?

If you're like most CEOs, your first instinct is to gather your team and figure out what this really means. You'll call a trusted advisor who can help you frame the threat. You'll analyze whether this is a real disruption or just noise. You'll debate response options with your leadership team.

But here's the problem: while you're trying to make sense of it, your competitor is already executing their next move. They're not smarter than you. They just have a better system for making strategic decisions – one that delivers both quality thinking and timely action.

Perhaps it's time to consider a different approach to strategy. One that produces better decisions, not just faster ones.

The Perfect Storm

We're living at the collision point of two forces that are reshaping business strategy:

First, traditional strategy tools are failing. The frameworks we learned in business school assume stable markets and predictable competition. But when **ByteDance** can create TikTok and reshape global media in five years,[1] those assumptions crumble.

Second, AI is accelerating everything. While companies debate digital roadmaps, **Moderna** designs vaccine candidates in 48 hours.[2] **Tesla** updates car capabilities overnight through software.[3]

The gap between companies using AI-enhanced decision making and those using traditional planning is widening every day. Once that gap gets wide enough, it becomes impossible to close. Not because AI is faster – because it enables better strategic thinking.

Meet Daniel Ross and Farella Foods

This book follows a real transformation story – one that shows exactly how to navigate this perfect storm.

Daniel Ross didn't come to **Farella Foods** [fictional example] to maintain the status quo. He was hired in early 2024 to save a company that was bleeding competitive advantage while looking stable on the surface.

DOI: 10.4324/9781003682455-1

The Hidden Crisis

Year	*Revenue ($M)*	*Gross Margin (%)*	*EBITDA ($M)*	*EBITDA Margin (%)*
2021	733	28.0	110	15.0
2022	726	26.9	95	13.1
2023	717	25.5	80	11.2
2024	707	24.0	65	9.2
2025	700	24.4	60	8.6

From the outside, Farella seemed fine. The **$700M** CPG company had been selling frozen meals, snack packs, and healthy bowls across America for 40 years. Revenue was holding steady. The brands were on shelves at **Walmart**, **Kroger**, **Costco**, and **Target**.[4]

But the financials told a different story:

EBITDA margin cut nearly in half in four years. The company had lost $50M in EBITDA while revenue stayed flat – the definition of value destruction. Gross margins compressed 360 basis points. The business was dying slowly, which is the most dangerous kind of corporate death because it feels manageable until it isn't.

The Product Portfolio Problem

Farella's 2025 reality across their three product lines painted a stark picture:

Frozen Meals (51% of revenue): The legacy cash cow was being milked dry. Average selling price of $6.00 faced constant pressure from private label. Volume declining 3% annually. Still profitable at 28% gross margin in retail, but that was down from 35% five years ago.

Snack Packs (20% of revenue): Growing 15% annually but burning cash. $4.00 price point meant razor-thin 20% gross margins. Every unit sold in retail lost money after trade spend. The "growth engine" was actually destroying value.

Healthy Bowls (12% of revenue): The innovation disaster. Despite three years and $30M invested, gross margins were an abysmal 16%. Premium positioning at $5.00 couldn't offset high ingredient costs and complexity. Losing money in every channel.

Three Wolves at the Door

While Farella's leadership team debated incremental improvements, three competitors were systematically dismantling their business:

Bravora Foods: This $3M private-label giant had turned cost advantage into an art form. Using AI-powered demand forecasting and a network of contract manufacturers, they could undercut Farella's prices by 30% while maintaining 5% points higher EBITDA margins. In frozen meals alone, they'd captured 400 basis points of market share in two years. Their strategy was brutally simple: offer retailers higher margins while giving consumers lower prices.

NüWave Naturals: The existential threat Farella didn't see coming. This AI-native startup went from zero to $200M in three years by completely reimagining the innovation cycle. Using social listening algorithms and rapid prototyping, they could identify trending ingredients on TikTok, develop products, and get to shelf in 12 weeks. Farella's innovation cycle? Eighteen months minimum. NüWave had launched 47 SKUs in the time it took Farella to launch 5.

BoxTop Kitchen: The B2B assassin. While Farella struggled with 94% on-time delivery, BoxTop guaranteed 99.5% with financial penalties for misses. Their secret: predictive analytics that anticipated demand spikes and automated production scheduling. They'd stolen three of Farella's largest school district contracts in the past year, representing $40M in lost revenue.

The Leadership Challenge

Ross inherited a capable but misaligned executive team:

- **Mark Chen** (COO): Deep operational expertise, but wedded to legacy processes
- **Jennifer Walsh** (CFO): Disciplined on costs, skeptical of any investment without guaranteed ROI
- **Sarah Martinez** (CMO): Creative brand builder, but disconnected from commercial reality
- **Dr. Raj Patel** (R&D): Technical brilliance trapped in slow commercialization cycles
- **Michael Thompson** (VP Strategy): Smart but buried in PowerPoint instead of driving decisions

Each executive ran their silo efficiently. But no one owned the enterprise strategy. Innovation wasn't talking to operations. Marketing wasn't connected to margin reality. Finance was saying no to everything.

Ross saw the truth immediately: "We had motion without momentum. Everyone was busy, but we weren't winning."

What Actually Works

After 25 years of working with leadership teams across four continents, the patterns are clear.[5] Many CEOs know their strategy process isn't delivering. They sit through quarterly reviews, sensing the disconnect between PowerPoints and reality. They watch competitors move faster while their teams debate.

Let's be honest – if you gave your executive team a pop quiz right now and asked them to write down your company's strategy or top three strategic bets, would you get the same answer from each person? Try it Monday morning. Ask them separately. Don't give them time to align. The results will be sobering.

Here's what's different about MOVE: over 95% of the strategies developed with these tools get implemented. Not because I'm brilliant at selling ideas, but because the teams own the thinking. They build it, they believe it, and they execute it.

Companies that win in fast markets share four behaviors:

1 **Make Thinking Visible**: Strategic logic everyone can see and act on
2 **Orient Around Advantage**: Ruthless focus on what truly differentiates
3 **Visibly Choose Bets**: Resources clearly aligned to strategic priorities
4 **Execute in Rhythm**: Decision cadence that matches market speed

These aren't new insights. They're what separates companies that execute from those that just plan.

The MOVE System

MOVE is a strategic decision-making system built on these proven patterns. Over 25 years, MOVE has helped clients realize over $2M in incremental EBITDA across more than 100 companies.[6] Not from reports or recommendations – from actual results. From $100M divisions to $1B+ enterprises, from software to steel to services.

The system is completely agnostic – if you have products, markets, capabilities, and a P&L to manage with competition breathing down your neck, MOVE works. The essential questions remain the same. What are we betting on? Where will we win? How do we get there?

MOVE works with or without AI. It worked before ChatGPT existed, and it will work regardless of what technology comes next. AI simply accelerates what MOVE already does well: force strategic clarity, align resources, and drive execution.

MOVE provides seven practical tools that create results, not reports:

Part I: Strategy (What): Five Core Tools

1 **Strategic Assumptions (SA)**: Identify external trends, constants, and implications
2 **Vision + Driving Force (VDF)**: Define, stretch, and score directional choices
3 3A. **Product-Market Matrix (PMM)**: Score product-market combinations to guide investment
3B. **Market Reality Check (MRC)**: Validate PMM choices using external market data
4 **Advantage + Future Capabilities (AFC)**: Clarify today's edge and future capabilities to build
5 **Strategic Numbers (SN)**: Track strategic impact using lead/lag indicators

Part II: Execution (How)

6 **Strategic Project Portfolio**: Prioritize and manage execution of strategic initiatives

Part III: Cadence (Why)

7 7A. **Root Cause Analysis (RCA)**: Diagnose what's behind missed results
7B. **Next Quarter Action Sheet (NQA)**: Capture three to five focused actions from each QBR

Each tool produces a one-page output driven by pragmatic questions. No endless analysis. No months of study. Just focused thinking that creates visible choices – and measurable EBITDA impact.

Think about what $2B+ in incremental EBITDA means: that's not cost cutting or financial engineering. That's real value creation from better strategic decisions, clearer focus, and faster execution. Results, not reports.

Who This Book Is For

CEOs and Executive Teams facing the reality that traditional strategy tools can't keep pace with AI-accelerated markets. You need to make better decisions faster without abandoning everything that got you here. Whether you run a division or an enterprise, if you have a P&L and competition, you need MOVE.

Business Unit Leaders and P&L Owners who want to think strategically before they reach the C-suite. You're tired of being handed strategies to execute. You want to shape them. MOVE gives you the tools to lead strategic discussions, not just attend them.

Rising Leaders who see the gap between business school theory and market reality. You want tools that work when the data is messy and the clock is ticking. MOVE provides the essential questions that cut through complexity to drive decisions.

Your Strategic Choice

The companies that recognize this shift early will own the next decade. Those that don't may well join **Kodak** and **Blockbuster** as cautionary tales.[7]

Here's what we're seeing: CEOs and their teams are learning how to leverage AI as it's unfolding. There's no final playbook yet – the technology is evolving too fast. But the leaders getting ahead aren't waiting for perfect answers. They're getting in the pool now, experimenting with [illegible]ir strategy process, seeing how AI can expedite both quality and speed of strategic thinking.

[illegible]'t have to abandon everything and start over. Start with pieces of your strategy. Use AI [illegible]ssumptions. Accelerate market analysis. Surface competitive blindspots. Build [illegible]e the tools evolve.

Every quarter you delay is a quarter your competitors pull further ahead. The gap between AI-enhanced decision making and traditional planning is widening exponentially. You can't afford not to take a hard look at how you're making strategic decisions.

Your CFO will appreciate the financial rigor – MOVE connects strategy directly to EBITDA impact. Your operators will love the clarity – one-page tools that show exactly what to do. Your board will love the results – measurable improvement in financial performance, not just strategic alignment.

That's what Daniel Ross discovered at Farella Foods. That's what this book will show you how to do.

The real danger isn't moving too fast. The real danger is being overtaken by those who do.

It's time to MOVE.

Notes

1 "ByteDance." Wikipedia. Accessed January 2025. https://en.wikipedia.org/wiki/ByteDance. ByteDance founded in 2012, launched TikTok internationally in September 2017, reaching 1 billion downloads by 2019.
2 "The Revolutionary Power of Bio Platforms - Or Why It Took Just 48 Hours to Develop the Covid-19 Vaccine." Nanowerk. Accessed January 2025. https://www.nanowerk.com/spotlight/spotid=57148.php.
3 "Software Updates." Tesla Support. Accessed January 2025. https://www.tesla.com/support/software-updates. Tesla pioneered automotive over-the-air updates in 2012.
4 Based on the author's 25+ years of consulting and client experience.
5 Based on the author's 25+ years of consulting and client experience.
6 Based on the author's 25+ years of consulting and client experience.
7 Clayton M. Christensen, *The Innovator's Dilemma: When New Technologies Cause Great Firms to Fail* (Boston: Harvard Business Review Press, 1997).

Part I

Perfect Storm

Why Strategy Breaks Down – and What's Coming Next

Chapter 1

Strategy's Slow Death

You wouldn't run your financials on software from the 1960s. So why are you running strategy on frameworks from the same era?

Walk into any corporate strategy session and you'll see the same tools that have dominated for 60 years. SWOT analysis. Porter's Five Forces. Growth-share matrices. Five year LRP plans with detailed financial projections.

These frameworks were revolutionary when created. They brought structure to chaos, turned gut feelings into analysis, made strategy teachable and repeatable. They worked brilliantly for the world they were designed for – a world that no longer exists.

The Mismatch That's Killing Companies

Traditional strategy tools seem to assume three things that are no longer true:

Assumption 1: Markets move predictably. When the growth-share matrix was created in 1968,[1] market leaders stayed on top for decades. **General Electric** dominated for 100 years.[2] Today? The average time in the S&P 500 has dropped from 60 years to under 20.[3]

Assumption 2: Industry boundaries are stable. Porter's Five Forces[4] assumes you know who your competitors are. But **Apple** wasn't a phone company until it was. **Amazon** wasn't a grocer until it bought Whole Foods.[5] The frameworks can't handle competitors you can't see coming.

Assumption 3: Planning cycles can match market speed. Long Range Planning made sense when markets evolved over decades. Today, **ChatGPT** has reached 100 million users in two months.[6] By the time traditional planning cycles complete, the market has moved three times.

Why We're Still Using Broken Tools

If these tools are failing, why does every company still use them? Three reasons:

1 **They're embedded in corporate DNA.** Annual planning cycles tie to budgets. Board reporting requires five-year outlooks. The entire corporate machinery is built around these tools.

2 **They feel rigorous.** A 200-page strategy document with detailed analysis feels substantial. But rigor isn't the same as results.

3 **We don't know what else to do.** Most executives learned these frameworks in business school. When you suggest abandoning SWOT analysis, the response is often: "What would we do instead?"

The Real Cost of Slow Strategy

The price of using outdated tools isn't just inefficiency. It's extinction.

DOI: 10.4324/9781003682455-3

Consider what traditional strategy processes actually cost:

- **6 months** average time for strategic planning cycles[7]
- **30%** of senior executive time spent in planning meetings[8]
- **$1.5M** average annual cost for large company strategy processes[9]
- **18 months** typical time from strategy to implementation[10]

But the real cost is opportunity. While **General Motors** spent years analyzing electric vehicles, **Tesla** built them.[11] While **Walmart** perfected retail operations, **Alibaba** created a new commerce ecosystem.[12]

You can't afford not to take a hard look at your strategy process. MOVE isn't additive – it replaces the strategy meetings you're already having with something that produces better outcomes. Same time investment, dramatically better strategic thinking and results.

What's Actually Working Now

Look at companies winning in fast markets. They don't have better frameworks or smarter people. They've simply figured out how to make better strategic decisions, not just faster ones.

Quality thinking at the right pace. While traditional retailers run annual merchandising reviews, **Zara** gets fashion from design to store in 15 days.[13] But speed isn't the point – they're responding to actual customer demand, not guessing what might sell.

Better questions over more analysis. Netflix doesn't pretend to know what content will succeed. They test constantly, measure religiously, adapt based on data. Their advantage isn't speed – it's learning what actually works.

Strategic adaptation over rigid planning. When **Microsoft** missed mobile entirely, they didn't double down on Windows phones. They pivoted to cloud and became a $2T company.[14] The strategy wasn't about moving fast – it was about making the right move.

The Two-Speed Problem

We're living in a two-speed world:

Traditional Speed

- Five-year LRP and strategy cycles strategy cycles
- Yearly strategy reviews business reviews
- 24-48 month innovation pipelines innovation pipelines

Market Speed

- **Shein** uploads 6,000 new products daily[15]
- **BYD** launches new car models in 18 months vs. 5 years for legacy auto[16]
- **Nubank** acquired 70 million customers in eight years[17]

The gap between these speeds is where companies die. And AI is making it exponentially worse.

Why AI Changes Everything

AI doesn't just make bad strategy faster – it makes the entire traditional approach obsolete.

While strategists build one scenario, AI can test thousands. While you analyze last quarter's data, AI spots patterns emerging now. While you plan for next year, AI helps competitors adapt daily.

The Recognition Moment

Every shift starts with recognition – The moment leaders realize their tools no longer fit their reality.

Let's be honest – you feel it in every strategy session. The frameworks from business school that once felt rigorous now feel like theater. The annual planning process that used to create alignment now creates frustration. You know something needs to change, but what?

Here's what's different now: we're working with CEOs and their teams to learn how AI can expedite the quality and speed of strategic thinking. Not replacing human judgment – augmenting it. Not automating strategy – accelerating it.

The companies that survive these recognition moments share one trait: they don't just acknowledge the problem. They act on it.

What Comes Next

This isn't about abandoning strategy. It's about evolving how we approach it.

The next two chapters will show you:

- How AI transforms strategic thinking from months to minutes
- Why the patterns that create competitive advantage remain constant even as tools change
- How companies worldwide are building strategic systems that move at market speed

The frameworks failing you weren't wrong. They were brilliant solutions to yesterday's problems. The question now is whether you'll keep using yesterday's solutions or build tomorrow's advantages.

The choice is yours. But while you're choosing, your competitors are already making better strategic decisions – and turning them into market advantage.

Notes

1 Bruce Henderson, "The Product Portfolio." Boston Consulting Group, 1970.
2 "General Electric." Wikipedia. Accessed January 2025. https://en.wikipedia.org/wiki/General_Electric. GE incorporated in 1892 and remained on the Dow Jones Industrial Average from 1907 to 2018.
3 "Creative Destruction." Innosight, January 24, 2024. https://www.innosight.com/insight/creative-destruction/. Average S&P 500 tenure declined from 33 years in 1964 to projected 12 years by 2027.
4 Michael E. Porter, *Competitive Strategy: Techniques for Analyzing Industries and Competitors*. New York: Free Press, 1980.
5 "Amazon to Acquire Whole Foods Market." Whole Foods Market, June 16, 2017. https://media.wholefoodsmarket.com/amazon-to-acquire-whole-foods-market/. Amazon acquired Whole Foods for $13.7B in June 2017.
6 "ChatGPT's on Track to Surpass 100 Million Monthly Users Faster than TikTok or Instagram: UBS." Yahoo Finance, February 2, 2023. https://finance.yahoo.com/news/chatgpt-on-track-to-surpass-100-million-users-faster-than-tiktok-or-instagram-ubs-214423357.html.
7 Based on the author's 25+ years of consulting and client experience.
8 Based on the author's 25+ years of consulting and client experience.
9 Based on the author's 25+ years of consulting and client experience.
10 Based on the author's 25+ years of consulting and client experience.
11 Based on the author's 25+ years of consulting and client experience.
12 Based on the author's 25+ years of consulting and client experience.
13 "ZARA'S CASE STUDY - The Strategy of the Fast Fashion Pioneer." ResearchGate, August 2022. https://www.researchgate.net/publication/362568585. Products take 10–15 days from design to reach stores.
14 "Microsoft Closes above $2 Trillion Market Cap for the First Time." *CNBC*, June 24, 2021. https://www.cnbc.com/2021/06/24/microsoft-closes-above-2-trillion-market-cap-for-the-first-time.html. Stock grew 600% under Satya Nadella's leadership since 2014.
15 "The Year Ahead: Deconstructing Fast Fashion's Future." Business of Fashion, July 2, 2024. https://www.businessoffashion.com/articles/professional/the-state-of-fashion-2024-report-fast-fashion-retail-customer-experience-regulation-shein-temu/. Shein adds between 2,000 and 10,000 items daily.
16 "Chart: BYD's Rapid Pivot to Electric Cars." Statista. https://www.statista.com/chart/30754/byd-passenger-car-sales/. BYD produced 5 million vehicles in 18 months.
17 "Nubank Reaches 70 Million Customers in Latin America." Nu International, October 25, 2022. https://international.nubank.com.br/company/nubank-reaches-70-million-customers-in-latin-america/. Reached 70 million in under ten years from 2013 launch.

Chapter 2

GenAI as Your Strategic Thinking Partner

I was sitting in a boardroom in New York with five executives who had just spent three hours mapping out their European expansion strategy. The flipcharts showed thorough analysis: market sizing, competitive positioning, channel strategies. They'd identified the key risks and opportunities. Good work, solid thinking.

Then the CEO paused. "We've covered a lot of ground, but what are we missing? How do we pressure-test these assumptions?"

That's when I asked them to imagine something different: "Picture your smartest relative – that wise uncle who's seen many patterns, knows the business world, but only speaks when asked. He's sitting quietly in the corner right now. Would you really ignore him?"

They smiled. The CFO nodded. "I'd definitely want to hear what he had to say."

"Not the uncle I'm thinking of," the head of marketing chuckled, and everyone laughed.

"Fair enough," I said. "But imagine if that uncle had analyzed thousands of market entries, seen what works and what doesn't, but only speaks when you ask. That's what AI can be."

I pulled out my laptop and suggested we use AI to explore their analysis – but first, I was clear: "We'll only use public information about your industry, market dynamics, and competitive landscape. Nothing proprietary from your flipcharts, nothing confidential."

The executives immediately raised the concern I expected. "What about our data?" the CFO asked.

"Exactly right," I said. "We keep your numbers out of it. Instead, we ask about patterns in your industry, what typically happens when companies like yours expand into markets like these."

They looked at each other. "Well, lunch is arriving in 15 minutes..."

"Perfect. That's enough time."

Using only publicly available context about their industry sector and the European market dynamics, we posed their strategic question to the AI. Within 90 seconds, we had three strategic options they hadn't considered. The AI identified market segments similar companies had successfully targeted without cannibalization, suggested partnership models that had worked in comparable situations, and highlighted precedents from adjacent industries.

Then someone asked: "What are we missing?"

The AI's response stopped the room cold. Based on patterns from other market entries, it flagged two types of regulatory changes that often impact companies 18 months after European expansion – something no one had mentioned in three hours of debate.

Ten minutes from start to finish. As lunch arrived, the CEO said: "We just got more strategic clarity in ten minutes than we got in the last ten weeks."

That's when I realized the game had changed forever.[1]

Understanding AI's Evolution

Understanding where AI came from helps us see where it's going – and why this moment is different from previous technology shifts.

DOI: 10.4324/9781003682455-4

The story starts in **1956** at Dartmouth College, where John McCarthy coined "artificial intelligence."[2] The pioneers asked a simple question: "Can machines think?" They believed they could simulate human intelligence within a generation. They were optimistic about the timeline – and right about the destination.

By the **1970s and 1980s**, AI moved from academic labs to corporate boardrooms. Expert systems gained traction across industries, helping companies automate decision making and capture expert knowledge.[3] These weren't just operational tools – they were early forms of strategic intelligence, showing that machines could help with complex business decisions.

The pattern recognition revolution came on **May 11, 1997**, when IBM's Deep Blue defeated world chess champion Garry Kasparov.[4] This wasn't just a technology demonstration – it proved machines could out-think humans in complex strategic situations. Chess requires planning multiple moves ahead, evaluating positions, and adapting to opponents. Sound familiar? That's what strategy is.

The **2010s** brought the deep learning breakthrough. In **2012**, Geoffrey Hinton's team used deep learning to win ImageNet, reducing image recognition errors by significant margins.[5] Each advancement proved the same point: AI wasn't just getting better at operational tasks – it was getting better at thinking itself.

Then came **2020** and GPT-3's launch.[6] For the first time, AI could engage in strategic reasoning that rivaled human experts. Many executives were still treating AI as a side project while AI-native companies were being born with strategic advantages that traditional firms couldn't match.

The Day Everything Changed

November 30, 2022 marked the strategic revolution. ChatGPT reached **1 million users in five days** – the fastest technology adoption in human history.[7] For comparison, it took Netflix 3.5 years, Facebook 10 months, and Instagram 2.5 months to reach the same milestone.[8]

The arc is clear:

- 1950s: Academic dream
- 1970s–1980s: Early business tools
- 1990s: Beating humans at chess
- 2010s: Deep learning breakthrough
- 2020s: Strategic reasoning
- 2022: **One million users in five days**

While committees formed to debate AI policies, the strategic revolution had already begun in boardrooms where executives were experimenting. This wasn't just another product launch. It was the day strategy evolved. Suddenly, executives with a laptop could access AI that could think, reason, and strategize. No coding required. No data science degree needed. Just questions and answers, at the speed of conversation.

What AI Actually Does for Strategy

Forget the hype. Here's what AI does today that transforms strategic thinking:

Let's be honest – AI creates a firehose of opportunities and data. Every vendor promises their AI will give you more insights, more analysis, more information. But you don't need more data. You need the right data faster with the right questions to build, implement, and sharpen your strategy.

Faster Analysis. In my experience working with executive teams, traditional market analysis takes two to three analysts working four to six weeks with limited scope. With AI, I've seen teams achieve comprehensive analysis in two to three hours with unlimited scope – but only when they know what to ask for.[9]

Broader Perspective. Where human teams typically track their direct competitors, AI can analyze patterns across thousands of companies, patents, and signals. The challenge isn't getting information, it's filtering for what matters.[10]

More Scenarios. Traditional planning explores three to five scenarios at most. With AI, I've watched teams test dozens of scenarios including edge cases – but without the right strategic questions, you're just creating more confusion.[11]

Three Ways AI Changes How We Work

1. **Everything Happens at Once:** Traditional strategy moves in order: gather data, analyze it, make decisions, and then execute. Each step waits for the previous one. AI lets you work on multiple things simultaneously – while you're testing one approach in market, AI is already analyzing results and suggesting five modifications.[12]
2. **Always-On Instead of Once-a-Year:** Annual planning assumes markets pause for your calendar. But ByteDance adjusts TikTok's algorithm continuously based on real-time engagement data.[13] Amazon's dynamic pricing system makes millions of price adjustments based on demand, competition, and inventory levels.[14] AI enables strategy that evolves as fast as your market.
3. **Seeing Around Corners:** Human teams naturally focus on direct competitors – the ones that look like you. AI excels at spotting threats from adjacent industries before they become obvious. I've seen companies identify disruption patterns by analyzing startups in seemingly unrelated sectors.[15]

Real Companies, Real Results

JPMorgan Chase invested $12B in technology in 2022, with significant portions dedicated to AI and machine learning. They use AI for fraud detection, risk assessment, and trading strategies, processing $5T in daily payments more efficiently.[16]

Stitch Fix built a data science team of over 145 professionals who use algorithms to personalize clothing recommendations. Their AI analyzes style preferences, body measurements, and feedback to drive inventory decisions and reduce return rates.[17]

Netflix uses machine learning algorithms to personalize content recommendations for over 230 million subscribers, driving 80% of viewing time through algorithmic suggestions rather than user browsing.[18]

John Deere acquired Blue River Technology for $305M to bring AI to agriculture, using computer vision to identify and spray weeds with precision, reducing herbicide use by up to 90%.[19]

Managing AI Risks

Every boardroom has the same concerns. Here's what we're learning:

Data Security: Keep proprietary data in secure environments. Use AI for market analysis with public data. I've seen executives get nervous about this, but think of it like email 20 years ago – you learned what to send and what to keep internal. Same principle.[20]

What Goes Wrong: The mistakes we're seeing are predictable but important. Executives sometimes share too much proprietary information, forgetting that what goes into AI becomes training data. Others accept AI-generated numbers without verification – the technology can sound confident even when it's making things up. We're all learning these boundaries through experience.[21]

The "AI Will Replace Us" Fear: In every session, someone asks this. Here's what I've observed: AI replaces tasks, not strategic thinking. The executives who thrive are using AI to test more scenarios, to spot patterns across industries they'd never have time to study. They're not being replaced – they're being amplified.[22]

Building Team Confidence: Start small. I've seen teams begin with simple market research questions, then gradually expand. One CFO told me: "First week, we were terrified. Second week, curious. By month two, we couldn't imagine working without it." Give people permission to experiment with non-sensitive topics first.[23]

Simple Governance That Works: The companies succeeding aren't creating 50-page AI policies. They have simple rules: No customer data. No financial details. No strategic plans. When in doubt, ask: "Would I post this on LinkedIn?" If no, keep it out of AI.[24]

What AI Can't Do (And Why That Matters)

We're all figuring out AI's boundaries together. Here's what I'm seeing:

AI can't read the room. When your biggest customer's CEO leans back and crosses his arms, when your team goes quiet after a proposal, when the energy shifts – that's strategic information AI will never capture. One executive told me: "AI gave me perfect analysis of our Asian expansion. But it couldn't tell me our partner was about to be acquired."[25]

AI can't make the hard calls. Should you exit a profitable but declining business? Should you bet the company on a new technology? AI can show you patterns and probabilities, but it can't weigh what matters to your specific situation. These decisions require wisdom, not just analysis.[26]

AI can't build trust. I've watched deals worth hundreds of millions get done because two CEOs trusted each other. No AI builds that. Strategic partnerships, key hires, critical negotiations – these still happen between humans who look each other in the eye.[27]

AI can't know what it doesn't know. It's confident even when it's wrong. It finds patterns in past data but can't imagine truly new possibilities. Marc Benioff didn't get the idea for cloud-based CRM from analyzing history – he imagined a different future.[28]

This isn't about protecting our egos. It's about using AI for what it does best – pattern recognition, scenario planning, broad analysis; while humans do what we do best: judge context, build relationships, imagine new possibilities, and make the calls that matter.

The executives winning with AI aren't trying to automate strategy. They're using it to see more, test faster, and decide better. But they're still the ones deciding.

Starting Tomorrow

Pick your biggest strategic question. Ask AI using only public context:

- "What strategies typically work for companies entering [market]?"
- "What are common failure patterns in [industry] transformations?"
- "How have companies successfully responded to [disruption]?"[29]

The New Strategic Reality

Companies using AI for strategic thinking aren't drowning in data – they're using focused questions to get precise answers:

- Spotting opportunities faster by knowing what signals matter
- Testing assumptions continuously with targeted queries
- Adapting before competitors by asking better questions[30]

They're not smarter. They're not processing more information. They're asking better questions and getting the right insights when they need them. And in strategy, the quality of your questions determines the quality of your outcomes – not the speed of your analysis.

The MOVE tools provide those questions. AI accelerates finding the answers. Together, they turn the firehose of possibilities into a focused stream of strategic advantage.

The Choice Ahead

Every leadership team faces the same decision: embrace AI as a strategic partner or compete against those who do.

This isn't about replacing strategic thinking with algorithms. It's about amplifying human insight with machine intelligence.

Your competitors have already decided. What's your move?

Notes

1 Based on the author's 25+ years of consulting and client experience.
2 John McCarthy et al., "A Proposal for the Dartmouth Summer Research Project on Artificial Intelligence." August 31, 1955, *AI Magazine* 27, no. 4 (2006): 12–14.
3 Edward A. Feigenbaum and Pamela McCorduck, *The Rise of the Expert Company: How Visionary Companies Are Using Artificial Intelligence to Achieve Higher Productivity and Profits* (New York: Times Books, 1988), 45–67.
4 IBM Corporation, "Deep Blue Defeats Kasparov." IBM Research, May 11, 1997, https://www.ibm.com/ibm/history/ibm100/us/en/icons/deepblue/.
5 Alex Krizhevsky, Ilya Sutskever, and Geoffrey E. Hinton, "ImageNet Classification with Deep Convolutional Neural Networks" In *Advances in Neural Information Processing Systems 25* (2012): 1097–1105.
6 Tom B. Brown et al., "Language Models Are Few-Shot Learners." In *Advances in Neural Information Processing Systems 33* (2020): 1877–1901.
7 Sam Altman, "ChatGPT." OpenAI Blog, December 5, 2022, https://openai.com/blog/chatgpt.
8 Business of Apps, "Time to One Million Users." Accessed January 2025, https://www.businessofapps.com/data/time-to-one-million-users/.
9 McKinsey Global Institute, "The Age of Analytics: Competing in a Data-Driven World." December 2016.
10 CB Insights, "The AI 100: The Most Promising Artificial Intelligence Startups of 2023." 2023 Report.
11 Based on the author's 25+ years of consulting and client experience.
12 MIT Sloan Management Review, "Winning With AI." Fall 2019.
13 ByteDance, "How TikTok Recommends Videos #ForYou." TikTok Newsroom, June 18, 2020. https://newsroom.tiktok.com/en-us/how-tiktok-recommends-videos-for-you.
14 Emek Basker, "Raising the Barcode Scanner: Technology and Productivity in the Retail Sector." *American Economic Journal: Applied Economics* 4, no. 3 (2012): 1–27.
15 Clayton M. Christensen, Michael E. Raynor, and Rory McDonald, "What Is Disruptive Innovation?" *Harvard Business Review* 93, no. 12 (December 2015): 44–53.
16 JPMorgan Chase & Co., "Annual Report 2022." 2023. https://www.jpmorganchase.com/content/dam/jpmc/jpmorgan-chase-and-co/investor-relations/documents/annualreport-2022.pdf.
17 Katrina Lake and Eric Colson, "Stitch Fix's CEO on Selling Personal Style to the Mass Market." *Harvard Business Review* 96, no. 3 (May-June 2018): 35–40.
18 Carlos A. Gomez-Uribe and Neil Hunt, "The Netflix Recommender System: Algorithms, Business Value, and Innovation." *ACM Transactions on Management Information Systems* 6, no. 4 (2015): 1–19.
19 John Deere, "John Deere Announces Agreement to Acquire Blue River Technology." Press Release, September 6, 2017. https://www.deere.com/en/our-company/news-and-announcements/news-releases/2017/corporate/2017sep06-blue-river-technology/.
20 World Economic Forum, "Global Risks Report 2023." January 2023.
21 Gary Marcus and Ernest Davis, "GPT-3, Bloviator: OpenAI's Language Generator Has No Idea What It's Talking About." *MIT Technology Review*, August 22, 2020.
22 Erik Brynjolfsson and Andrew McAfee, "The Business of Artificial Intelligence." *Harvard Business Review*, July 2017.
23 Based on the author's 25+ years of consulting and client experience.
24 National Institute of Standards and Technology, "AI Risk Management Framework." NIST AI 100–1, January 2023.
25 Based on the author's 25+ years of consulting and client experience.
26 Daniel Kahneman, Olivier Sibony, and Cass R. Sunstein, *Noise: A Flaw in Human Judgment* (New York: Little, Brown Spark, 2021), 234–245.
27 Francis Fukuyama, *Trust: The Social Virtues and the Creation of Prosperity* (New York: Free Press, 1995), 89–102.
28 Marc Benioff and Carlye Adler, *Behind the Cloud: The Untold Story of How Salesforce.com Went from Idea to Billion-Dollar Company* (San Francisco: Jossey-Bass, 2009), 45–52.
29 Based on the author's 25+ years of consulting and client experience.
30 Andrew McAfee and Erik Brynjolfsson, *Machine, Platform, Crowd: Harnessing Our Digital Future* (New York: W.W. Norton, 2017), 156–178.

Chapter 3

Visible Truths That Always Show Up

Daniel Ross's first Monday at Farella Foods [fictional example] started with a question that would define his entire turnaround.

"Tell me our strategy," he said to the assembled leadership team.

What followed was 90 minutes of PowerPoint presentations. The CMO talked about brand positioning. The CFO discussed cost optimization. R&D presented the innovation pipeline. Operations outlined efficiency initiatives.

Everyone had a strategy. No one had the strategy.

"Let me ask differently," Daniel tried. "What are we betting on to win?"

Silence.

This wasn't about intelligence – these were seasoned executives. It was about visibility. Strategy lived in different heads, different spreadsheets, and different assumptions. The company was bleeding $50M in EBITDA over four years while everyone executed their own version of success.

Here's what most teams miss: if your executives can't articulate the same strategy in the same way, you don't have a strategy. You have a collection of hopes organized by function.

The Pattern Recognition

After 25 years working with leadership teams, the patterns are unmistakable. Companies that consistently outperform share four behaviors. Not sometimes. Always.[1]

Pattern 1: Make Thinking Visible

Companies that execute don't hide their strategic logic. They make it explicit, testable, and clear to everyone who needs to act on it.

TSMC publishes technology roadmaps so detailed that Apple designs chips years in advance, knowing exactly what manufacturing capabilities will exist. No surprises. No hidden assumptions.[2]

Amazon's "Day 1" mentality isn't just a slogan – it's visible in every decision. Customer obsession, long-term thinking, eagerness to invent. These aren't buried in strategy documents. They're encoded in how every team operates.[3]

Contrast with Theranos: $945M raised while keeping their technology assumptions invisible even from board members. When the hidden logic finally surfaced, the company vaporized.[4]

Making thinking visible isn't about transparency theater. It's about speed. When everyone sees the strategic logic, decisions happen in days not months.

Pattern 2: Focus Ruthlessly on Advantage

Companies that win pick one genuine advantage and align everything around it. Not seventeen "competitive advantages" listed in a strategy deck. One real edge that matters.

DOI: 10.4324/9781003682455-5

Nvidia spent years focused solely on parallel processing for graphics while Intel chased dozens of markets. When AI needed exactly what Nvidia had built, they captured 80% market share almost overnight.[5]

The companies that struggle try to be best at everything. GE under later-stage Jack Welch claimed leadership in financial services, media, healthcare, aviation, and energy. Each business was good. None were great.[6]

Pattern 3: Commit Resources Visibly

Focus without resources is just wishful thinking. Winners don't just declare priorities – they fund them visibly.

Microsoft's transformation under Satya Nadella wasn't just cultural – it was visible in resource allocation. Cloud infrastructure investment jumped from $4B to $19B annually. Employees could see where the company was heading.[7]

Hidden bets create hidden failures. Boeing's 737 MAX disaster revealed years of obscured trade-offs between safety investment and cost reduction. When strategic bets aren't visible, organizations optimize locally without seeing global consequences.[8]

Pattern 4: Execute in Rhythm

Winners establish execution rhythms that match or exceed market speed. Your strategic heartbeat must be faster than your market's pulse.

ByteDance reviews TikTok algorithm performance daily, not quarterly.[9] Tesla pushes over-the-air updates monthly while traditional automakers plan model years.[10]

Meanwhile, companies operating on annual planning cycles in monthly markets inevitably lose.

How Daniel Ross Discovered the Need

Back at Farella Foods [fictional example], Daniel's journey to these realizations unfolded week by painful week.

Week 1: The Assumption Crisis. In the first leadership meeting, a seemingly simple question about digital investment revealed a deeper problem. The CFO, Jennifer Walsh, pushed back hard: "Our retail partners will never change their ordering systems. We've been doing EDI the same way for 20 years."

The head of digital disagreed: "Walmart just announced mandatory migration to their new AI-powered inventory system. We have 18 months to comply or lose preferred vendor status."

They were making million-dollar decisions based on opposite assumptions about the future. Without surfacing and aligning on what they believed would happen, every strategic choice became a battle of unstated beliefs.

Week 3: The Focus Vacuum. Daniel asked each executive to write down Farella's competitive advantage. The responses revealed the heart of their problem:

- Mark Chen (COO): "Operational excellence and reliability"
- Jennifer Walsh (CFO): "Cost leadership through scale"
- Sarah Martinez (CMO): "Most trusted heritage food brand"
- Dr. Raj Patel (R&D): "Innovation pipeline and speed-to-market"
- Michael Thompson (Strategy): "Retail relationships and shelf space"

Five executives, five different strategies. No wonder the company was losing ground – they were fighting seven different wars with one army.

Be more specific, Daniel thought. If everyone thinks we have a different advantage, we have no advantage.

Week 5: The Resource Reality. The monthly P&L review exposed the strategic dysfunction in black and white:

- Frozen meals: Generated 70% of profits but received 30% of innovation investment
- Snack packs: Contributed 12% of profits but consumed 45% of marketing spend
- Healthy bowls: Lost money on every unit but was labeled "strategic priority #1"

"Show me where we're actually placing our bets," Daniel challenged. The room fell silent. Resources were scattered across 47 different initiatives, with the top 10 consuming only 40% of discretionary spending. They weren't making strategic bets – they were making invisible bets.

The MOVE System Emerges

These four patterns: visible thinking, focused advantage, committed resources, matched rhythm; aren't just observations. They're the foundation of the MOVE system.

MOVE provides seven interconnected tools organized in three parts:

Strategy (What): Five tools that clarify your strategic choices

- Strategic Assumptions (SA) surfaces hidden beliefs about the future
- Vision + Driving Force (VDF) creates directional clarity
- Product-Market Matrix (PMM) and Market Reality Check (MRC) work together: PMM shows where you're placing bets internally, MRC validates those bets against external market reality
- Advantage + Future Capabilities (AFC) identifies which capabilities deserve investment
- Strategic Numbers (SN) tracks whether strategy is working

Execution (How): One tool that turns strategy into action

- Strategic Project Portfolio transforms strategic choices into funded initiatives with clear owners and deadlines

Cadence (Why): Two Interlocked Tools that create strategic rhythm

- Root Cause Analysis (RCA) diagnoses why results miss expectations
- Next Quarter Action (NQA) Sheet captures specific actions to close gaps

The beauty is how they connect. SA inform your Vision. Vision guides your Product-Market bets. MRC validates those bets. Capabilities enable execution. Projects deliver results. Strategic Numbers track progress. When numbers miss, RCA reveals why, and NQA closes the gap.

It's a complete system, not a collection of frameworks.

The Transformation Begins

Six months later, Farella Foods [fictional example] was a different company:

- Strategic assumptions visible on one page, updated monthly
- Focused on "convenient nutrition" as their driving force
- Resources visibly shifted: 60% to core renovation, 30% to adjacent growth, 10% to experiments
- Monthly innovation sprints replacing annual planning cycles

Revenue grew 4%. More importantly, EBITDA margin stopped declining and started climbing.

Your Path Forward

Every company eventually discovers these patterns. The question is whether you build them in systematically or stumble into them through crisis.

Strategy isn't what you plan – it's what you do. And what you do must be visible, focused, funded, and fast.

Daniel Ross stopped hoping and started building. The next chapters will show you exactly how.

Sidebar: Strategy Before It Was Cool – Lessons from Shell

When I was living in Italy in the early 2000s, I had the pleasure of talking freely with Arie de Geus, the head of Shell's Strategic Planning Group during the 1970s. He shared how they approached strategy when few companies were thinking beyond annual budgets. De Geus and his team didn't start with elaborate tools – they started with questions about the external environment that no one else was asking.[11]

Shell pioneered scenario planning because they realized they were living in an increasingly volatile world and needed a way to test assumptions and prepare for unexpected futures. Instead of betting everything on a single five-year forecast, they developed multiple scenarios: What if oil prices quadrupled? What if Middle East conflicts disrupted supply chains?[12]

This approach proved prescient during the 1973 oil crisis. While competitors scrambled to respond to the supply shock, Shell had already war-gamed this scenario and positioned themselves accordingly.[13]

What struck me most was how de Geus described their approach: "We didn't wait for perfect data or the 'right' framework – we built the tools we needed from scratch, because the external forces were already moving faster than traditional plans could handle."

Shell's breakthrough reveals something crucial: even in the 1970s, the most successful strategic thinkers were already moving beyond traditional planning. They understood that rigid frameworks couldn't handle an uncertain world. But most companies missed this lesson entirely, doubling down on the very tools that Shell had moved beyond.

Arie saw the tea leaves – he recognized that the world was changing faster than traditional planning could handle and that companies needed new tools. Now, 50 years later, we're seeing it again. The acceleration isn't just continuing; it's exponential.

Sidebar: The Practitioner's Path to Strategy

That conversation with Arie de Geus stayed with me. It confirmed what I'd been discovering in my own journey – that the best strategic thinking happens when you make assumptions visible, focus ruthlessly, and move faster than traditional planning allows.

When CEOs look me up before our first meeting, they don't find the typical strategy consultant background. I did go to business school. I did work at a major consulting firm. I worked for a company in Princeton. But my real education in strategy began differently – at 19, sitting across from CEOs, asking questions about how they really make decisions.

This path – 38 years of being in the room when strategy actually happens – shaped everything about how I approach strategy and ultimately why MOVE exists.

Starting Where Strategy Lives

My strategy education happened in boardrooms from Veneto to Shanghai, from São Paulo to Stockholm. I've been on planes with clients flying to make-or-break decisions. I've been in sessions where CEOs have fired team members on the spot. I've had executives throw paper balls at me when discussions got heated. I once asked a Chairman why he'd acquired 12 companies that didn't seem to fit – his response: "It was the '80s, kid. Everyone was doing it." This is where strategy really lives – not in case studies but in the messy reality of competitive pressure.[14]

Living and working across Europe, the United States, and Canada taught me that while business contexts vary, the fundamental challenges of strategy remain consistent. Whether in Nordic minimalism or South American passion, executives face the same core problems: how to see clearly, choose wisely, and execute effectively.

I studied Porter's Five Forces like everyone else – and liked it.[15] The frameworks from business school provided valuable structure. But watching CEOs wrestle with real competitive dynamics taught me that frameworks alone aren't enough when time is short and stakes are high.

What Current Books Offer – And Where They Stop

My office has the same strategy shelf as most executives. The classics written by academics and former CEOs each offer valuable perspectives. They explain concepts brilliantly. They provide mental models. They inspire with success stories.

But when executives finish reading, they often ask: "Now what do I actually do Monday morning?" The gap between understanding strategy conceptually and building it practically remains vast.

The latest wave tackles AI's impact on strategy. These books help executives understand what's coming – the economics of prediction, the transformative power, the competitive implications.[16] But understanding isn't strategy. When a CEO asks, "How do I use AI to make better strategic decisions tomorrow?" vision isn't enough. They need tools.

Where Practice Taught Me Differently

My wife often asks why I stay behind the scenes when the executives I work with go on to great success. The answer is simple: it's not about me. It's about results. My job is to help executives deliver, not to build my own brand.

This approach focusing on client outcomes rather than personal visibility taught me what actually drives strategic success:

Consistent Results: Strategy isn't about one brilliant insight. It's about building a repeatable capability for making good decisions. The executives who succeed develop systematic approaches they can use again and again.

Team Buy-In: The best strategy means nothing if the team doesn't own it. Real buy-in happens when people help build the strategy, not when it's handed to them. Making thinking visible transforms passive recipients into active architects.

Leveraging Everyone's Intelligence: Every executive team has untapped strategic thinking. The question is whether you have tools to surface it. When you do, the quiet engineer often has the breakthrough insight.

Engaging the Next Generation: The leaders below your senior team will inherit whatever you build. Involving them in strategic thinking develops capability while improving strategy. They see possibilities that experience might blind you to.

Building What Works, Step by Step

Over decades, working with over 100 CEOs, patterns emerged. The same challenges appeared repeatedly: hidden assumptions derailing alignment, resources spread thin across too many initiatives, execution failing because implementers weren't involved in planning.[17]

These patterns showed up everywhere from rope manufacturing to pharmaceuticals, from farm equipment to furniture, from medical devices to elevators. I've worked with family offices protecting wealth, PE firms driving returns, multinationals navigating complexity, and mid-cap companies fighting for growth. CPG companies, heavy industry, retail, injection molding; the industries vary, but the strategic challenges remain remarkably consistent.

I've had my fair share of executives look at me after the first hour and say, "I guess we need flipcharts." Yep. Because whether you're making paper or pharmaceuticals, strategy becomes real when it becomes visible.

Solutions developed organically, one client challenge at a time. A tech company struggling with alignment led to making assumptions visible. A consumer goods company unable to see resource flows led to mapping products and markets differently. Each solution built on the last, creating an integrated system.

The tools weren't designed in isolation they emerged from real sessions with real consequences. Each iteration made them simpler and more immediately useful. Complexity got stripped away, leaving only what drove decisions.

The Real Competition

The competition isn't other strategy books or frameworks. The real competition is getting consistent results when markets move fast and disruption is constant. It's getting your team to buy in when they've been through countless strategy processes before. It's leveraging their skills and thinking when traditional planning exhausts them.

Most importantly, it's resetting the table because of AI and accelerating competition. The executives who win aren't waiting for perfect frameworks – they're building strategic capability that adapts as fast as their markets.

MOVE works with or without AI because it's question-driven and initiative-focused. AI amplifies the process but doesn't replace strategic judgment. The tools force clarity whether you're using cutting-edge technology or just markers and flip charts.

Your Strategic Choice

Here's something I always say: if you're wondering whether to pick up this book or use these tools, ask yourself two questions:

What's your criteria for making decisions right now? What are your options for improving how strategy happens in your organization?

If your current approach delivers consistent results, creates genuine buy-in, and adapts as fast as your market – keep it. Don't fix what's working.

But if you're seeing the patterns I've seen across hundreds of companies – strategies that live in PowerPoints but not in decisions, teams that comply but don't commit, planning cycles that can't match market speed – then you need different tools.

MOVE isn't about ego. It's about what I've learned from executives who had to deliver results: that strategy works when thinking is visible, when teams build it together, when tools drive action not just analysis.

It's a privilege to walk into these rooms and work with executives. They're sharing the good, the bad, and the ugly – their real challenges, not polished cases. That's why my role is to quietly support and challenge, to help them see what's not being said, and build something they believe in.

After 25+ years in strategy sessions across the globe, from calm boardrooms to heated debates where paper balls fly, I've learned that sustainable strategic success comes from systematic approaches that engage everyone's best thinking.[18]

The question is simply whether you're ready to work differently. Whether you're willing to make thinking visible, even when it's uncomfortable. Whether you can let your team truly own the strategy, not just execute your vision.

These tools have helped generate over $2B in EBITDA improvements.[19] Not because they're revolutionary, but because they're practical. Not because they're complex, but because they're clear. Not because they come from prestigious institutions, but because they come from the room where strategy actually happens.

Now it's your choice. What's your criteria? What are your options?

The executives who create extraordinary value aren't necessarily the smartest or best resourced. They're simply the ones willing to change how strategy happens.

Your move.

Notes

1 Based on the author's 25+ years of consulting and client experience.
2 Mark Liu, "TSMC Technology Symposium 2023," Taiwan Semiconductor Manufacturing Company, June 2023. https://www.tsmc.com/english/news-events/blog.
3 Jeff Bezos, "2016 Letter to Shareholders," Amazon.com, Inc., April 12, 2017. https://www.aboutamazon.com/news/company-news/2016-letter-to-shareholders.
4 John Carreyrou, *Bad Blood: Secrets and Lies in a Silicon Valley Startup* (New York: Alfred A. Knopf, 2018), 298–301.
5 Dylan Patel and Afzal Ahmad, "Nvidia's Dominance in AI Chips," SemiAnalysis, March 2023. https://www.semianalysis.com/p/nvidias-dominance.
6 Geoffrey Colvin, "What Were They Thinking?" *Fortune*, November 28, 2022, 112–118.
7 Microsoft Corporation, "Annual Report 2023," Form 10-K, July 27, 2023, 24–26.
8 House Committee on Transportation and Infrastructure, "Final Committee Report: The Design, Development & Certification of the Boeing 737 MAX," September 2020, 15–42.
9 Eugene Wei, "TikTok and the Sorting Hat," *Remains of the Day* (blog), August 3, 2020, https://www.eugenewei.com/blog/2020/8/3/tiktok-and-the-sorting-hat.
10 Fred Lambert, "Tesla Releases Big Holiday Software Update with Apple Music, Improved Autopilot Visualizations, and More," *Electrek*, December 21, 2022.
11 Based on the author's 25+ years of consulting and client experience.
12 Arie de Geus, "Planning as Learning," *Harvard Business Review* 66, no. 2 (March-April 1988): 70–74.
13 Pierre Wack, "Scenarios: Uncharted Waters Ahead," *Harvard Business Review* 63, no. 5 (September-October 1985): 73–89.
14 Based on the author's 25+ years of consulting and client experience.
15 Michael E. Porter, *Competitive Strategy: Techniques for Analyzing Industries and Competitors* (New York: Free Press, 1980).
16 Ajay Agrawal, Joshua Gans, and Avi Goldfarb, *Power and Prediction: The Disruptive Economics of Artificial Intelligence* (Boston: Harvard Business Review Press, 2022).
17 Based on the author's 25+ years of consulting and client experience.
18 Based on the author's 25+ years of consulting and client experience.
19 Based on the author's 25+ years of consulting and client experience.

Part II

BRIDGE

From Patterns to Practice

You've seen the problem. Traditional strategy tools built for stable markets can't handle the speed of modern competition. Companies using 1960s' frameworks are losing to AI-native competitors who move 10× faster.

You understand the opportunity. AI transforms strategic thinking from months to minutes – but only if you know how to use it as a thinking partner, not just another analytics tool.

You've discovered the patterns. The four behaviors that separate companies that win from those that struggle: visible thinking, focused advantage, committed resources, and matched rhythm.

Now comes the practical question every CEO asks: "How do I actually implement this?"

The Cost of Invisible Thinking

Right now, in companies around the world, critical strategic decisions are being made on invisible assumptions. Marketing believes the market is moving toward premiumization. Operations believes it's commoditizing. Finance believes it's consolidating. Sales believes it's fragmenting.

They're all smart. They're all experienced. They're all wrong – because they're operating in different realities without knowing it.

This invisible thinking creates invisible costs:

- **Wasted investment** when initiatives built on conflicting assumptions collide
- **Delayed decisions** as teams debate without understanding why they disagree
- **Failed execution** when strategies that made sense in the boardroom hit market reality
- **Talent frustration** as A-players waste energy on internal alignment instead of external competition

The most dangerous part? You can't fix what you can't see. Traditional planning processes actually make this worse by layering analysis on top of invisible assumptions, building elaborate strategies on foundations of sand.

Daniel's Moment of Recognition

That's exactly what Daniel Ross discovered after three months at Farella Foods. He'd done the executive tour – met with every division, reviewed every strategy document, analyzed every P&L. The business was underperforming, but the reasons seemed to shift depending on who he talked to.

Then came the moment that changed everything.

During a heated strategy session about their frozen meals division, Daniel asked each executive to write down what they believed would happen to consumer behavior over the next three years. Simple question. Revealing answers.

DOI: 10.4324/9781003682455-6

His CMO wrote: "Consumers will pay more for clean labels and transparency." His COO wrote: "Price pressure will intensify as private label quality improves." His CFO wrote: "Retail consolidation will squeeze all margins." His head of innovation wrote: "Meal kits will make frozen food obsolete."

Daniel stared at the flip chart. "We're not debating strategy," he said quietly. "We're debating reality. And we don't even know it."

The room went silent as the implications sank in. Every strategic debate, every resource battle, every execution failure traced back to this: they were operating on different assumptions about the future without realizing it.

"How do we fix this?" Sarah Martinez asked.

Daniel's answer would transform how Farella made every strategic decision: "We make our thinking visible. All of it. Starting with what we actually believe about the future."

He didn't need more analysis. He needed a systematic way to: Surface hidden assumptions before they derailed decisions; Focus resources on advantages that actually mattered; Make strategic bets visible to everyone who had to execute; Create rhythm that matched market speed.

Traditional Approaches vs. Visible Thinking

Traditional planning approaches often make the problem worse. They start with internal analysis: strengths, weaknesses, capabilities, finances. They build elaborate frameworks that impress boards but confuse operators. They produce thick documents that few read and fewer act on.

Most damaging of all, they keep the real drivers of strategy – the assumptions about what's changing, the bets being placed, the advantages being built – buried beneath layers of analysis and abstraction.

MOVE takes the opposite approach. It makes the invisible visible through simple one-page tools that force clarity. Instead of hiding complexity in 100-page decks, it exposes the critical choices that actually drive success or failure.

The answer is the MOVE system – seven interconnected tools that force these patterns into practice (Figure II.1).

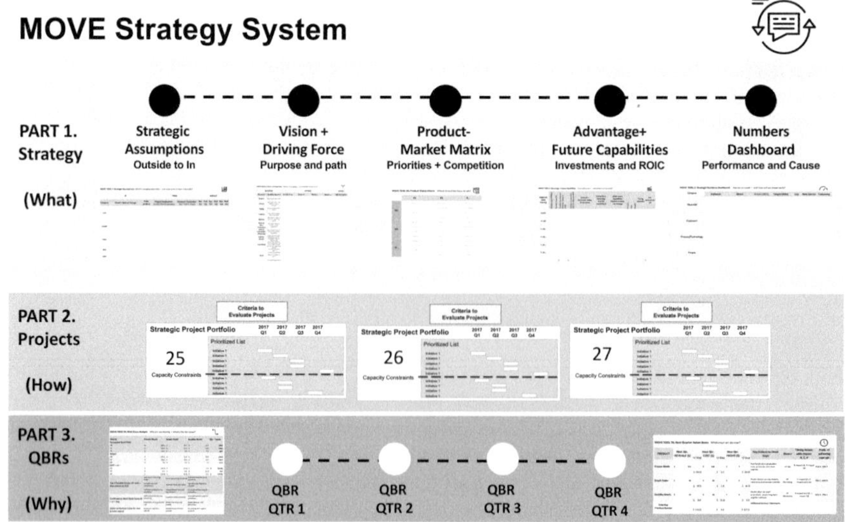

Figure II.1 MOVE Strategy System Map

MOVE STRATEGY SYSTEM VISUAL HERE – showing the complete system:

1 Strategy (What): Strategic Assumptions → Vision + Driving Force → Product-Market Matrix → Advantage+ Future Capabilities → Strategic Numbers
2 Projects (How): Strategic Project Portfolios for Years 202X, 202Y, 202Z
3 QBRs (Why): Quarterly Business Reviews Q1–Q4

What Makes MOVE Different

MOVE isn't another framework to add to your collection. It's a complete system that replaces complexity with clarity, analysis with decisions, planning with momentum.

Each tool: **Produces one-page outputs**: Not decks, just decisions; **Driven by one pragmatic question**: Cut through to what matters; **Forces visible choices**: Everyone sees the same strategy; **Integrates AI naturally**: Accelerate insight without adding risk; **Creates immediate clarity**: Know what to do Monday morning.

Think about what this means: instead of months building strategy documents that few read and fewer act on, you get visible choices on single pages that drive immediate action. Instead of strategic planning seasons that exhaust your best people, you get focused sessions that energize them. Instead of alignment meetings that go in circles, you get visible assumptions that reveal why people disagree.

Most importantly, the tools work together as a complete system to decide, execute, and adjust strategy. Each one-pager builds on the previous one, creating compound clarity that traditional approaches never achieve. From small divisions to global enterprises, these are the essential tools for anyone managing products, markets, and P&L in competitive environments.

Part II: The MOVE System: Strategy Tools

The next six chapters give you the five strategy tools that make thinking visible:

Chapter 4: What's Next? See Around Corners

Surface what you really believe about the future. Most strategy fails because teams operate on different assumptions without realizing it. This one-pager is driven by one essential question: "What's changing in our external environment that will impact our strategy?" The tool makes hidden beliefs visible in under an hour. You'll discover why your smartest executives disagree – and more importantly, how to harness those different perspectives into strategic advantage rather than internal friction.

Chapter 5: Vision + Driving Force: Surface, Stretch, Select

Define where you're going and the single capability that gets you there. Without this clarity, organizations pursue dozens of directions simultaneously, exhausting resources and confusing customers. VDF forces you to choose: What's your destination, and what's the one driving force that will get you there? Most executive teams can't answer this consistently – which explains why execution feels so hard.

Chapters 6 & 7: The Two Sides of Strategic Bets

Chapter 6: Make Bets Visible: Where Strategy Gets Real – Transform strategy into visible bets across products and markets. See exactly where resources are flowing versus where they should flow. Most companies discover they're funding 20+ experiments when they think they have 3 strategic priorities.

Chapter 7: Market Reality Check: Pressure-Test Your Bets – Validate those bets against what customers actually value. The brutal truth: half your strategic bets are based on what you wish customers wanted, not what they'll actually pay for.

These tools are two sides of the same coin: PMM shows your internal strategic logic; MRC tests it against external market truth. Together, they prevent the most common strategic failure – beautiful strategies that customers ignore.

Chapter 8: Build the Capabilities to Win: Invest in What Matters

Clarify your current edge and identify which future capabilities deserve investment. Most companies spread capability investments like peanut butter, building nothing to competitive standards. AFC forces concentration: What are the two to three capabilities that will determine whether you win or lose? Everything else is a distraction.

Chapter 9: Measure What Moves the Needle – Strategic Numbers

Track what actually drives results using leading and lagging indicators that matter. Replace your 47-metric dashboard that measures everything and manages nothing with six to eight numbers that actually predict success. You'll know you've found the right ones when your operators start managing them without being asked.

These aren't theoretical frameworks. Each tool has been refined through hundreds of working sessions with executives who had real P&Ls to protect and grow. They're one-page tools that force you to think differently about how strategic decisions get made in your organization.

You're not adding to your workload. You're replacing unproductive strategy meetings with focused sessions that produce decisions, not decks.

What's Coming in Part III

But here's what Daniel discovered – and what you'll discover too: having clarity isn't enough. The best strategy means nothing if it doesn't translate into funded projects and maintained rhythm.

That's why Part III: Strategy to Action will show you how to turn these strategic choices into reality:

- How to consolidate dozens of initiatives into three to four signature programs that actually move the needle
- How to create quarterly rhythm that catches problems before they become crises
- How to adjust when reality doesn't match plan (because it never does)

The companies that win don't just have better strategies. They execute those strategies with better focus and rhythm than their competitors can match.

Your Journey Starts Now

Each chapter in Part II includes: the Farella team discovering why they need this tool; step-by-step instructions for using it; AI prompts that accelerate insights; real examples from companies worldwide; common mistakes and how to avoid them.

By the end of Part II, you'll have a complete strategic foundation that moves faster than your competitors can plan. More importantly, you'll have tools that your entire organization can use to make better decisions every day.

Ready to see how strategic decisions really get made in your organization? Let's start with the tool that changes everything: making your assumptions visible ...

Chapter 4

What's Next? See Around Corners

If Each Executive Wrote Down Your Top Three Market Trends, How Many Would Match?

Daniel Ross leaned back in his chair at the end of Farella Foods' [fictional example] quarterly operating review. Revenue was flat at $700M. Margins were compressed. Their frozen meals line, once the profit engine, was losing shelf space. On paper, they were surviving.

But survival wasn't the mandate.

The board hadn't hired him to manage decline. They'd hired him to find growth. Yet the leadership conversation felt oddly disconnected from market reality. No one mentioned the private-label surge. No one talked about retail buyers changing the rules. No one raised questions about what was coming around the corner.

Daniel broke the silence. "Let's try something. What are the three biggest external changes hitting our business right now?"

The room froze.

Sarah Martinez, CMO, glanced at her phone. Mark Chen, COO, studied his operations report. Jennifer Walsh, CFO, kept her eyes on the P&L.

"This isn't a test," Daniel continued. "I'm genuinely asking – what forces are reshaping our industry?"

The Hidden Problem with How We Plan

Sarah finally spoke. "Well, Walmart just told us they're moving to performance-based shelf fees. If our SKUs don't hit specific turn rates, we pay penalties."

"When did you learn this?" Daniel asked.

"Last week. They're piloting now. Full rollout in 18 months."

"Is anyone else tracking this?" Daniel scanned the room.

Blank looks.

Jennifer jumped in. "Actually, I've been tracking something different. Private label is exploding in snacks – Kroger's new line looks exactly like ours but sells for 30% less."

"That's interesting," Mark said, looking up. "Because I'm seeing pressure from a different angle. Foodservice customers are cutting frozen SKUs. They want heat-and-serve, not prep-and-cook. We could lose 10% of our SKU count."

"And I'm worried about regulations," added Dr. Raj Patel from R&D. "FDA is tightening sodium and sugar disclosure. We'll need to reformulate half our products in the next 18 months."

Michael Thompson, VP of Strategy, shook his head. "So we have five different views of what matters most. No wonder our strategic planning feels disconnected."

Daniel walked to the whiteboard. "This is exactly why traditional strategy tools fail us. We all learned SWOT analysis in business school – great framework for the 1960s when markets were

DOI: 10.4324/9781003682455-7

predictable. But SWOT assumes we agree on what the opportunities and threats actually are. We clearly don't."[1]

"It's like what happened with Peloton and Mirror," Sarah offered. "Both companies built their entire strategy on assumptions about post-pandemic fitness behavior. Peloton assumed people would keep riding at home forever. Mirror assumed virtual group fitness was the future. Same market data, completely different assumptions about what it meant."[2]

"Exactly," Daniel said. "Peloton's valuation dropped 95% when their assumption proved wrong.[3] Mirror got sold for parts.[4] The lesson? Invisible assumptions kill companies."

He drew five boxes on the whiteboard: Customer, Competition, Technology, Regulatory, Constants.

"Think about OpenAI and Google right now," Daniel continued. "They have access to the same AI research, same talent pools, same computing resources. But OpenAI assumed speed matters more than perfection – ship fast, learn, and iterate. Google assumed reputation risk requires careful, slow deployment. Those different assumptions led to ChatGPT capturing 100 million users in two months while Google scrambled to respond."[5]

Jennifer nodded. "So it's not about having better information. It's about making our assumptions visible so we can debate them and align."

"Precisely. And that's what we're going to do right now."

Strategic Assumptions: Making the Invisible Visible

Daniel pulled out a single sheet of paper. "This is how we're going to align on external reality. One page. Five categories. Every assumption connected to action and financial impact."

What Strategic Assumptions Does

SA is MOVE Tool #1: the external intelligence system that makes invisible market beliefs visible and connects trends to specific strategic options with measurable impact.

The One Question It Answers: ***What external forces are changing our competitive environment, and what specific strategic moves should we consider in response?***

The Framework:

- IF [market change] happens
- THEN we can [build/buy/partner]
- IMPACT [$revenue/profit estimate]

Why It Works: Instead of debating opinions, you're debating evidence. Instead of listing trends, you're choosing moves. Instead of analysis paralysis, you get clear options with dollar values attached (Figure 4.1).

"The beauty is its simplicity," Daniel explained. "We're going to work through each category, surface our assumptions, and immediately connect them to moves we could make. No hundred-page reports. Just visible choices."

How to Build Strategic Assumptions

Here's the process for building your SA:

Step 1: Gather Your Strategic Intelligence

Bring together people who understand different aspects of your business and external environment. Include your leadership team, those with direct market contact and diverse perspectives that will challenge conventional thinking.

MOVE TOOL 1: Strategic Assumptions: What's changing externally— and what does it mean internally?

	IF		THEN		IMPACT					
Category	Trend + Rate of Change	Prob. (H-M-L)	Organic Implication (Product-Market-Capabilities)	Inorganic Implication (Buy - Partner - Divest)	Rev Yr1	Prof Yr1	Rev Yr2	Prof Yr2	Rev Yr3	Prof Yr3
CUS										
COMP										
TECH										
REG										
CON										

Figure 4.1 MOVE Tool #1: Strategic Assumptions Blank Template.

Step 2: Work Through Five Categories

Use these specific questions to surface meaningful trends:

CUSTOMER (Demand Power)

- ***Primary question:*** "What are customers starting to demand that they didn't care about 18 months ago?"
- ***Follow-up questions:***
  - Which expectations are becoming non-negotiable?
  - What purchasing criteria are changing?
  - Which customer segments are growing or shrinking fastest?
  - How are buying processes evolving?

COMPETITION (Supply Power)

- ***Primary question:*** "Who's winning share in our space and what are they doing differently?"
- ***Follow-up questions:***
  - Which new entrants are gaining traction?
  - What business models are disrupting traditional approaches?
  - Where are competitors investing that we're not?
  - How is the basis of competition shifting?

TECHNOLOGY (Enabling Power)

- ***Primary question:*** "What technology is moving from 'nice-to-have' to 'table stakes' in our industry?"
- ***Follow-up questions:***
  - What capabilities are becoming expected by customers?

- Which technologies enable new business models?
- What are early adopters using to gain advantage?
- How is technology changing customer expectations?

REGULATORY (Rule-Setting Power)

- ***Primary question:*** "What new rules or social pressures will become requirements?"
- ***Follow-up questions:***
  - Which compliance changes are definitely coming?
  - What social movements are driving new standards?
  - Where are regulators focusing enforcement?
  - What incentives or penalties are emerging?

CONSTANTS (Strategic Stability)

- ***Primary question:*** "Despite all the change, what customer needs or behaviors haven't changed in ten years?"
- ***Follow-up questions:***
  - Which patterns always repeat in our industry?
  - What do customers always value regardless of trends?
  - Which competitive dynamics remain stable?
  - What can we count on continuing?

Focus on trends that would significantly impact your business if they accelerate. Aim for four to six critical assumptions total. You can have more but more as an initial pass.

Step 3: Generate Strategic Options

For each trend, force the "So what?" conversation:

The Three-Part Question Sequence:

1 "If this trend accelerates, what happens to our business?"
2 "What could we do about it?" (Push for multiple options)
3 "Should we build, buy, or partner?"

Organic Options (Build):

- New products or services
- New market entry
- Process improvements
- Capability development
- Business model changes

Inorganic Options (Buy/Partner):

- Acquisitions for instant capability
- Partnerships for market access
- Joint ventures for risk sharing
- Licensing for speed
- Strategic alliances

Push beyond obvious answers. If someone says, "improve our product," ask: "What specifically? Which products? What capabilities would we need? How would this create advantage?"

Step 4: Estimate Financial Impact

Attach revenue and profit estimates to create accountability:

Revenue Impact Questions:

- "If we capture this opportunity, what revenue could we generate in Year 3?"
- "If we ignore this threat, what revenue is at risk?"
- "What's the total addressable market?"
- "What share could we realistically capture?"

Profit Impact Questions:

- "Will this improve or hurt our margins?"
- "What's the required investment?"
- "What's the expected return?"
- "How does this compare to other options?"

Use ranges if needed. These aren't budget commitments – they're directional estimates that enable prioritization. The combined opportunities should represent a meaningful portion of your growth goals.

The goal: Transform vague external concerns into specific strategic choices with quantified impact.

Building Strategic Assumptions: The Farella Example

"Let's build this together," Daniel said. "We'll start with customers since Sarah already surfaced a critical trend."

Customer Trends: What's Changing in Demand?

"Tell us more about these performance-based shelf fees," Daniel prompted.

Sarah pulled up an email on her laptop. "Walmart's pilot reportedly covers 15 categories. If products don't hit specific turn rates – which they're setting 20% higher than current – we pay penalties equal to the margin on those units. It completely changes the economics."

"What's the probability this spreads?" Daniel asked.

"High," Sarah said without hesitation. "Target's already asking about it. Kroger's interested. For retailers, it's brilliant – shifts all inventory risk to suppliers."

Mark leaned forward. "This could kill our health bowls. They're already our slowest movers."

"So what do we do about it?" Daniel pressed. "Let's think beyond the obvious."

The room went quiet. Then Mark spoke. "We need to completely redesign those SKUs. Not just smaller pack sizes – rethink the entire value proposition. Make them impulse-friendly. Create variety packs. Design for velocity, not just health claims."

"Organic option," Daniel said, writing on the template. "What else?"

Michael jumped in. "What if we partnered with a meal kit company? Get our health bowls included in their weekly deliveries? Bypass the shelf velocity issue entirely?"

"Good. That's an inorganic option. Jennifer, what's the financial impact if we don't act?"

Jennifer pulled up a spreadsheet. "If this spreads to our top five retailers, we're looking at \$3–4M in annual penalties. But if we fix the velocity issue, we protect \$15M in revenue and \$3.1M in profit by year three."

Daniel captured it all on the template.

"What else with customers?" he asked.

Dr. Patel raised his hand. "Can we talk about foodservice? Mark mentioned the frozen SKU cuts. It's worse than that. I was at the National Restaurant Association show last month. Every operator talked about labor shortages. They need products that require zero prep – literally heat-and-serve. Our frozen entrées take 8–12 minutes of active prep time."[6]

"How many SKUs are at risk?" Daniel asked.

"Forty percent of our foodservice frozen portfolio," Mark admitted. "About $12M in revenue."

Sarah saw an opportunity. "But wait – this could be good news. What if we rationalize the portfolio? Kill the complex SKUs that barely sell anyway, and redeploy those resources into simple, high-velocity items?"

"I can model that," Jennifer said, typing rapidly. "If we cut the bottom 30% of SKUs and reinvest in the top performers... we'd save $2M in complexity costs and protect $7M in revenue. Net profit impact of $1.7M by year three."

The energy in the room shifted. They were turning threats into opportunities.

Competition: Who's Changing the Rules?

"Let's talk about competition," Daniel said. "Jennifer, you mentioned private label growth."

"It's not just growth – it's the quality leap," Jennifer explained. "Kroger's new private label snacks are indistinguishable from ours. Same taste profile, similar packaging, 30% lower price. They're gaining 15% share annually in key categories."[7]

"This is like Netflix versus traditional studios all over again," Michael observed. "The studios assumed their content quality and brand relationships were unbeatable moats. Netflix assumed convenience and value would win. We all know how that ended."[8]

Sarah bristled. "But we're not a movie studio. We have real brand equity."

"Do we?" Daniel challenged. "When was the last time we measured brand preference at shelf? When a mom is choosing between our snacks at $4.99 and Kroger's at $3.49, what wins?"

Silence.

Mark broke it. "We need to give them a reason beyond price. Either we reinvest heavily in brand differentiation – better packaging, clearer quality cues, emotional connection – or we find a different game to play."

"Like what?" Sarah asked.

"Partner with regional distributors who specialize in premium products," Michael suggested. "Create bundled offerings. Position ourselves as part of a curated selection rather than competing item-by-item on shelf."

"Or both," Daniel said. "These aren't mutually exclusive. Jennifer, impact?"

"Each option protects about $7M in revenue and $1.7M in profit if we move fast. The partnership route might actually have higher margins since we'd avoid slotting fees."

Technology: What New Capabilities Matter?

"Technology trends?" Daniel prompted. "What's changing the game?"

Dr. Patel perked up. "Ingredient traceability. It sounds boring, but it's exploding. Gen Z consumers want to scan a QR code and see exactly where ingredients came from, how they were processed, what the carbon footprint is. Adoption is doubling every 18 months."[9]

"Is this real demand or just noise?" Mark asked skeptically.

"Real," Sarah confirmed. "Whole Foods just made it mandatory for all new organic products. It's coming whether we like it or not." [10]

"So what's our move?" Daniel asked.

Dr. Patel had clearly thought about this. "We could add QR codes to our health SKUs. Build a simple web interface showing sourcing data. Not that complex technically."

"Or," Michael said, "there's a startup in Austin – TracePath – that does exactly this. Full farm-to-fork transparency platform. They're raising Series A funding. We could acquire them before someone else does."

"Cost versus build?" Daniel asked.

"Build internally: maybe $500K investment," Dr. Patel estimated. "Acquire: probably $5–8M based on similar deals."

"But acquisition gets us there two years faster," Michael argued. "And we'd own the IP."

"Revenue impact?" Daniel pressed.

Jennifer worked through the numbers. "If this becomes table stakes for health-conscious consumers, it protects our premium positioning. Call it $5M revenue and $1.4M profit by year three. More if we can charge a premium for transparency."

Regulatory: What Rules Are Changing?

"Raj, you mentioned FDA disclosure requirements," Daniel said.

"It's coming fast," Dr. Patel confirmed. "Full sodium and sugar transparency on front-of-pack labeling. Plus new requirements for 'natural' claims. We have 12–18 months before it's mandatory."[11]

"Threat or opportunity?" Daniel asked.

Dr. Patel smiled. "Opportunity, actually. Our R&D pipeline already has clean-label reformulations for 60% of our products. We developed them for European markets. We just need to accelerate the rollout here."

"So while competitors scramble, we're ready?" Sarah asked.

"If we move now, yes. But it requires investment to scale up production and reformulate the remaining 40%."

"Impact?"

"$3M in revenue from being first to market with compliant products," Jennifer calculated. "Plus $1M in profit from avoiding reformulation rush costs that competitors will face."

Constants: What Won't Change?

"Last category," Daniel said. "In all this change, what stays the same?"

Mark didn't hesitate. "Value-conscious families still need to feed their kids for under $10. That hasn't changed in 20 years and won't change in the next 20."

"Interesting," Sarah mused. "While we're all chasing premium and health trends, the core frozen meal business remains stable."

"More than stable," Mark corrected. "It's defensible if we position it right. Reemphasize value. Bigger portions. Family sizes. Make it about feeding your family affordably, not about gourmet aspirations."

"Like Costco's strategy," Michael noted. "They've kept their rotisserie chicken at $4.99 for over a decade. It's not about margin on that item – it's about what it represents."[12]

"Exactly," Daniel said. "So our move?"

"Reposition our core frozen line around unbeatable value," Sarah suggested. "New packaging that emphasizes portion size and price per serving. Maybe even create a 'Feed Your Family' campaign."

"Revenue protection?" Daniel asked.

"$8M defended revenue and $2M profit by year three," Jennifer confirmed. "Maybe more if we can take share from competitors who abandon the value segment."

From Assumptions to Aligned Action

By session end, they'd identified six major assumptions with eight strategic options worth $57M in revenue and $14M in profit by year three (Figure 4.2).

MOVE TOOL 1: Strategic Assumptions: What's changing externally— and what does it mean internally?

IF			THEN		IMPACT					
Category	Trend + Rate of Change	Prob. (H-M-L)	Organic Implication (Product-Market-Capabilities)	Inorganic Implication (Buy - Partner - Divest)	Rev Yr1	Prof Yr1	Rev Yr2	Prof Yr2	Rev Yr3	Prof Yr3
CUS	Retail buyers accelerating shift to performance-based shelf fees (esp. for health SKUs); +25% shift projected in 3 yrs	H	Reprice and redesign snack and health SKUs to meet shelf ROI hurdles		$ 5.0	$ 1.2	$ 12.0	$ 2.5	$ 15.0	$ 3.1
	Foodservice customers reducing frozen SKUs due to prep time constraints; -10% in SKU count forecasted	M	Rationalize slow-selling frozen SKUs and relaunch core prep-efficient bundles		$ 2.0	$ 0.4	$ 5.0	$ 1.2	$ 7.0	$ 1.7
COMP	Private labels gaining 15% share in snacks across North America driven by cost-conscious consumers	H	Reinvest in branded equity and quality cues in retail snack packaging		$ 4.0	$ 0.8	$ 6.0	$ 1.5	$ 7.0	$ 1.7
				Partner with regional distributors for bundle placement	$ 4.0	$ 0.8	$ 6.0	$ 1.5	$ 7.0	$ 1.7
TECH	Ingredient traceability tech adoption expected to double (esp. Gen Z pull on sustainability)	M	Digitize labeling across health SKUs; integrate QR-based sourcing info		$ 1.0	$ 0.2	$ 3.0	$ 0.8	$ 5.0	$ 1.4
				Acquire compliance/traceability startup	$ 1.0	$ 0.2	$ 3.0	$ 0.8	$ 5.0	$ 1.4
REG	Nutritional disclosure tightening; sodium and sugar transparency regs coming in 12–18 months	H	Advance R&D pipeline for clean label re-formulations		$ 1.0	$ 0.2	$ 2.0	$ 0.6	$ 3.0	$ 1.0
CON	Frozen meals remain household staples for < $10 dinners among cost-sensitive segments	H	Defend frozen by repositioning core SKUs on value + portion size		$ 6.0	$ 1.5	$ 7.0	$ 1.7	$ 8.0	$ 2.0

Figure 4.2 MOVE Tool #1: Strategic Assumptions Farella Foods Example.

"Look what just happened," Daniel said. "We've identified strategic options worth $57M in revenue and $14M in profit by Year 3. As a first pass, this gives us something substantial to work with – these assumption-based moves could contribute over half our growth target. And we haven't even built our product-market strategy or identified capability investments yet."

Jennifer studied the numbers. "So this is just the beginning. We'll find more opportunities as we work through the other tools?"

"Exactly," Daniel confirmed. "Strategic Assumptions gives us the external foundation. The rest of the MOVE system will reveal additional growth levers – from portfolio optimization to new capabilities. But now we have a solid starting point grounded in market reality."

"The retail shelf fee change is still our biggest risk," she noted.

"Which is exactly why we surfaced it," Daniel said. "Now when we build our vision and strategic bets, we'll be working from the same understanding of what's changing."

"What about validating these?" Mark asked. "Some of these trends feel certain to me, but we might be missing something."

"That's our next step. Each of you owns validating your assumptions with real data. And here's where it gets interesting – we can use AI to accelerate this process dramatically."

Making Strategic Assumptions Stick

DO:

- Test assumptions with external data, not internal opinions
- Connect every assumption to specific strategic options
- Force probability assessments to prioritize resources
- Update quarterly as markets accelerate
- Include contrarians who challenge comfortable thinking

DON'T:

- List generic trends without implications
- Create assumptions that justify what you're already doing
- Skip financial estimates because they're "too early"
- Ignore assumptions that threaten existing business
- Let assumptions survive without evidence

The MOVE+AI Advantage

Traditional SA sessions required extensive preparation and follow-up research. Teams would surface assumptions, then spend weeks gathering market data and validating trends.

Sarah remembered their last planning cycle. "We identified e-commerce growth as a key trend. Took us six weeks to gather data, analyze implications, and size the opportunity. By the time we had answers, two competitors had already launched direct-to-consumer platforms."

"That's the old way," Daniel said. "Today, AI transforms this into a dynamic, real-time strategic conversation. While we're debating a trend, we can validate it. While we're estimating market size, we can get current data. While we're generating options, we can see what others have tried."[13]

Security Note

Never input sensitive company data, financial information, or strategic plans into public AI tools. Use generic descriptions to get insights while protecting confidential information.

AI Prompts That Accelerate Strategic Assumptions

Assumption Validation

- ***Prompt:*** "What evidence from the last 12 months supports or contradicts the assumption that retailers are shifting to performance-based shelf fees in CPG categories? Include specific examples and adoption rates."
- ***What you'll get:*** Current market data testing your assumption
- ***How to use it:*** Adjust probability ratings based on evidence

Competitive Intelligence

- ***Prompt:*** "Which CPG companies have successfully defended against private label competition through brand differentiation or partnerships in the last three years? What specific strategies worked?"
- ***What you'll get:*** Proven strategic options with real examples
- ***How to use it:*** Expand your option set beyond obvious moves

Market Sizing

- ***Prompt:*** "What is the current market size and growth rate for ingredient transparency solutions in food CPG? Include adoption rates by retailer and consumer demographics."
- ***What you'll get:*** Quantified market opportunity
- ***How to use it:*** Refine revenue projections and prioritize investments

Scenario Modeling

- ***Prompt:*** "If performance-based shelf fees become standard across major retailers, model three scenarios for a mid-sized CPG company: optimistic, realistic, and pessimistic. What factors drive the variance?"
- ***What you'll get:*** Range of potential outcomes with key variables
- ***How to use it:*** Stress-test your strategies and identify critical success factors

Regulatory Tracking

- ***Prompt:*** "What FDA labeling requirements are changing in the next 24 months for packaged foods? Include implementation timelines and compliance requirements."
- ***What you'll get:*** Specific regulatory changes and deadlines
- ***How to use it:*** Prioritize compliance investments and identify first-mover opportunities

How Farella Validated Their Assumptions

The next day, Sarah used AI to verify the shelf fee trend. She prompted: "What evidence supports retailers shifting to performance-based shelf fees in CPG categories?"

The results were eye-opening. Beyond Walmart, six other major chains were piloting similar programs. But the AI also revealed something they'd missed small and mid-sized retailers were resisting due to system complexity.

"This changes our approach," Sarah reported to the team. "We should focus innovation on large retail partners first, but maintain our current approach with regional chains. It's not one-size-fits-all."

Mark investigated the private-label threat: "Show examples of CPG brands that successfully defended against private label through premiumization or partnerships."

The AI surfaced fascinating cases:

- KIND bars maintained premium positioning through founder storytelling and social mission[14]
- Blue Buffalo pet food created an "ingredient deck" that private labels couldn't match[15]
- Several snack brands succeeded through exclusive regional partnerships

"Look at this," Mark said. "The winners didn't compete on price. They changed the game entirely. We need to think beyond just 'better packaging.'"

Dr. Patel validated the traceability trend with specific data: "What percentage of Gen Z consumers actively use QR codes to check product information, and what's the year-over-year growth?"

The results: 47% of Gen Z consumers had scanned a food product QR code in the last month, up from 28% the previous year. More importantly, 73% said they'd pay up to 15% more for products with full transparency.

"This isn't a nice-to-have," Dr. Patel concluded. "It's becoming table stakes for anyone under 35."

Using AI, Farella [fictional example] accomplished in three days what traditionally took weeks:

- Validated six assumptions with current market data
- Identified 12 additional strategic options they hadn't considered
- Refined financial projections based on real benchmarks
- Discovered two blind spots in their original thinking

"AI didn't make our decisions," Daniel emphasized in their follow-up session. "But it made us smarter about them. We still chose what mattered, but with better evidence and more options to consider."

Your Move: Surface Assumptions Before Markets Surprise You

Every strategic decision in your company rests on assumptions about external reality. When those assumptions remain invisible, each executive operates on different beliefs. You fund contradictory initiatives. You miss obvious shifts. You react to change instead of leading it.

Consider what happened to Shopify and Amazon in e-commerce infrastructure. Amazon assumed merchants wanted simplicity use our fulfillment, our customer base, our rules. Shopify assumed merchants wanted independence their own brand, their own customer relationships, their own rules. That different assumption led Shopify to a $150B valuation while Amazon scrambled to create "Buy with Prime" to compete.[16]

The difference wasn't capability. It was clarity about assumptions.

SA forces that clarity: What's changing? So what? How much is it worth?

If your leadership team can't agree on the five biggest external trends affecting your business, you don't have a strategy problem you have an assumption problem. Fix that first.

Quick-Action Checklist

- ☐ Block three hours with your leadership team this week
- ☐ Have each executive bring their top three external trends
- ☐ Build the one-page SA tool together
- ☐ Assign owners to validate each assumption with data

Next: Once you know what's changing in your environment, Chapter 5 shows you how to craft a Vision and Driving Force that focuses your entire organization on winning moves.

Notes

1 Albert S. Humphrey, "SWOT Analysis for Management Consulting." SRI Alumni Newsletter (December 2005).
2 Lauren Thomas, "Peloton Shares Tank 24% as Company Cuts Revenue Outlook, Warns of Slowing Growth." *CNBC*, November 4, 2021.
3 Sara Ashley O'Brien, "Peloton's Market Value Has Shrunk by More Than 90%." *CNN Business*, January 20, 2022.
4 Sara Ashley O'Brien, "Lululemon to Shutter Mirror Stores Less Than 18 Months After Acquisition." *CNN Business*, March 22, 2022.
5 Rowan Curran, "ChatGPT Gained 1 Million Users in Under a Week." *Forrester*, December 5, 2022.
6 National Restaurant Association, "State of the Restaurant Industry Report 2023." 2023.
7 Private Label Manufacturers Association, "Private Label Today 2023." PLMA, 2023.
8 W. Chan Kim and Renée Mauborgne, *Blue Ocean Strategy, Expanded Edition* (Boston: Harvard Business Review Press, 2015), 189–195.
9 IBM Institute for Business Value, "Meet the 2020 Consumers Driving Change." IBM, June 2020.
10 Whole Foods Market, "Whole Foods Market Announces Top 10 Food Trends for 2023." Press Release, October 18, 2022.
11 U.S. Food and Drug Administration, "Food Labeling: Revision of the Nutrition and Supplement Facts Labels." Federal Register, May 27, 2016.
12 Brad Tuttle, "The Costco Rotisserie Chicken Mystery: Actually Less Than $5." Money, October 11, 2022.
13 Based on the author's 25+ years of consulting and client experience.
14 Daniel Lubetzky, *Do the KIND Thing* (New York: Ballantine Books, 2015), 112–125.
15 General Mills, "General Mills to Acquire Blue Buffalo Pet Products for $8 Billion." Press Release, February 23, 2018.
16 Tobi Lütke, "The Future of Commerce Has Arrived." Shopify Blog, January 2023.

Chapter 5

Vision + Driving Force

Surface, Stretch, Select

If You Removed Your Company Name, Would Anyone Recognize Your Strategy?

Daniel Ross watched his leadership team debate resource allocation for the third consecutive meeting. They'd successfully identified $57M in opportunities through SA. They agreed on external trends. But every discussion about where to invest ended in stalemate.

The breaking point came when Sarah Martinez requested $8M for health food innovation while Mark Chen wanted the same amount for frozen meal automation. Both made sense. Both addressed trends they'd identified. Both promised strong returns.

"Time out," Daniel said. "Before we debate another investment, answer this: What business are we actually in?"

He went to the whiteboard. "Someone give me one clear statement about what Farella is becoming. Not what we do today, but what we're building toward."

The responses revealed the problem:

Jennifer Walsh (CFO):	"We're a quality-focused food manufacturer protecting margins through operational excellence."
Sarah Martinez (CMO):	"We're becoming the trusted health transformation partner for conscious consumers."
Mark Chen (COO):	"We're the frozen meal category leader expanding into adjacent opportunities."
Michael Thompson (VP Strategy):	"We're building a data-driven food platform that personalizes nutrition."
Dr. Raj Patel (R&D):	"We're the innovation leader bringing fresh culinary experiences to shelf-stable formats."

Five executives. Five different strategies. Each consuming resources. Each pulling the organization in different directions.

Daniel captured each response, then stepped back. "No wonder every investment decision becomes a political battle. We're not debating priorities within one strategy – we're debating between different strategies."

The room fell silent. They'd discovered something profound: they weren't running one company with five departments. They were running five different companies that happened to share overhead.

When Strategic Confusion Destroys Value

The problem wasn't communication. It was strategic fragmentation – different leaders running different companies under the same logo.

DOI: 10.4324/9781003682455-8

Why This Matters

Executive teams often run multiple different strategies without realizing it. That's why execution feels impossible – you're not executing one strategy, you're executing fragments of several. This invisible fragmentation destroys more value than any competitor.

The Hidden Cost of Multiple Strategies

Consider what happened to GE in the 2010s. By 2017, GE was simultaneously pursuing:

- Industrial Internet leadership (Predix platform)
- Financial services expansion (GE Capital)
- Healthcare technology innovation (GE Healthcare)
- Traditional manufacturing excellence (Power, Aviation)
- Media and entertainment (NBC Universal)

Each division had compelling logic. Each showed growth potential. Each demanded billions in investment. But pursuing all strategies meant mastering none. While GE spread resources across multiple futures, focused competitors dominated each space. The result: GE's value collapsed from $400B to under $100B as the company frantically shed businesses to find focus.[1]

Or look at Yahoo in the mid-2010s. Yahoo tried to be:

- A media company competing with traditional publishers
- A technology platform competing with Google
- A social network competing with Facebook
- An email service competing with Gmail
- A finance portal competing with Bloomberg

Each strategy required different capabilities, metrics, and resource allocation. Board meetings became battles between competing visions. Talent didn't know which skills to develop. Customers didn't know what Yahoo represented. While Yahoo debated what business they were in, focused competitors captured each market.[2]

IBM faced similar fragmentation in the 2010s. Three distinct strategies competed for resources:

- Hardware defending mainframe and server leadership
- Software pushing cloud and AI platforms
- Services selling transformation consulting

Each division ran its own strategy. Hardware protected margins on legacy systems. Software chased growth through acquisitions. Services sold whatever generated fees. The result: IBM lost position in all three areas to focused competitors. Only when they explicitly chose hybrid cloud as their unified direction did performance stabilize.[3]

Even retail giants struggle with strategic fragmentation. Sears simultaneously tried to be:

- Discount retailer competing with Walmart on price
- Middle-market department store competing with Macy's
- Premium appliance destination competing with Home Depot
- Financial services provider through Sears Credit

Four strategies. Four investment requirements. Four cultures. While Sears tried to be everything, focused retailers picked apart each business. The company that once defined American retail died from strategic confusion, not market changes.[4]

Why Traditional Vision Exercises Fail

Many companies try to solve this with vision statements. They hire consultants, run workshops, wordsmith inspirational language. But vision exercises typically produce one of two outcomes:

Generic Aspiration: "Be the leading provider of innovative solutions that exceed customer expectations." Could describe any company in any industry. Provides no guidance for real decisions.

Kitchen Sink Strategy: "We will lead in products, services, experiences, and platforms across all markets we serve." Trying to be everything means being nothing distinctive.

The problem isn't the words – it's the lack of integrated strategic choice. Real strategy requires choosing what business you're in, what you offer, who you serve, and how you win. Most vision exercises avoid these choices.

How Vision Lost Its Strategic Power

To understand why, we need to see how vision statements became disconnected from strategy.

In the 1960s and 1970s, vision wasn't a separate exercise – it was embedded in strategy. Companies knew exactly what business they were in and why. General Motors had "a car for every purse and purpose" – clear choices about serving every income segment with distinct brands. IBM meant "nobody gets fired for buying IBM" – explicit focus on enterprise reliability over innovation.

These weren't just slogans. They drove decisions. When GM evaluated opportunities, they asked: "Does this fit our ladder of aspiration?" When IBM allocated resources, they asked: "Does this strengthen enterprise trust?" Vision and strategy were one.

Then came the 1980s' vision movement. Tom Peters and Robert Waterman's "In Search of Excellence" (1982) celebrated companies with strong cultures and clear purpose. Suddenly every company needed an inspiring vision statement.[5]

The concept exploded with Jim Collins and Jerry Porras's research. Their 1994 book *Built to Last* made vision statements mandatory for any company claiming to be "visionary." They distinguished between:

- Core ideology (who you are)
- Envisioned future (what you aspire to become)[6]

Good concepts, but implementation went sideways. Companies spent months crafting perfect vision statements while avoiding hard strategic choices. They hired consultants to facilitate visioning retreats. They formed committee after committee to wordsmith inspiring language.

Jack Welch at GE popularized being "#1 or #2 in every market" – which sounded strategic but actually enabled GE to define markets narrowly enough to claim leadership while losing focus.[7]

By the 2000s, vision statements had devolved into generic aspirations:

- "Be the most trusted provider of..."
- "Enable customer success through..."
- "Deliver innovative solutions that..."

Interchangeable. Meaningless. Divorced from real strategic choice.

Meanwhile, each executive interpreted the vision differently. The CMO read "innovative solutions" as digital transformation. The COO read it as operational excellence. The CFO read it as margin improvement. Same words, different strategies.

Making Strategic Direction Visible and Complete

After decades of strategic consulting, one pattern emerges: winning companies answer the complete strategic question:

> **"What is your purpose and path relative to products, customers, and capabilities to deliver your goals relative to competition?"**

This isn't about inspiration – it's about integration. Every element must connect and reinforce the others.

Think about Netflix's clarity when they shifted from DVDs to streaming: "Become the best entertainment distribution service globally – licensed content in one market, original content in multiple markets." Every word drove decisions. "Distribution" meant they were a platform, not a studio. "Licensed then original" sequenced investments. "Multiple markets" justified global infrastructure spending.[8]

Or consider Zara's integrated strategy: "Make fashion trends accessible to everyone through vertical integration enabling two-week design-to-shelf cycles at affordable prices." This drives everything from real estate (high-traffic locations) to manufacturing (owned facilities) to inventory (small batches).[9]

These companies don't run multiple strategies in different divisions. They run one integrated strategy that everyone executes.

Vision + Driving Force: MOVE Tool #2

VDF transforms strategic confusion into strategic clarity by forcing complete, integrated choices across ten connected parameters.

What Vision + Driving Force Does

VDF is MOVE Tool #2: the strategic direction system that unifies fragmented strategies into one complete answer everyone can execute.

The One Question It Answers: "What is our complete strategy that connects purpose, products, markets, capabilities, and competitive advantage into one coherent direction?"

Why It Works: Instead of wordsmithing vision statements, you're making integrated strategic choices. Instead of avoiding trade-offs, you're making them explicit. Instead of allowing multiple interpretations, you're creating shared understanding.

The Ten-Parameter Framework

1. **Mission**: Why do we do what we do? (purpose beyond profit)
2. **Nature:** What are we today – and what do we need to become? (transformation journey)
3. **Timing:** What is our strategic time frame? (horizon for change)
4. **Products:** What products should we offer and not offer? (portfolio choices)
5. **Markets:** What customer segments should we serve and not serve? (customer choices)
6. **External Value Proposition:** Why should customers choose us over the competition? (customer view)
7. **Internal Competitive Advantage:** What capabilities allow us to deliver on our value proposition? (internal view)
8. **Path for Growth:** Which moves from the Ansoff matrix makes the most sense now? (expansion logic)

MOVE TOOL 2: Vision + Driving Force - Where are we going — and what will we say no to?

QUESTIONS		OPTIONS				CHOICE
Parameter	**Clarifying Question**	**Current State**	**Option 1**	**Option 2**	**Option ...**	**Selected Option**
Mission	*Why do we do what we do?*					
Nature	*What are we today — and what do we need to become?*					
Timing	*What is our strategic time frame?*					
Products	*What products should we offer and not offer?*					
Markets	*What customer segments should we serve and not serve?*					
External Value Proposition	*Why should customers choose us over the competition?*					
Internal Competitive Advantage	*What capabilities allow us to deliver on our value proposition?*					
Path for Growth	*What is our growth path? Which moves from the Ansoff matrix make the most sense now?*					
Capabilities	*What current capabilities must we protect and what future capabilities should we build, buy, or partner to succeed?*					
Goals	*What are our Revenue Goals $*					
	What are our profit goals					
	What are our capability goals?					
	What are our people goals?					

Figure 5.1 MOVE Tool #2: Vision and Driving Force Blank Template.

9 **Capabilities:** What current capabilities must we protect and what future capabilities should we build, buy, or partner? (investment priorities)
10 **Goals:** What are our revenue, profit, capability, and people targets? (measurable outcomes)

The power comes from completion and connection. Every parameter must be filled. Every choice must reinforce the others.

If this seems like a lot, here's the key: most teams can't even agree on these basics for their CURRENT strategy. That diagnostic alone is worth the exercise (Figure 5.1).

How to Build Vision + Driving Force

Phase 1: Surface Current Reality

Start with brutal honesty about what strategy you're actually running based on resource allocation, not rhetoric.

Have each executive complete the ten parameters independently for your current strategy. Compare answers. The differences reveal strategic confusion that explains execution struggles.

Phase 2: Stretch to Create Alternatives

Develop two to three genuinely different strategic futures. Not variations of today, but fundamentally different directions you could take.

Critical rule: complete all ten parameters for each alternative. No blanks. No hedging. Force complete thinking.

Phase 3: Select Based on Evidence

Use structured evaluation criteria tied to SA from Tool #1. This connects your internal strategic choices to external market reality.

Evaluation Framework with Weights:

- Market Trends Alignment (25%): How well does each alternative use the trends you identified?
- Growth Potential (30%): What revenue and profit can each realistically deliver?
- Competitive Advantage (30%): How strong and lasting is each alternative's advantage?
- Execution Risk (15%): What are capability gaps and implementation challenges?

Building Vision + Driving Force: The Farella Example

"Let's fix our strategic fragmentation," Daniel said the next morning. "We'll use Vision + Driving Force to create one integrated strategy we all execute."

Phase 1: Surfacing Farella's Current Reality

"First, let's see if we even agree on our current strategy," Daniel suggested. "Everyone take 10 minutes to fill out the 10 parameters for what you think we're doing today."

The results exposed the confusion:

Mission Divergence

- Jennifer: "Deliver quality food products with strong margins"
- Sarah: "Transform how people think about nutrition"
- Mark: "Be the operational leader in frozen foods"

Multiple Blanks

- No one could articulate their current competitive advantage
- Growth path had three different answers
- Value proposition was generic platitudes

Heated Debates

- "We ARE investing in innovation!" Sarah insisted
- "No, we're dabbling in innovation while focusing on operations," Mark countered
- "Our real strategy is margin protection," Jennifer added

"Look at this mess," Daniel said. "We can't even agree on current reality. Half the parameters have multiple answers. Some are just blank. No wonder execution feels impossible – we're not executing one strategy, we're executing fragments of several."

Dr. Patel studied the responses. "I couldn't even fill out our growth path. Are we penetrating current markets? Developing new products? Expanding geographically? We're doing all three with no clear priority."

"That's exactly the problem," Michael confirmed. "We have initiatives everywhere but excellence nowhere. We're spreading ourselves thin trying to be everything."

Sarah defended her view. "But we need to innovate! The market is moving toward health and wellness. We can't just optimize frozen meals forever."

"And we can't chase every trend," Mark shot back. "Our strength is operational efficiency. We should build on that, not abandon it for some health transformation fantasy."

The debate escalated, proving Daniel's point. Without aligned vision, every discussion became a battle between competing worldviews.

Phase 2: Stretching to Create Strategic Alternatives

"Now let's channel this energy productively," Daniel said. "We'll create three genuinely different futures for Farella [fictional example]. Not tweaks to today, but fundamentally different strategic directions."

After hours of structured debate, they developed three distinct options:

Option 1: "Wide Portfolio for Scale" **Stay broad, compete on scale**

- **Mission**: Stick with wide portfolio for scale
- **Nature**: Generalist food producer → Multi-brand aggregator
- **Timing**: Take longer-term bets (five plus years)
- **Products**: Keep all products and try to optimize
- **Markets**: Invest evenly in all channels
- **External Value Proposition**: Low price, high distribution
- **Internal Competitive Advantage**: Outsource innovation
- **Path for Growth**: New products in same channels
- **Capabilities**: Add more capacity and expand ops footprint
- **Goals**: $750M revenue, $65M EBITDA, basic eComm capability, generalist hiring

"This maintains our current approach," Mark argued. "We don't disrupt anything. We just optimize what we have and rely on scale. It's the lowest risk path."

But Sarah challenged immediately: "Low risk? This guarantees we lose to focused competitors. Scale without differentiation is a recipe for commoditization."

Option 2: "Premium Health Convenience Brand" **Go premium, shrink to grow**

- **Mission**: Reposition as premium health convenience brand
- **Nature**: Food producer → Functional expert
- **Timing**: Immediate turnaround (one to two years)
- **Products**: Drop tail SKUs, invest in hero lines
- **Markets**: Exit Foodservice, focus on DTC
- **External Value Proposition**: Exclusive ingredients, niche positioning
- **Internal Competitive Advantage**: Invest in digital marketing engine
- **Path for Growth**: Same products into new countries
- **Capabilities**: Build influencer partnerships, expand supply chain automation
- **Goals**: $850M revenue, $70M EBITDA, supply chain automation, external ops hires

"This takes us premium," Sarah advocated. "We become the health brand for conscious consumers willing to pay more. We'd finally have a clear identity."

Mark shook his head. "And abandon our core customers? Exit foodservice where we have decades of relationships? This is strategic suicide disguised as transformation."

Dr. Patel added technical concerns: "The R&D requirements for truly premium health products are massive. We'd need to rebuild our entire innovation capability from scratch."

Option 3: "Win with Focus" Focus smartly, transform steadily

- **Mission**: Win with focus: simplify portfolio, prioritize advantage zones
- **Nature**: Fragmented producer → Category-led growth business
- **Timing**: Focused transformation by 2028 (three years)
- **Products**: Focus on Frozen and Healthy, reduce SKU clutter
- **Markets**: Double down on retail; selectively optimize foodservice
- **External Value Proposition**: Best-tasting, clean-label convenience for modern retail consumer
- **Internal Competitive Advantage**: Speed-to-market in innovation; scalable supply chain
- **Path for Growth**: Penetrate and expand in core categories and growth regions
- **Capabilities**: Build category-led innovation, consumer-led marketing, digital ops foundation
- **Goals**: $800M revenue, $75M EBITDA, modernize innovation & marketing engine, upskill key teams

"This is the balanced path," Daniel suggested. "We focus without going to extremes. We simplify but keep our strengths. We transform but at a measured pace."

Jennifer studied the numbers. "Option 3 gives us the highest EBITDA margin. That's interesting – not the highest revenue, but the best profitability."

"Because focus drives margin," Michael explained. "Less complexity, better execution, higher realization."

The Strategic Debate

The room erupted in discussion as each option sparked new insights and disagreements.

"Option 1 is corporate death by a thousand cuts," Sarah argued passionately. "We'd be choosing to remain mediocre at everything rather than excellent at something. In five years, we'll be a low-margin commodity player begging for shelf space."

Mark defended it: "At least we'd still exist. Option 2 is a fantasy. Premium health brands take years to build. We don't have the credibility, the capabilities, or the capital to pull it off."

"But Option 3 asks us to exit profitable businesses," Jennifer noted. "Yes, they're low margin, but they're still contributing. Can we really afford to shrink our way to growth?"

Dr. Patel brought technical perspective: "From an R&D standpoint, Option 3 finally gives us focus. Instead of spreading innovation across 200 SKUs, we could actually develop category leadership in Frozen and Healthy. We might actually create products that matter instead of line extensions nobody wants."

"And from a marketing perspective," Sarah added, warming to Option 3, "we could finally tell a coherent story. Not 'we make everything,' but 'we're the best at these specific things.'"

Michael Thompson, who'd been quietly analyzing, spoke up: "There's something else to consider. Look at our Strategic Assumptions from last quarter. Retail consolidation, private label growth, demand for speed – Option 3 directly addresses every trend we identified. Options 1 and 2 largely ignore them."

The debate continued for another hour, each executive gradually seeing how their functional perspective fit into the broader strategic choices.

Understanding Growth Paths

Dr. Patel raised a crucial point: "I'm still confused about growth paths. What exactly does 'penetrate and expand in core categories' mean?"

Daniel explained using Ansoff's framework: "Every company has four fundamental ways to grow:[10]

- **Market Penetration**: Current products to current customers – going deeper
- **Product Development**: New products to current customers – innovation
- **Market Development**: Current products to new customers – expansion
- **Diversification**: New products to new customers – transformation

The key insight: pursuing multiple paths simultaneously splits focus and resources. You need one primary path."

"So Option 1 tries Product Development – new products in same channels," Michael clarified. "Option 2 pursues Market Development – same products to new countries. Option 3 focuses on Penetration first – going deeper in core categories before expanding."

"Exactly," Daniel confirmed. "And that's why Option 3 makes sense. We master our core before we expand. We earn the right to grow by becoming excellent first."

Phase 3: Selecting Based on Evidence

"Let's evaluate systematically," Daniel suggested. "We'll use the criteria that connect back to our Strategic Assumptions."

They evaluated each option against four weighted criteria:

Market Trends Alignment (25%)

- Option 1: 3/10: Ignores all trends identified in Strategic Assumptions
- Option 2: 7/10: Addresses premium trends but ignores retail consolidation
- Option 3: 8/10: Balances focus with retail requirements

Growth Potential (30%)

- Option 1: 4/10: Minimal growth ($750M barely moves needle)
- Option 2: 8/10: Highest revenue ($850M) but execution risk
- Option 3: 7/10: Solid growth ($800M) with higher EBITDA margin

Competitive Advantage (30%)

- Option 1: 2/10: No real differentiation
- Option 2: 6/10: Premium positioning but narrow
- Option 3: 8/10: Speed and focus create sustainable advantage

Execution Risk (15%)

- Option 1: 8/10: Easy but leads nowhere
- Option 2: 4/10: Radical shift, high risk
- Option 3: 7/10: Manageable transformation

The Strategic Choice

The weighted scores revealed:

- Option 1: 4.35/10 (status quo trap)
- Option 2: 6.55/10 (aggressive but risky)
- Option 3: 7.45/10 (balanced winner) (Figure 5.2)

"Option 3 wins because it balances ambition with reality," Daniel noted. "We transform but don't try to become something we're not."

Sarah initially preferred Option 2's premium positioning. "But I see why Option 3 works better. We can still elevate our brand while keeping retail relationships strong."

MOVE TOOL 2: Vision + Driving Force - Where are we going — and what will we say no to?

QUESTIONS		OPTIONS				CHOICE
Parameter	**Clarifying Question**	**Current State**	**Option 1**	**Option 2**	**Option 3**	**Selected Option**
Mission	*Why do we do what we do?*	Broad-based food company chasing multiple segments	Stick with wide portfolio for scale	Reposition as premium health convenience brand	Win with focus: simplify portfolio, prioritize advantage zones	Win with focus: simplify portfolio, prioritize advantage zones
Nature	*What are we today — and what do we need to become?*	Generalist food producer, fragmented identity	Multi-brand aggregator	Functional expert (e.g., ops or supply chain play)	Category-led growth business	Category-led growth business
Timing	*What is our strategic time frame?*	5+ years with no specific targets	Take longer-term bets (5+ years)	Immediate turnaround (1–2 years)	Focused transformation by 2028 (3 years)	Focused transformation by 2028 (3 years)
Products	*What products should we offer and not offer?*	All current SKUs including low-performing	Keep all and try to optimize	Drop tail SKUs, invest in hero lines	Focus on Frozen & Healthy, reduce SKU clutter	Focus on Frozen & Healthy, reduce SKU clutter
Markets	*What customer segments should we serve and not serve?*	Retail, Foodservice, and DTC without clarity	Invest evenly in all channels	Exit Foodservice, focus on DTC	Double-down on Retail; selectively optimize Foodservice	Double-down on Retail; selectively optimize Foodservice
External Value Proposition	*Why should customers choose us over the competition?*	Inconsistent brand pull	Low price, high distribution	Exclusive ingredients, niche positioning	Best-tasting, clean-label convenience for modern retail consumer	Best-tasting, clean-label convenience for modern retail consumer
Internal Competitive Advantage	*What capabilities allow us to deliver on our value proposition?*	Efficient plants but slow innovation	Outsource innovation	Invest in digital marketing engine	Speed-to-market in innovation; scalable supply chain	Speed-to-market in innovation; scalable supply chain
Path for Growth	*What is our growth path? Which moves from the Ansoff matrix make the most sense now?*	Undefined; some adjacencies explored	New products in same channels	Same products into new countries	Penetrate and expand in core categories and growth regions	Penetrate and expand in core categories and growth regions
Capabilities	*What current capabilities must we protect and what future capabilities should we build, buy, or partner to succeed?*	Traditional manufacturing, limited brand innovation	Add more capacity and expand ops footprint	Build influencer partnerships	Build category-led innovation, consumer-led marketing, and digital ops foundation	Build category-led innovation, consumer-led marketing, and digital ops foundation
Goals	*What are our Revenue Goals $*	Not clear	$750M	$850M	$800M	$800M
	What are our profit goals	Not clear	$65M EBITDA	$70M EBITDA	$75M EBITDA	$75M EBITDA
	What are our capability goals?	Not clear	Build basic eComm capability	Expand supply chain automation	Modernize innovation & marketing engine	Modernize innovation & marketing engine
	What are our people goals?	Not clear	Generalist hiring	External hires in ops	Up-skill key teams in category marketing and ops speed	Up-skill key teams in category marketing and ops speed

Figure 5.2 MOVE Tool #2: Vision and Driving Force Farella Foods Example.

Mark appreciated the measured approach: "Option 3 gives me a clear path. Reduce complexity without destroying capabilities. Focus without abandoning everything."

Jennifer confirmed the financial logic: "$800M with $75M EBITDA gives us the highest margin percentage – 9.4%. Option 2's higher revenue comes with lower margins at 8.2%. That's the wrong trade-off. Focus drives profitability."

The board discussion that followed tested their conviction. One director challenged: "Why not stay broad and optimize? Option 1 seems safer."

Daniel presented the evaluation: "Safe for whom? Our analysis shows Option 1 leads to gradual irrelevance. We scored it lowest on every criterion that matters for future success. Option 3 balances transformation with execution reality."

Another director worried about focus. "Won't we lose revenue by narrowing our portfolio?"

"Short term, possibly," Jennifer acknowledged. "But we'll more than compensate through better margins and focused growth. Option 3 delivers the highest EBITDA percentage – that's what creates enterprise value."

From Choice to Clarity

With Option 3 selected – "Win with Focus" – the team understood the strategic implications.

"This Vision gives us clear direction without extreme disruption," Daniel said. "We're choosing to simplify and focus on Frozen & Healthy, but we're not abandoning our retail strength or operational capabilities."

Sarah saw how this would reshape her approach: "I need to think about marketing fewer brands more powerfully. Not 200 SKUs with diluted support, but focused investment in categories where we can win."

Mark understood the operational path: "This means SKU rationalization, but thoughtfully. We keep what works, exit what doesn't, and optimize our supply chain for speed rather than just cost."

Dr. Patel saw the innovation opportunity: "With focus on Frozen & Healthy, we can actually build category leadership instead of being mediocre everywhere. Speed-to-market becomes our innovation edge."

Jennifer modeled the transformation: "The path to $800M and $75M EBITDA requires both growth and margin improvement. Focus enables both – less complexity, better margins, clearer growth."

"Exactly," Daniel confirmed. "This Vision choice will guide every subsequent tool. When we build our Product-Market Matrix, we'll map opportunities in Frozen and Healthy. When we identify capabilities, we'll prioritize category-led innovation and modern marketing. Our Strategic Assumptions revealed the opportunities. Our Vision commits us to a specific way of capturing them."

Michael captured the strategic shift: "We're transforming from a broad generalist into a focused category leader. Not as radical as Option 2, not as static as Option 1. It's ambitious but achievable."

The team left with clarity. They would become a category-led growth business focused on winning in Frozen and Healthy through speed and innovation. The transformation would take three years, but the direction was set.

Using AI to Pressure-Test Vision + Driving Force

Two weeks into their strategic planning, competitive intelligence revealed a troubling development. A major competitor was launching a premium frozen line with celebrity chef partnerships.

"Should we reconsider our strategy?" Sarah asked in the emergency meeting.

"Let's use AI to pressure-test our choice," Daniel suggested.

AI Prompts for Vision Testing

Competitive Response Analysis *Prompt*: "If an established frozen food manufacturer chooses to focus exclusively on premium frozen meals through speed-to-market innovation, how would major competitors likely respond? What defensive or offensive moves would they make?"

AI Output: Competitors would likely:

- Acquire premium frozen brands defensively (most probable)
- Launch copycat premium lines (6–12 month lag)
- Focus on value segments you're abandoning
- Partner with meal kit companies for fresh alternatives

Insight: The competitor's move validates our direction. They see the same premium opportunity. But their celebrity chef approach differs from our speed and innovation advantage.

Capability Gap Assessment *Prompt*: "What specific capabilities distinguish winning premium frozen meal brands from commodity players? Rank by importance and difficulty to build."

AI Output:

1 Speed-to-market innovation process (critical, 18 months to build)
2 Consumer insight engine (important, 12 months)
3 Premium sourcing at scale (required, six months)
4 Brand storytelling authenticity (valuable, ongoing)
5 Digital marketing expertise (helpful, can partner)

Insight: Our focus on speed-to-market addresses the most critical capability. The competitor's celebrity approach skips the fundamental innovation capability.

Growth Path Validation *Prompt*: "Analyze success factors for food companies pursuing Market Penetration (deeper in current markets) vs. Market Development (expansion to new markets) as primary growth strategy. Include examples and key success factors."

AI Output: Market Penetration in food typically shows higher success when:

- Building on core category strength
- Leveraging existing customer relationships
- Using proven distribution channels
- Focusing resources on innovation

Market Development typically requires:

- New channel capabilities
- Different customer understanding
- Modified operations
- Higher investment

Insight: Our Penetration-first approach aligns with established success patterns.[11]

Security Note

Never input actual company strategies, financial data, or competitive intelligence into public AI tools. Use generic industry descriptions to get insights while protecting confidential information.

The AI-Enhanced Decision

The team adjusted their planning based on AI insights:

- Prioritized category-led innovation in capability planning
- Identified speed-to-market as critical success factor
- Mapped innovation engine requirements
- Designed marketing transformation approach

"The AI analysis confirms we're on the right path," Daniel said. "The competitor's celebrity approach validates the premium opportunity, but our focus on speed and innovation creates deeper advantage."

Sarah saw it differently now. "They're playing catch-up with marketing. We're planning to build fundamental capability. That's the difference between strategy and tactics."

Michael added, "This also shows why Option 3 works. We don't need to be the most premium like Option 2 suggested. We need to be the fastest and most focused."

Dr. Patel appreciated the validation: "The capability ranking shows we're investing in what matters most. Speed-to-market innovation is harder to copy than celebrity endorsements."

Your Move: From Strategic Confusion to Strategic Clarity

Right now, your leadership team is probably running multiple strategies without realizing it. Your resource battles aren't about priorities – they're about competing visions. Your execution struggles aren't about capability – they're about direction.

VDF forces the strategic clarity that enables true execution. One integrated strategy. Ten connected parameters. Clear trade-offs made visible.

If your executives can't agree on what business you're in, how can your organization execute effectively?

Quick-Action Checklist

- □ Have each executive complete the ten parameters for current strategy
- □ Compare answers to reveal strategic fragmentation
- □ Create two to three genuinely different strategic alternatives
- □ Evaluate using weighted criteria tied to market assumptions

Next: Chapter 6 shows how to transform your chosen Vision into specific strategic bets across products and markets through the Product-Market Matrix tool.

Notes

1 Thomas Gryta and Ted Mann, *Lights Out: Pride, Delusion, and the Fall of General Electric* (Boston: Houghton Mifflin Harcourt, 2020), 245–267.
2 Nicholas Carlson, *Marissa Mayer and the Fight to Save Yahoo!* (New York: Twelve, 2015), 189–203.
3 IBM Corporation, "IBM Annual Report 2020." Accessed January 2025, https://www.ibm.com/annualreport/2020.
4 Donald Katz, *The Big Store: Inside the Crisis and Revolution at Sears* (New York: Penguin Books, 2023), 312–329.
5 Tom Peters and Robert Waterman, *In Search of Excellence: Lessons from America's Best-Run Companies* (New York: Harper & Row, 1982).
6 James C. Collins and Jerry I. Porras, *Built to Last: Successful Habits of Visionary Companies* (New York: HarperBusiness, 1994), 220–239.
7 Jack Welch and John A. Byrne, *Jack: Straight from the Gut* (New York: Warner Books, 2001), 157–162.
8 Reed Hastings and Erin Meyer, *No Rules Rules: Netflix and the Culture of Reinvention* (New York: Penguin Press, 2020), 89–104.
9 Enrique Badía, *Zara and Her Sisters: The Story of the World's Largest Clothing Retailer* (London: Profile Books, 2019), 145–156.
10 H. Igor Ansoff, "Strategies for Diversification." *Harvard Business Review* 35, no. 5 (September-October 1957): 113–124.
11 Based on the author's 25+ years of consulting and client experience.

Chapter 6

Make Bets Visible

Where Strategy Gets Real

> "If you had to bet the company on three product-market combinations, which would you choose and why---and can you show exactly where your current resources are actually flowing?"

Daniel Ross gathered his executive team at Farella Foods [fictional example] for their strategic planning session. They'd completed SA and Vision work – unprecedented clarity about external trends and strategic direction. The flipcharts from previous sessions lined the walls. Everyone felt aligned.

They'd just selected their "Win with Focus" vision – becoming a category-led growth business focused on Frozen and Healthy through speed and innovation. Clear purpose. Clear direction. Clear transformation path.

But when Daniel asked them to place their top growth opportunities on a simple product-market grid, everything changed.

"Let's try something," Daniel said, drawing a 3×2 matrix on the whiteboard. "Write your top three growth opportunities on Post-it notes and place them where they belong – which product for which market."

The executives dove in with confidence. They knew their business. They'd been doing this for years.

Mark Chen went first, placing his yellow Post-its: "Frozen Meal automation for Retail," "Supply chain optimization across all Foodservice," "New snack formats for convenience stores." All in different cells across the matrix.

Sarah Martinez added her blue notes: "Premium Healthy Bowls for upscale Retail," "Marketing campaign for all products," "Digital engagement platform." She placed them in completely different cells from Mark.

Dr. Raj Patel contributed his green notes: "Clean-label Frozen innovation," "Snack Pack reformulation," "Next-gen Healthy Bowl ingredients." Not one overlapped with the others.

Twenty minutes later, Daniel stepped back to view the board. Six executives. Eighteen growth opportunities. One company.

The matrix looked like chaos – colored Post-its scattered across every cell, overlapping ideas, conflicting priorities, zero coherence. Not one executive placed a note in the same cell as another.

Daniel stared at the board. His face changed as the reality sank in. "This is our current strategy, isn't it? Six leaders running six different businesses."

The room went silent. Then Jennifer Walsh spoke up: "But these are all good opportunities. We discussed them in our planning sessions."

"That's exactly the problem," Daniel responded. "They're all good ideas. But good ideas without strategic focus is how companies slowly bleed to death. We're spreading resources so thin that nothing gets the critical mass needed to win."

DOI: 10.4324/9781003682455-9

Daniel walked closer to the whiteboard, studying the scattered Post-its. "We've been doing this for years, haven't we? Everyone fighting for their piece of the budget, no one asking if the pieces add up to a winning strategy."

Jennifer did quick math. "If we're pursuing eighteen opportunities with our available capital... that's less than $4M per initiative. No wonder nothing ever seems to get traction."

Daniel turned to his team. "We just discovered we've been funding chaos, calling it strategy."

The Invisible Decision Making Already Happening

Daniel's discovery wasn't unique. In company after company, the same reality emerges: resource allocation happens through an invisible operating system that no one can see or control.

As we discussed in Chapter 5, Igor Ansoff pioneered the systematic approach to growth decisions with his 2×2 framework, showing four paths: Market Penetration, Market Development, Product Development, and Diversification.[1] But here's what executives often miss – this framework isn't just a planning tool. It's already operating in your company right now.

Think about it: every dollar you spend, every person you hire, every project you approve is going toward some combination of products and markets. Your resources are already flowing through a PMM. It's happening right now. Like gravity – you don't have to believe in it, but drop something and see which way it goes.

The question isn't WHETHER you have a PMM. The question is whether you can SEE it and manage it strategically.

The Pattern That Emerges

Everyone with a P&L is already managing a version of the company PMM. The regional VP managing retail operations is managing a piece of the PMM. The product manager running your frozen meals line is managing a piece. The foodservice director handling institutional accounts is managing a piece.

They're all making resource allocation decisions within their PMM cell – but they can't see how their piece connects to the whole, whether their segmentation makes strategic sense, or if their performance criteria aligns with company strategy.

A Japanese food manufacturer discovered this problem dramatically. Their retail manager was investing heavily in premium products for grocery chains. Meanwhile, their product head was cutting features to compete on price. Both were managing their piece of the PMM brilliantly – in opposite directions. The PMM wasn't visible, so $50M of investment was fighting against itself.[2]

Some combinations generate massive returns. Others are budget incinerators disguised as strategic investments. Many executives struggle to distinguish between them because they've never made their PMM visible.

Three Assumptions Leadership Teams Make

Assumption #1: "Our leadership team understands our business the same way." Reality: The Post-it exercise typically reveals complete misalignment. A European food company discovered their German operations head focused on technical innovation, their Italian sales head on geographic expansion, and their British CFO on service revenue. Three executives, three different businesses in their minds.[3]

Assumption #2: "We segment our business strategically." Reality: Most segment by accounting convenience – how sales territories were carved up or factories organized. A Mexican food company segmented by product type (frozen, fresh, packaged) because of factory structure, missing that real profit pools were need-based: convenience seekers, health optimizers, budget families.

Assumption #3: "We allocate resources based on strategic priorities." Reality: The loudest voice often wins. A South African retailer's $200M growth capital went 40% to their largest region ("can't ignore our biggest business"), 30% to the best presenter, and the rest carved up to avoid conflict. Strategy had nothing to do with it.[4]

When Companies Can't See Where Money Goes

Bed Bath & Beyond vs. Target: The Cost of Invisible Allocation

Bed Bath & Beyond had the ingredients to dominate home retail: massive stores, loyal customers, famous coupons, trusted brand. But their resource allocation was invisible and scattered.

From 2019 to 2023, Bed Bath & Beyond was simultaneously investing in:

- Store renovations across 1,500 locations
- Private-label brand development
- BuyBuy Baby expansion
- Digital transformation and e-commerce
- New store concepts and formats

Each initiative made sense in isolation. Together, they created strategic chaos. Resources spread thin across everything meant nothing achieved critical mass. Meanwhile, Target focused relentlessly on one thing: affordable style for the home through limited-time designer partnerships and exclusive brands.[5]

By 2022, Bed Bath & Beyond was investing across dozens of initiatives with declining returns. Target was concentrating resources on curated home collections that drove traffic and margins.

Result: Bed Bath & Beyond filed for bankruptcy in April 2023 with $5.2B in debt.[6] Target's home category grew to $20B+ with expanding margins.[7]

Disney+ vs. Netflix: Same Streaming Wars, Different Resource Choices

When Disney entered streaming in 2019, both companies faced similar challenges. The difference was how they allocated resources.

Netflix's focused allocation:

- Global content production across all genres
- Technology platform and recommendation engine
- International expansion with local content
- Building streaming-first culture

Disney's scattered approach:

- Protecting theatrical release windows
- Maintaining cable networks
- Building streaming while preserving traditional distribution
- Balancing parks, products, and media

Result: Netflix maintained streaming leadership with 240+ million subscribers.[8] Disney+ grew fast but at massive losses – bleeding $4B in 2022 alone as they tried to serve multiple masters.[9] Only when Bob Iger returned and focused resources did Disney's streaming strategy stabilize.

The lesson repeats across industries: companies trapped in invisible PMMs consistently lose to competitors who make strategic bets visible and systematic. They're fighting themselves while focused competitors capture the market.

The Core Problem

Executive teams can't see where their budget actually generates competitive returns. They're making coordinated decisions based on completely uncoordinated assumptions about which product-market combinations matter most.

Without visible PMMs, companies spread time, budget, and effort across conflicting priorities that satisfy everyone internally but optimize nothing externally. While leadership teams debate which initiatives to fund, competitors with visible PMMs are making systematic moves that capture market position and pricing power. They're not smarter – they're just more focused.

The hidden cost compounds: when your competitors make faster decisions using clear frameworks, they capture opportunities while you're still debating. One telecommunications company lost three major enterprise deals in six months – not because their technology was inferior, but because their competitor could approve strategic pricing moves in 48 hours using their PMM criteria while they needed three weeks of executive debate.

Here's what many companies miss – your PMM isn't separate from your budget, it IS your budget made strategic. When you build your PMM from the outside-in (starting with SA, then Vision, then segmentation), the sum of all PMM cells should equal your fiscal year budget.

Companies that maintain separate processes for strategy (PMM) and budgeting are running two different businesses – one they talk about in strategy sessions and one they actually fund. Strategic thinking should drive budget targets, not the other way around. The PMM becomes the bridge between strategic intent and financial truth.

Back in Farella's conference room, Daniel knew they had to make their resource allocation visible. The Post-it chaos on the wall proved they were funding 18 different experiments instead of one focused strategy. It was time to see exactly where their money was actually going – and where it should go instead.

The MOVE Solution: Product-Market Matrix

PMM is the first half of MOVE Tool #3: a two-part system for making and testing strategic bets. The PMM makes your resource allocation visible and systematic by connecting products and markets to financial reality and competitive advantage. Its companion tool, MRC, pressure-tests these bets against external market forces. Two sides of the same strategic coin: first you see where you're placing bets, then you validate whether those bets will win.

The One Question It Answers: "Which specific product-market combinations generate the highest competitive returns, and how should we allocate resources accordingly?"

Why This Tool Creates Breakthrough Value

You stop spreading budget across everything. Instead of allocating time, budget, and effort to every good idea, teams invest systematically in combinations that generate measurable competitive returns. Resource efficiency improves dramatically through strategic focus.

But here's the real breakthrough: when everyone uses the same basket of criteria to evaluate opportunities, strategic alignment happens automatically. Political battles get exposed for what they are – territorial fights, not strategic debates. Teams make visible bets based on shared criteria.

The magic isn't in the criteria themselves – it's that everyone uses THE SAME criteria. This transforms resource allocation from political negotiation to strategic discipline. Your board sees clear rationale for every investment. Your leadership team can respond to competitive moves in days, not months. Your best talent knows exactly where to focus their energy.

A Brazilian pharmaceutical company used to spend months debating which therapeutic areas to pursue. Each executive brought different arguments: market size, competitive landscape, regulatory pathway, development costs. With their PMM visible and everyone using the same MOVE criteria, the debates shifted from opinion to evidence. Investment decisions became faster and more strategic.[10]

How to Build Your Product: Market Matrix

Framework: Strategic Segmentation → Financial Reality → MOVE Evaluation → Resource Allocation

[Products × Markets from Vision] → [Revenue/Margin/Profit/Volume] → [Advantage Scoring] → **[GREEN/YELLOW/BLUE priorities]**

Here's what a blank PMM looks like before you fill it with your strategic bets (Figure 6.1):

Each cell represents a strategic bet – a specific product offered to a specific market. The power comes from seeing all your bets at once and evaluating them with consistent criteria.

Step 1: Build Your Product-Market Matrix

Start with how you currently segment products and markets – probably by product line and channel. These come directly from the Vision you selected in Chapter 5 – you're working backward from your strategic direction. Then challenge whether these segments reveal where you can actually win.

MOVE TOOL 3A: Product-Matrix Matrix Where should we focus to win?

	P1	P2	P...
M1	$ Revenue % Gross Margin $ Profit # Volume	$ Revenue % Gross Margin $ Profit # Volume	$ Revenue % Gross Margin $ Profit # Volume
M2	$ Revenue % Gross Margin $ Profit # Volume	$ Revenue % Gross Margin $ Profit # Volume	$ Revenue % Gross Margin $ Profit # Volume
M...	$ Revenue % Gross Margin $ Profit # Volume	$ Revenue % Gross Margin $ Profit # Volume	$ Revenue % Gross Margin $ Profit # Volume

Figure 6.1 MOVE Tool #3A: Product-Market Matrix Blank Template.

Ask yourself:

Products

- What offerings enable premium pricing vs. price competition?
- What capabilities create customer dependency vs. easy switching?
- What solutions solve problems vs. provide commodities?

Markets

- What customer behaviors create profit vs. consume resources?
- What decision processes enable premium pricing vs. force bidding?
- What customer needs create loyalty vs. price sensitivity?

Step 2: Fill in the Numbers

Each PMM cell must contain four critical metrics that, when combined across all cells, represent 100% of your business:

- Revenue ($): Current annual revenue from this combination
- Margin (%): Gross margin or contribution margin percentage
- Profit ($): Absolute profit dollars generated (e.g., EBITDA, Operating Income)
- Volume (#): Units, customers, or transactions driving numbers

Start by filling in what numbers you have. Many companies find their data isn't organized by product-market combinations – use estimates where needed. The exercise often sparks valuable discussions, especially around cost allocation. Get something in every cell, even if it's initial estimates. You can refine numbers as you go.

Step 3: Strategic Evaluation Using MOVE Criteria

This is where strategic alignment becomes visible. Everyone evaluates every cell using the exact same criteria. No more sales pushing revenue while finance pushes margins while operations pushes safety. One basket of criteria oriented around competitive advantage.

MOVE Scoring Criteria

Score each cell using business essentials every executive understands:

Criteria	*Weight*	*Focus*
Profit $	35%	"Will this make money?"
Advantage (GP %)	30%	"Do I have an edge?"
Revenue $	20%	"Can I sell this?"
Growth %	10%	"Will this grow?"
Execution Risk	5%	"What's my risk?"

We allocate resources and focus business energies on Product-Market cells that best satisfy the **COMBINED criteria** – not individual executive preferences.

These weights aren't sacred – adjust based on your strategic context. Growth companies might weight Growth % higher. Turnarounds might weight Profit $ at 50%. The key is consistency: everyone uses the same weights for every decision.

How the scoring works: each cell gets scored 1–10 on each criterion. Multiply by the weight and add them up. See Farella's detailed scoring below for a complete example.

Total Score = (Profit × 35%) + (Advantage × 30%) + (Revenue × 20%) + (Growth × 10%) + (Risk × 5%)

Scoring Guidelines:

- Profit $: Based on absolute profit contribution and margin quality
- Advantage: Your competitive edge vs. alternatives (technology, brand, relationships)
- Revenue $: Market size and revenue potential
- Growth %: Expected annual growth rate over three years
- Execution Risk: Capability gaps, resource needs, complexity (10 = easy, 1 = very hard)

Based on the total score, cells fall into three categories:

- **GREEN (7.0–10.0):** Highest strategic priority: concentrate resources here
- **YELLOW (4.0–6.9):** Medium strategic priority: maintain and selectively invest
- **BLUE (1.0–3.9):** Low priority: minimize resources or consider exit

This isn't about good or bad. BLUE cells might be profitable – they're just not strategic. They don't build competitive advantage. They don't deserve growth investment.

Build one PMM for each fiscal year to see how your bets evolve. A cell that's BLUE today might turn YELLOW next year as you invest, then GREEN by year three as it gains traction. This multi-year view transforms PMM from a budget tool into a strategic roadmap – you can see which bets need patience vs. which should deliver immediately. Color-code the progression so the evolution becomes visible at a glance.

Think about what this means: your head of sales can no longer argue for low-margin revenue. Your CFO can't kill growth investments purely on risk. Your regional managers can't claim special circumstances. Everyone evaluates opportunities against the same visible scorecard.

Step 4: Ensure Cells Total 100% of Your Business

Double check that your PMM cells combined represent 100% of revenue, profit, and volume. If you're missing pieces, you're not seeing your complete resource allocation picture.

SIDEBAR: Cascading Product-Market Matrix Throughout the Organization

After building the corporate PMM, work with Regional Managers, Product Directors, Channel Leaders – they each build their own version of the PMM for their piece of the business.

This creates strategic alignment at scale:

- High-potentials learn to think strategically using the same methodology the CEO uses
- When someone who runs Retail Frozen Meals retires, you hand their replacement the PMM – they can see exactly what strategic bets were working, which weren't, and why
- Succession planning becomes strategic knowledge transfer, not just relationship handoffs
- Drives accountability – each leader owns their cells' performance
- Builds P&L acumen throughout the organization
- Creates foundation for quarterly business reviews – every QBR tracks cell performance

The power multiplies when every P&L owner uses the same framework. A regional manager's PMM rolls up into the corporate PMM. Their strategic bets align with corporate priorities because they're using the same criteria, same scoring, and same language. No translation needed between levels.

When evaluating internal promotions, look at how well managers improved their cells' colors. Did they move BLUE to YELLOW? YELLOW to GREEN? That's strategic leadership in action. This becomes your talent development system – identifying who can see and capture opportunity.

Strategic Segmentation: The Hidden Key to PMM Success

Most companies segment their business the way they always have – by product category and channel. That's accounting segmentation, not strategic segmentation.

Strategic segmentation reveals different opportunities. Take Farella Foods:

- Traditional (Legacy) Segmentation:
- By product line: Frozen, Snacks, Healthy
- By channel: Retail, Foodservice
- By geography: Regional divisions

Strategic Alternatives That Reveal Different Opportunities:

- By customer wellness journey: Prevention-focused, convenience-driven, price-conscious
- By purchase occasion: Planned meals, impulse snacks, health routines
- By price sensitivity: Premium seekers, value optimizers, price fighters
- By innovation adoption: Early adopters, fast followers, traditionalists

Each segmentation tells a different story and suggests different strategic moves. Power comes from testing multiple views before selecting the ONE that best reveals competitive advantage opportunities.

Process for Finding Your Strategic Segmentation:

1 Create three to four different segmentation approaches
2 Build a quick PMM for each to see what it reveals
3 Select the segmentation that best shows where you can win
4 Use that ONE segmentation to drive resource allocation

Trap: Many executives want to use multiple segmentations simultaneously. When marketing uses one view and sales uses another, you're pulling your company apart. Pick ONE strategic segmentation and align everyone around it.

This isn't academic theory – it's about preventing the "why are we doing both?" confusion that kills execution.

Putting Product-Market Matrix Into Practice: The Farella Journey

Back in the conference room, Daniel knew it was time to move from scattered Post-its to systematic resource allocation. They'd selected their "Win with Focus" vision. Now they needed to see where their resources would actually create competitive advantage.

Daniel stood at the front of the room, studying the scattered Post-it chaos on the matrix. Eighteen growth ideas, zero alignment. Time to translate this mess into strategic reality.

"Let's build our actual PMM with real numbers," he said. "Revenue, margin, profit, volume – by product and market. And we'll build it for each year through 2028 to see how our strategy evolves."

Jennifer Walsh resisted. "Our systems don't report this way. We track by product line and region, not strategic combinations."

Mark Chen, the COO, added his concern. "We're already stretched thin. How do we focus when every product contributes something?"

"That's exactly why we need this," Daniel countered. "Budgets show accounting structure. PMM shows strategic bets."

He paused, then added a crucial point. "Remember, we chose Market Penetration as our growth path in our Vision work. We're going deeper with current products in current markets. In strategy, it's smart to clean up your house first before thinking you need some eureka moment. Most companies have 20–30% improvement opportunity just by focusing on what they already do – they just can't see it because their bets aren't visible."

Over the next four hours, they built their strategic view of the business for 2025–2028. Dr. Raj Patel pulled technical data. Sarah validated market segments. Jennifer worked through margin calculations. The picture that emerged shocked them.

2025 PMM: Current State ($700M Total Revenue)

"Look at this reality," said Jennifer, studying the numbers. "Frozen Meals in Retail – $360M revenue at 28% margin. That's over half our revenue and profit. But we're treating it like a legacy business."

Sarah pointed to another revelation. "Snack Packs are 20% gross margin in Retail. We're barely breaking even after trade spend. Why are we investing there?"

The team scored each cell using MOVE criteria:

Frozen Meals:

- Retail: $360M revenue, 28% margin, $33M EBITDA – **YELLOW (6.2 score)**
- Foodservice: $120M revenue, 26% margin, $9M EBITDA – **YELLOW (5.8 score)**

Snack Packs:

- Retail: $100M revenue, 20% margin, $12M EBITDA – **BLUE (3.9 score)**
- Foodservice: $40M revenue, 18% margin, $2.5M EBITDA – **BLUE (3.2 score)**

Healthy Bowls:

- Retail: $50M revenue, 16% margin, $3M EBITDA – **YELLOW (4.5 score)**
- Foodservice: $30M revenue, 14% margin, $0.5M EBITDA – **BLUE (2.8 score)**

"We have zero GREEN cells," Michael observed. "Nothing we're doing today qualifies as high strategic priority. We're running a portfolio of mediocre bets."

"But look closer," Daniel said. "Frozen Meals has strong margins and scale. Healthy Bowls has growth potential despite current margins. Those align with our 'Win with Focus' strategy. Snack Packs? All BLUE cells – that's where we need to make hard choices."

The Strategic Debate

Mark defended Snack Packs: "They're 20% of revenue. We can't just abandon them."

"Watch what happens if we don't," Daniel projected the next slide. "If we keep investing equally everywhere, here's 2028."

He showed a scenario where they maintained current allocation patterns:

- Total Revenue: $750M (7% growth)
- Total EBITDA: $65M (8.7% margin)
- Still zero GREEN cells
- Continued margin pressure across all products

"Now watch what happens if we execute our 'Win with Focus' strategy," Daniel continued.

2026 PMM: Transition Year ($732M Total Revenue)

"Here's year two with focused investment in Frozen and Healthy, reduced support for Snacks."

Frozen Meals (Growing):

- Retail: $376M (+4.6%), maintaining 28% margin
- Foodservice: $126M (+4.6%), maintaining 26% margin
- Innovation investment starting to show

Snack Packs (Maintaining):

- Retail: $105M (+4.6%), margins flat
- Foodservice: $42M (+4.6%), margins flat
- Minimal investment, harvesting cash

Healthy Bowls (Accelerating):

- Retail: $52M (+4.6%), margins still low but volume growing
- Foodservice: $31M (+4.6%), building presence

"Notice what's happening," Jennifer calculated. "We're growing revenue to $732M while improving EBITDA to $64M. That's 8.7% margin vs. 8.6% today – but we're building momentum."

The scoring evolution showed progress:

- Frozen Meals Retail: Moving toward **GREEN (6.8)**
- Healthy Bowls Retail: Improving to **YELLOW (5.2)**
- Snack Packs: Remaining **BLUE**

2027 PMM: Acceleration ($765M Total Revenue)

"Year three is where the strategy really takes hold," Daniel continued.

Frozen Meals (Category Leader):

- Retail: $394M – Speed-to-market paying off – **GREEN (7.2)**
- Foodservice: $131M – Operational excellence showing – **YELLOW (6.5)**

Snack Packs (Optimized):

- Retail: $109M – Reduced SKUs, better margins
- Foodservice: $44M – Focused on profitable segments

Healthy Bowls (Breakthrough):

- Retail: $55M – Innovation engine working – **YELLOW (6.8)**
- Foodservice: $33M – Selected accounts only – **YELLOW (5.5)**

"By 2027, we have our first GREEN cell," Sarah noted. "Frozen Meals Retail becomes our growth engine at scale."

2028 PMM: Vision Realized ($800M Total Revenue)

"This is our destination," Daniel said, revealing the final PMM.

Strategic Portfolio:

- **Frozen Meals:** $549M total (69% of business) – Both cells **GREEN**
- **Snack Packs:** $160M total (20% of business) – Maintained but not grown
- **Healthy Bowls:** $91M total (11% of business) – Retail approaching **GREEN**

Financial Transformation:

- **Revenue: $800M** (14% total growth from 2025)
- **EBITDA: $73M** (9.2% margin vs. 8.6% in 2025)
- **3 GREEN cells, 2 YELLOW cells, 1 BLUE cell**

"**We've transformed from scattered mediocrity to focused excellence**," Daniel summarized. "Same products, same markets, but completely different resource allocation and strategic focus."

Jennifer added the critical insight for the board (Figure 6.2): "This 60 basis point margin improvement translates to roughly 15–20% higher enterprise value. We're not just improving operations – we're building a more valuable company."[11]

MOVE Criteria Scoring Applied

Michael Thompson pushed deeper. "Let's validate the scoring logic. Why does Frozen Meals Retail become GREEN?"

They worked through the scoring:

Frozen Meals Retail 2028 Score: 7.8 (GREEN)

- Profit $: $39M absolute profit (Score: 9/10 × 35% = 3.15)
- Advantage: Speed + clean label leadership (Score: 8/10 × 30% = 2.40)
- Revenue $: $411M scale matters (Score: 7/10 × 20% = 1.40)
- Growth %: 14% over 3 years (Score: 6/10 × 10% = 0.60)
- Execution Risk: Proven capabilities (Score: 7/10 × 5% = 0.35)
- Total: 7.9 = GREEN

"Compare that to Snack Packs Retail," Jennifer noted:

MOVE TOOL 3A: Product-Matrix Matrix Where should we focus to win?

Farella Foods PMM 2025-2028		2025			2026			2007			2028		
		Frozen Meals	Snack Packs	Healthy Bowls	Frozen Meals	Snack Packs	Healthy Bowls	Frozen Meals	Snack Packs	Healthy Bowls	Frozen Meals	Snack Packs	Healthy Bowls
Retail	Revenue ($MM)	$ 360	$ 100	$ 50	$ 376	$ 105	$ 52	$ 394	$ 109	$ 55	$ 411	$ 114	$ 57
	Gross Margin (%)	28	20	16	28	20	16	28	20	16	28	20	16
	EBITDA ($MM)	$ 33	$ 12	$ 3	$ 35	$ 14	$ 3	$ 37	$ 15	$ 3	$ 39	$ 17	$ 4
	Volume (MM units)	60	25	10	63	26.5	10.5	66	28	11	69	29.5	12
Foodservice	Revenue ($MM)	$ 120	$ 40	$ 30	$ 126	$ 42	$ 31	$ 131	$ 44	$ 33	$ 137	$ 46	$ 34
	Gross Margin (%)	26	18	14	26	18	14	26	18	14	26	18	14
	EBITDA ($MM)	$ 9	$ 3	$ 1	$ 10	$ 3	$ 1	$ 10	$ 3	$ 1	$ 11	$ 3	$ 1
	Volume (MM units)	20	10	6	21	10.5	6.5	22	11	7	23	11.5	7.5
Segment TOTAL	Revenue ($MM)	$ 480	$ 140	$ 80	$ 502	$ 146	$ 84	$ 525	$ 153	$ 88	$ 549	$ 160	$ 91
	Gross Margin (%)												
	EBITDA ($MM)	$ 42	$ 15	$ 4	## $ 44	$ 16	$ 4	# $ 47	$ 18	$ 4	# $ 50	$ 20	$ 4
	Volume (MM units)	80	35	16	0 84	37	17	0 88	39	18	0 92	41	19.5
Fiscal TOTAL	Revenue ($MM)			$ 700			$ 732			$ 765			$ 800
	EBITDA ($MM)			$ 60			$ 64			$ 69			$ 73

Priority and Emphasis

Criteria	Weight
Profit $	35%
Advantage (GP %)	30%
Revenue $	20%
Growth %	10%
Execution Risk	5%

High Priority | Medium Priority | Low Priority

Color scores reflect weighted evaluation across a basket of strategic criteria. Each Product - Market Combination is a Strategic Scenario

Figure 6.2 MOVE Tool #3A: Product-Market Matrix Farella Foods 2025–2028 Progression.

Snack Packs Retail 2028 Score: 3.8 (BLUE)

- Profit $: $16.5M with thin margins (Score: 4/10 × 35% = 1.40)
- Advantage: No differentiation (Score: 3/10 × 30% = 0.90)
- Revenue $: $114M modest scale (Score: 5/10 × 20% = 1.00)
- Growth %: 14% but from low base (Score: 4/10 × 10% = 0.40)
- Execution Risk: Easy but why bother (Score: 2/10 × 5% = 0.10)
- Total: 3.8 = BLUE

"The scoring makes our choices crystal clear," Mark admitted. "I was defending Snack Packs on revenue. But when you factor in advantage and profit quality, the strategic logic is undeniable."

Sarah saw the talent implications: "We need our best innovation people on Frozen Meals and Healthy Bowls. Why waste A-players on BLUE cells?"

Michael added the competitive insight: "If a competitor attacks our Frozen Meals Retail cell – our future GREEN engine – we need to respond fast. The PMM tells us exactly what to defend and what to let go."

Making your PMM visible transforms how you allocate resources. But static analysis in a dynamic market leaves you vulnerable. That's where AI changes the game – turning your PMM from an annual planning exercise into a living strategic system.

DO's and DON'Ts

DO:

- Segment by competitive advantage potential, not operational convenience
- Force financial reality into every cell with actual numbers
- Apply consistent MOVE criteria across all combinations
- Concentrate resources on GREEN cells ruthlessly
- Update PMM quarterly as market conditions change

DON'T:

- Accept generic segmentation that could apply to any company
- Hide poor performance behind complex allocation schemes
- Fund BLUE cells out of political courtesy
- Create PMM cells that can't be measured financially
- Let PMM become static planning document instead of dynamic allocation tool

Enhancing Your Product-Market Matrix with AI

PMM creates unprecedented visibility into your resource allocation. You've made your bets visible using shared criteria that align your entire organization. Now AI can help you test alternative segmentations, model resource scenarios, and optimize your PMM performance in real-time.

MOVE is your executive insights and judgment (INPUT) + systematic strategic questions (PROCESS) = better customer value and sustainable profit (OUTPUT). AI enhances PMM from annual planning exercise into real-time competitive advantage system.

How AI Magnifies Strategic Clarity

Once the scoring exercise was complete, Daniel stood at the edge of the room, arms crossed, taking it all in – four years of PMM, scored, structured, and sequenced. Each cell now told a story. Not just about potential, but about pressure. Investment. Timing. Trade-offs.

It was Michael Thompson who finally said what no one else had yet voiced.

"You know, this is the first time I've seen us move from slides to actual strategic clarity. We didn't just analyze – we can see exactly where to place our bets."

The group turned. Daniel gestured for him to elaborate.

Michael continued. "Think about how AI could enhance this. We could:

- Test alternative segmentations – maybe by customer wellness journey instead of just channel
- Forecast volume based on category growth patterns
- Benchmark margins against best-in-class competitors
- Identify risks we haven't considered
- Validate our Frozen Meals growth assumptions"

Important: Never input actual company strategies, financial data, or strategic plans into public AI tools. Use generic descriptions and anonymized examples to get insights while protecting confidential information.

AI Prompt Guidance

For Segmentation Intelligence: ***Prompt:*** "A food company currently segments by product type (frozen, snacks, healthy) and channel (retail, foodservice). What alternative segmentation approaches might reveal different strategic priorities? Consider customer behavior and competitive advantage."

- ***What you'll get:*** Hidden opportunity spaces and new ways to view your business
- ***How to use it:*** Test three to four segmentations before selecting the ONE that reveals where you can win

For PMM Construction: ***Prompt:*** "Help organize P&L data into a strategic product-market matrix showing Revenue, Margin %, Profit $, and Volume for each cell. My business has [X products] and [Y markets]. Score using criteria: Profit $ (35%), Advantage (30%), Revenue $ (20%), Growth % (10%), Risk (5%)."

- ***What you'll get:*** Structured framework with consistent scoring methodology
- ***How to use it:*** Create your initial PMM with clear evaluation criteria

For Scenario Testing: ***Prompt:*** "Model 3-year scenarios showing how cells evolve from low-priority to high-priority as investment shifts. What's the financial impact of moving 30% of resources from low-margin to high-margin cells?"

- ***What you'll get:*** Financial projections and risk flags for resource reallocation
- ***How to use it:*** Validate your strategic bets before committing capital

For Performance Tracking: ***Prompt:*** "Our frozen meals category is growing 4% annually below the 7% category average. Based on similar company patterns, should we double down, maintain, or reduce investment? What moves do patterns suggest?"

- ***What you'll get:*** Pattern-based recommendations from comparable situations
- ***How to use it:*** Make better decisions on underperforming cells

How Farella Applied AI to Their PMM

After building their initial PMM, Daniel's team used AI to pressure-test and optimize their resource allocation decisions.[12]

Their Segmentation Analysis: "We've segmented by product category and channel. What alternative segmentations might reveal different opportunities?"

AI's analysis suggested three alternatives they hadn't considered:

- By wellness journey stage (prevention, management, optimization)
- By purchase frequency (daily, weekly, monthly, special occasion)
- By price elasticity (premium insensitive, value conscious, price fighters)

"The wellness journey segmentation was eye-opening," Dr. Raj noted. "It showed that our Healthy Bowls and premium Frozen Meals serve the same 'optimization' customer. We should cross-sell, not compete internally."

Their Resource Reallocation Modeling: The team asked AI to model shifting resources from BLUE to GREEN cells over three years.

The analysis revealed:

- Year 1: $5M EBITDA impact as Snack Pack resources reduce
- Year 2: Break-even as Frozen and Healthy gain scale
- Year 3: $8M EBITDA gain from focused investment

"But look at this risk flag," Jennifer pointed out. "If we cut Snack Packs too fast, we lose shelf space that competitors capture. We need to manage the transition carefully."

Their Competitive Threat Assessment: AI identified three emerging threats to their GREEN cells:

1 Private-label frozen meals improving quality (high probability)
2 Meal kit companies adding frozen options (medium probability)
3 QSR chains expanding frozen retail (low but high-impact)

This shaped their execution timing. "We have a window," Daniel said, "but it's closing. We need to build our Frozen Meals advantage fast – speed-to-market becomes critical."

Their M&A Screen: The team asked AI to identify acquisition targets that would strengthen their GREEN cells.

"Look for companies with capabilities in clean-label frozen meals or innovative healthy bowls," they prompted. "Must have strong retail relationships and gross margins above 25%."

The analysis surfaced three regional brands that could accelerate their transformation. "Instead of building capabilities from scratch, we could acquire and scale," Jennifer noted. "The PMM scoring gives us clear acquisition criteria."

The AI-enhanced PMM transformed from a static planning tool into a dynamic decision system. Monthly updates, competitive alerts, and scenario modeling meant they could adjust resource allocation based on real market movements, not annual planning cycles.

Your Move

Right now, your executives are probably funding different strategies without realizing it. Resource allocation happens through political battles between competing priorities. Customers receive mixed signals. Execution feels hard because you're executing several strategies at once.

PMM makes your resource allocation visible and strategic. Instead of funding everything that sounds good, you invest systematically in combinations that generate competitive returns. But the real power comes from strategic alignment – when everyone uses the same criteria to make visible bets.

Daniel looked at the four PMMs his team had built.

"This is the first time in my career where I can see exactly where every dollar creates value. Not hoped-for value. Not political value. Real competitive advantage we can measure and manage."

Sarah nodded. "And everyone's using the same scorecard. No more fighting about my marketing priorities vs. Mark's operational needs. We all see which cells deserve investment."

Jennifer added the financial perspective: "Our 9.2% EBITDA target suddenly looks achievable. Not through cost cutting, but through strategic focus. We know exactly which cells drive margin improvement."

As they prepared to move to the next tool, Daniel made one final point:

"Most companies fund chaos and call it strategy. They spread resources across dozens of initiatives because they lack visible criteria for making hard choices. We just changed that. Our PMM doesn't just show where we're spending money – it shows whether those bets will actually win."

The breakthrough isn't having criteria – it's having SHARED criteria.

But even the best internal analysis needs external validation. You've made your bets visible with the PMM. Now you need to test whether those bets align with market reality.

Quick-Action Checklist

- □ Have each executive write their top 3 growth priorities
  Compare where they think resources should go
- □ Compare where executives think resources should go
  Look for alignment or chaos in priorities
- □ Map one product-market combination completely
  Revenue, margin, profit, volume for one cell
- □ Test if your budget categories match strategic priorities
  Do accounting lines match strategic bets?
- □ Identify which resource decisions took longest last cycle
  These reveal where alignment is weakest

Next: Chapter 7 introduces MRC – the second half of Tool #3 – showing you how to pressure-test your PMM bets against external market forces. Because making bets visible is only half the battle; validating they'll win is what separates strategy from hope.

Notes

1 H. Igor Ansoff, "Strategies for Diversification." *Harvard Business Review* 35, no. 5 (September-October 1957): 113–124.
2 Based on author's 25+ years consulting and client experience.
3 Based on author's 25+ years consulting and client experience.
4 Based on author's 25+ years consulting and client experience.
5 Target Corporation, "Annual Report 2022." Accessed January 2025, https://investors.target.com/annual-reports.
6 Bed Bath & Beyond Inc., "Form 8-K Bankruptcy Filing." U.S. Securities and Exchange Commission, April 23, 2023.
7 Target Corporation, "Q4 2022 Earnings Call Transcript." February 28, 2023.
8 Netflix Inc., "Q4 2023 Letter to Shareholders." January 23, 2024.
9 The Walt Disney Company, "Fiscal Year 2022 Annual Report." Accessed January 2025.
10 Based on author's 25+ years consulting and client experience.
11 Aswath Damodaran, "The Value of Control: Implications for Control Premiums, Minority Discounts and Voting Share Differentials." *NYU Stern School of Business*, June 2012.
12 Based on author's 25+ years consulting and client experience.

Chapter 7

Market Reality Check

Pressure-Test Your Bets

"You've built your strategy thinking as a management team – which is good. But do you have the customers and competition in the room to pressure-test your ideas?"

The Farella Foods [fictional example] executive team had just finished their PMM work. After intense debate and analysis, their PMMs for 2025 through 2028 were complete. Each cell – a specific product in a specific market – now held concrete financials: revenue, margins, EBITDA, and volume. They'd scored every combination using shared criteria: profit, advantage, revenue, growth, and risk.

The final step had been color-coding – GREEN for highest strategic priority, YELLOW for medium, BLUE for minimize or exit. For the first time in years, Daniel Ross could see exactly where their $700M in revenue was going and where it should go.

"This is what we've needed," Daniel said, studying the 2028 projection on the screen. "We're transforming from zero GREEN cells today to three GREEN cells by 2028. It's not just gut instinct anymore. Every choice has logic behind it."

Jennifer Walsh, who had initially resisted the PMM process, nodded. "Building these matrices forced us to confront reality. Frozen Meals in Retail becomes our growth engine. Healthy Bowls gains traction. Snack Packs... we maintain but don't invest. The path is clear."

But Michael Thompson, VP of Strategy, raised his hand.

"Can I share a concern?" Michael's voice was steady but serious. "We've built a beautiful internal view. But how much reflects what's actually happening out there?"

Daniel turned. "What specifically worries you?""We just labeled Frozen Meals Retail as GREEN – our biggest bet going forward. But based on what? Do we really know if private label is about to destroy our margins? What if Bravora launches a premium frozen line? Or if meal kits make frozen meals obsolete?"

The room fell silent.

Michael continued.

"We've all seen this movie before. Management team agrees in the conference room, makes big bets, then discovers the market moved in a different direction. I suggest we do something different: pressure-test each PMM cell against market reality. No PowerPoint decks. Just one sheet per cell. Hard questions. Real answers."

Daniel studied the PMM on the wall – six cells representing their entire business. "If we're betting our transformation on Frozen Meals and Healthy Bowls, we better validate those assumptions."

He made the call. "We're doing a Market Reality Check – MRC for short. Every cell gets external validation. Michael, you coordinate. I want real intelligence, not internal opinions. Tap

DOI: 10.4324/9781003682455-10

whatever sources we need – industry reports, customer feedback, competitive intelligence. But I want truth, not narrative."

The room's energy shifted. This wasn't about slowing down – it was about getting smarter before placing bigger bets.

Daniel ended with clarity: "We're not running a strategy exercise. We're allocating real capital. Let's act like it."

Why Smart Teams Build Strategy in Echo Chambers

For decades, companies relied on internal analysis because external intelligence was expensive and slow. Teams defaulted to internal assumptions because external validation took months and cost millions.

But here's what makes this dangerous: internal thinking creates blind spots no matter how smart your team is. You get ten executives agreeing in a conference room and everyone feels aligned. But that's not strategy – that's an echo chamber.

This pattern plays out predictably. A consumer goods company invests heavily in premium products because executives agree "consumers are trading up." Then Nielsen data reveals their target customers are actually trading down due to inflation. The market moved while they were agreeing with each other.

Having worked with leadership teams across industries, one pattern stands out: experienced executives sometimes mistake their expertise for market reality. That CEO who built the business over 20 years brings invaluable wisdom but also carries assumptions that may no longer hold.[1]

The most painful part? By the time companies get comprehensive market studies, competitors have already moved. You spend six months on research only to confirm what your sales team has been saying all along.

When Market Validation Saves Companies – And When Its Absence Destroys Them

Best Buy's Reality Check (2012)

Best Buy faced existential threat from "showrooming" – customers browsing in-store then buying on Amazon. Internal analysis suggested matching Amazon's prices and cutting costs.

CEO Hubert Joly insisted on validating assumptions with customers:

- **Market Reality**: Customers wanted expertise and immediate gratification, not just price
- **Competitor Blind Spot**: Amazon couldn't provide hands-on help or same-day availability
- **Customer Truth**: They'd pay more for service and convenience

Strategic Pivot: Instead of competing on price, Best Buy transformed stores into experience centers. Added services Amazon couldn't match – installation, tech support, and immediate pickup.

Result: Stock price increased 600% from 2012 to 2019 while Circuit City and others died. They won by checking what customers actually valued, not what executives assumed.[2]

Quibi's Reality Avoidance (2020)

Quibi executives built strategy on internal conviction: mobile-first premium content would revolutionize entertainment. They raised $1.75B based on founder credibility.

If they'd validated market assumptions:

- **User Behavior**: People watch mobile video during commutes – which disappeared during COVID
- **Competition**: TikTok and YouTube already owned short-form; Netflix owned premium
- **Value Proposition**: No clear reason to pay for what was free elsewhere
- **Market Size**: Their projected audience didn't exist

But they avoided external validation. When skeptics questioned assumptions, leadership dismissed concerns.

Result: Shut down after six months, losing $1.75B. All because assumptions went untested.[3]

The Hidden Cost of Internal-Only Strategy

Companies skipping external validation pay for it in other ways. While you perfect internal analysis, competitors who check market reality capture emerging opportunities. You fund bets based on beliefs while they invest based on evidence. Most painful: you optimize for yesterday's reality while markets evolve around you.

Retail pharmacy chains learned this lesson painfully. They identified convenience as their advantage – thousands of locations, quick service, trusted pharmacists. They invested billions in store expansion.

What they missed: convenience was redefined by Amazon and mail-order pharmacies. Those physical locations became liabilities. "Quick service" meant same-day delivery, not ten-minute drives. The competitive advantage they optimized for had already expired.

By the time they recognized this external reality, significant share was lost to digital players.

The MOVE Solution: Market Reality Check

(MRC) overlays external market intelligence on your PMM to validate or challenge strategic bets before major resource commitments.

The One Question It Answers: "Does external market evidence support our strategic bets, or are we making expensive assumptions about market reality?"

Framework: Same PMM Structure + Market Questions = External Validation

[Your existing GREEN/YELLOW/BLUE priorities] + [Market intelligence] = [Validated or adjusted bets]

Why This Creates Breakthrough Value

Systematically checking external reality functions as an early warning system. It surfaces market shifts before they hit your P&L.

Food manufacturers provide clear examples. Many identify foodservice as stable, reliable revenue – long contracts, predictable volumes, good relationships. When they validate against market data, they discover that segment is actually shrinking as on-site dining decreases while delivery explodes.

Companies that reallocate early capture the delivery opportunity. Those that don't wonder why their "stable" business keeps missing targets. The difference? Checking assumptions against reality.

How to Build Your Market Reality Check

Step 1: Start with Your PMM Structure

Take your completed PMM exactly as built – same products, same markets, same GREEN/YELLOW/BLUE designations. Don't modify anything. You're about to overlay market reality on internal assessments.

This sequencing matters: start with what you believe internally, then test it externally. If you begin with external data, you'll rationalize why your internal view is still correct. Starting with internal beliefs makes gaps impossible to ignore (Figure 7.1).

Step 2: Apply Market Questions to Each Cell

For each cell in your PMM, gather intelligence on:

1 **Market Size:** What's the total addressable market?
2 **Growth Rate:** Is it expanding or contracting?
3 **Market Share:** What's your current position?
4 **Why Customers Buy:** What really drives decisions?

MOVE TOOL 3B: Market Reality Check Do our bets match the market?

Color should match PMM - shown Black and White here	Question	Frozen Meals	Snack Packs	Healthy Bowls
Retail	*1. Estimated market size and revenue opportunity ($)*			
	2. Growth rate for this product/segment			
	3. Farella revenue estimate and market share			
	4. Why the customer buys?			
	5. Who are the top 3 current competitors?			
	6. Top 2 future competitors (names or types)			
	7. Risks shaping demand			
	8. Market or buyer dynamics influencing vendor preference or loyalty			
	9. Who is the customer buyer (economic or decision maker)			
Foodservice	*1. Estimated market size and revenue opportunity ($)*			
	2. Growth rate for this product/segment			
	3. Farella revenue estimate and market share			
	4. Why the customer buys			
	5. Who are the top 3 current competitors?			
	6. Top 2 future competitors (names or types)			
	7. Risks shaping demand			
	8. Market or buyer dynamics influencing vendor preference or loyalty			
	9. Who is the customer buyer (economic or decision maker)?			

Figure 7.1 MOVE Tool #3B: Market Reality Check Blank Template.

5 **Current Competition:** Who are you actually competing against?
6 **Future Competition:** Who could enter this space?

These questions need specificity. Don't ask "Who are our competitors?" Ask "Which specific companies are targeting frozen meals in retail?" or "What three startups could disrupt healthy bowls in foodservice?" The specificity forces better thinking and prevents consolidated responses like "everyone in food."

For future competition, push further: "What would the ideal business model look like for this cell?" or "Which companies from adjacent industries have the capabilities to win here?" This reveals threats you might miss by only watching current competitors.

7 **Market Risks**: What could disrupt demand?
8 **Buyer Dynamics:** What influences loyalty and switching?
9 **Decision Makers:** Who actually controls the purchase?

These nine questions form your baseline. But you can have fewer or different questions – just know what you're trying to answer and how it supports better decision making. Software companies might focus on technology adoption rates. Healthcare companies track regulatory approvals. Retailers monitor e-commerce penetration.

The key isn't the number of questions – it's asking the right ones for your business. Start with market size and growth (fundamental economics), add competitive dynamics (who you're fighting), then layer in customer behavior (why they choose). Additional questions should address your specific strategic uncertainties.

Reality Check: Most companies already have competitive intelligence they barely use. Market reports sitting unread. Industry subscriptions on auto-renew that no one accesses. Before seeking new data, check what you already own. You probably have more intelligence than you think.

Step 3: Compare Internal Confidence vs. External Reality

You've already gathered external intelligence in SA (Tool #1). Your Vision reflects outside-in thinking. Your PMM cells were scored using those insights.

So why do MRC? Because markets move. Competitors act. New data emerges. You need to verify whether your specific bets – your actual resource allocation – align with current reality, not the snapshot from months ago.

The Linked Logic of MOVE: This isn't a random check – it's the critical third validation in your strategic logic chain:

- **MOVE 1 (SA)**: You started outside-in, identifying external trends and market realities
- **MOVE 2 (VDF)**: You built strategic options grounded in those realities, then selected one
- **MOVE 3A (PMM)**: You made that Vision tangible – specific bets by product and market, year by year
- **MOVE 3B (MRC)**: Now you pressure-test those specific bets against current market evidence

By this point, your Vision has taken on a life of its own. Executives can see it unfolding year by year in the PMM. But that clarity can create blinders – you fall in love with your own strategy. The MRC forces you back outside the office walls to check: Are we missing something? Have markets shifted? Who's coming after our specific bets?

This linked logic matters enormously for board conversations. When directors ask about competition, you're not scrambling for generic answers. You can say: "For our Frozen Meals Retail bet, we face Bravora moving upmarket and Trader Joe's premium private label. Here's our specific response...." You're explaining competition relative to your actual resource allocation, not giving a general market overview.

Systematically compare:

- Do your GREEN cells still align with the external trends you identified?
- Have market dynamics shifted since you built your Vision?
- Which PMM cells have market evidence supporting your scores?
- Where does internal confidence contradict external data?
- Which assumptions need urgent revalidation?

This isn't starting over – it's confirming your strategic logic still holds. **You're looking for holes in your strategy before competitors find them.**

Prioritizing Your Market Reality Check Effort

Here's what many executives miss: **not every PMM cell deserves equal validation effort**. Your GREEN cells – where you're betting millions in growth investment – need deep, continuous validation. Your BLUE cells – where you're harvesting cash with minimal investment – need basic monitoring at most.

Think about it strategically:

- **GREEN cells**: Full MRC with all questions, monthly updates, senior team ownership
- **YELLOW cells**: Standard MRC, quarterly updates, delegate to directors
- **BLUE cells**: Light validation, annual check-ins, operational monitoring

This prioritization serves multiple purposes. First, it focuses effort where money flows. Why spend weeks validating a BLUE cell you're planning to exit? Second, it creates development opportunities. Assigning YELLOW cell MRCs to high-potentials lifts their thinking from functional silos to strategic integration – they start seeing **products × markets × capabilities × competition** as an integrated system.

With GenAI, this tiered approach becomes even more powerful. Instead of buying market reports that are outdated on arrival, you can get real-time intelligence on your GREEN cells while automating basic monitoring for BLUE cells. One CPG executive told us: "We used to buy $2M in market reports annually that no one read. Now we spend $200K on AI tools that give us daily updates on what actually matters."[4]

The transformation goes beyond efficiency. When functional leaders build MRCs for their cells, they stop thinking just about their department and start thinking about competitive dynamics, market evolution, and capability requirements. A head of sales analyzing their cell suddenly sees why R&D capabilities matter. An operations leader recognizes how customer preferences drive complexity. The MRC becomes a strategic development system, not just a validation tool.

Putting Market Reality Check into Practice: The Farella Journey

Two weeks after launching the MRC, Daniel reconvened the team. The results were in – six MRCs, one for each Product-Market cell. Each contained field intelligence from customer interviews, industry reports, store visits, and competitive analysis.

"Let's go cell by cell," Daniel said. "And remember – we want truth, not confirmation of what we already believe."

Cell 1: Frozen Meals: Retail

Their future GREEN cell. The MRC revealed complex dynamics.

Market Intelligence

- **Market Size**: $5.5B in retail frozen meals
- **Growth**: 3% annually – steady but not spectacular
- **Share**: Farella at 6.5% (#4 player)
- **Why Customers Buy**: Convenience, price, brand familiarity
- **Current Competition**: Bravora Foods, Nestlé, ConAgra
- **Future Threats**: Specific companies like Freshly (acquired by Nestlé), Factor (HelloFresh), and, surprisingly, Trader Joe's private label moving upmarket
- **Key Risk**: Margin compression from private label

"The specificity helps," Jennifer noted. "It's not just 'private label threat.' It's **Bravora launching 'Chef-Inspired' line and Trader Joe's adding premium frozen at $4.99** vs. **our $6.00.**"

Michael added insights from AI analysis: "The ideal attacker for this cell would have automated production, direct-to-store delivery, and influencer marketing. **That describes Amazon's Fresh brand perfectly.** They're not here yet, but they have every capability needed."

Sarah shared store intelligence: "**Wegmans is testing a 'fresh-frozen' concept** – made daily, frozen same day, premium pricing. If that model works, every regional grocer could become a competitor."

Strategic Insight: Market supports GREEN designation but specific competitive threats require faster innovation. **Watch Trader Joe's model closely – they're teaching consumers that private label can be premium.**

Cell 2: Frozen Meals: Foodservice

Currently YELLOW, trending stable.

Market Intelligence

- **Market Size**: $2.5B institutional frozen
- **Growth**: 2% – basically inflation
- **Share**: Farella at 4.8%
- **Why They Buy**: Bulk value, consistency, operational simplicity
- **Current Competition**: BoxTop Kitchen, Sysco, US Foods
- **Future Threats**: Ghost kitchens, fresh-prepared alternatives
- **Key Risk**: Contract consolidation

Mark Chen shared operational reality: "BoxTop just won two districts we've served for ten years. Their 99.5% on-time delivery guarantee beat our 94% track record."

Strategic Insight: Confirms YELLOW status. Reliable cash flow but not strategic. BoxTop's operational excellence is hard to match without major investment.

Cell 3: Snack Packs: Retail

Currently BLUE in their PMM.

Market Intelligence

- **Market Size**: $2.0B and fragmented
- **Growth**: 5% but volatile by segment
- **Share**: Farella at 5%
- **Why They Buy**: Portability, kid-friendly, value multi-packs

- **Current Competition**: Bravora, Kraft Heinz, Mondelez
- **Future Threats**: DTC snack brands, healthy alternatives
- **Key Risk**: High SKU churn, promotional intensity

"This validates our BLUE designation," Dr. Raj observed. "Innovation cycles are six months, margins are terrible, and every competitor is fighting for the same shelf space."

Strategic Insight: MRC confirms minimize investment. Harvest cash but don't chase growth.

Cell 4: Snack Packs: Foodservice

Small but stable BLUE cell.

Market Intelligence

- **Market Size**: $1.0B vending and cafeteria
- **Growth**: 4% driven by convenience locations
- **Share**: Farella at 4%
- **Why They Buy**: Compliance packaging, extended shelf life, portion control
- **Current Competition**: BoxTop, Aramark, Compass
- **Future Threats**: Healthier vending options, fresh alternatives

"Surprising stability," Michael noted. "Not exciting but predictable revenue with decent margins in vending channels."

Strategic Insight: Keep as cash generator. Minimal investment, maximum efficiency.

Cell 5: Healthy Bowls: Retail

Currently YELLOW with growth potential.

Market Intelligence

- **Market Size**: $1.2B and expanding
- **Growth**: 8% – fastest growing segment
- **Share**: Farella at 4.2%
- **Why Customers Buy**: Health trends, Instagram-worthy, clean labels
- **Current Competition**: NüWave Naturals, Amy's, Luvo
- **Future Threats**: Sweetgreen launching frozen line, Daily Harvest expanding from smoothies, Whole Foods 365 brand moving into bowls
- **Key Risk**: Trend volatility, high development costs

Sarah's eyes lit up. "This specificity changes everything. It's not 'meal kit competition' – it's **Sweetgreen specifically taking their restaurant bowls to freezer.** They have brand permission we don't."

Dr. Raj analyzed the threat: "**Daily Harvest has subscription model mastery and vertical integration** from farm to freezer. But they're venture-funded and burning cash. We could outlast them with patience."

Michael shared AI findings: "The ideal business model for this cell combines fresh restaurant credibility with frozen convenience. **That's why Chipotle and Cava are both exploring frozen.** They have health halos we'd need years to build."

Strategic Insight: Upgrade to potential GREEN but watch specific restaurant-to-retail moves. **Partner with a fast-casual brand before they go alone?** NüWave's freshness complexity creates opportunity, but restaurant brands entering frozen pose real threat.

Cell 6: Healthy Bowls: Foodservice

Small but interesting YELLOW cell.

Market Intelligence

- **Market Size**: $800M corporate wellness
- **Growth**: 6% as employers focus on health
- **Share**: Farella at 3.75%
- **Why They Buy**: Employee wellness programs, nutrition requirements
- **Current Competition**: NüWave, BoxTop, custom integrators
- **Future Threats**: Tech-enabled nutrition platforms
- **Key Risk**: Customization demands

"Corporate cafeterias want healthy options but need operational simplicity," Mark observed. "Our frozen format actually advantages us over NüWave's fresh complexity."

Strategic Insight: Confirms YELLOW trending GREEN. Underexploited opportunity aligned with capabilities.

Strategic Realignment Based on Reality

Daniel summarized what the MRC revealed:

> Our core thesis holds – Frozen Meals Retail can be our growth engine, but we need innovation speed to combat private label. The surprise is Healthy Bowls growing faster than modeled, with competition more vulnerable than we thought.

The team had learned something else critical: they didn't need perfect data on every cell. Their BLUE Snack Packs cells needed basic monitoring – why overanalyze what you're not investing in? But their future GREEN cells (Frozen Meals Retail, potentially Healthy Bowls Retail) needed continuous intelligence.

"Let's be smart about follow-up," Michael suggested. "Monthly updates on GREEN cells using AI monitoring. Quarterly checks on YELLOW. Annual review for BLUE unless something dramatic changes."

Sarah saw the development opportunity: "Can we assign each YELLOW cell to a high-potential manager? Building an MRC forces you to think strategically – understanding market dynamics, competitive moves, capability requirements. It's perfect development."

"Exactly," Daniel agreed. "And it lifts people out of functional thinking. When you own a cell, you can't just think about marketing or operations. You have to integrate everything – products, markets, capabilities, competition."

The MRC crystallized strategic priorities:

Validated Bets:

- Frozen Meals Retail as GREEN – but requires constant innovation
- Snack Packs as BLUE – harvest cash, minimize investment
- Healthy Bowls undervalued – consider accelerating

Adjusted Actions:

- Accelerate clean-label frozen innovation to combat Bravora
- Exploit NüWave's fresh complexity in Healthy Bowls
- Improve foodservice delivery metrics to defend against BoxTop

Jennifer calculated impact: "If we shift resources based on these insights – accelerate Healthy Bowls, defend Frozen margins through innovation – we could exceed our 9.2% EBITDA target."

"More importantly," Daniel added (Figure 7.2), "we've validated our transformation with market evidence, not just internal conviction. When the board asks about our strategy, I can explain exactly who threatens each bet and how we'll respond."

The consensus was clear: PMM gave them strategic focus. MRC gave them strategic confidence – and board-ready answers about competitive reality.

Other Success Stories

Domino's Pizza Reality Check (2010)

Domino's faced brutal reality: last in taste tests, losing share, stock at $7. Internal view suggested improving marketing and promotions.

CEO Patrick Doyle demanded honest customer feedback:

- **Market Reality**: "Your pizza tastes like cardboard"
- **Competition**: Local pizzerias winning on quality
- **Customer Truth**: They'd forgiven taste for convenience – until delivery apps made everyone convenient

MOVE TOOL 3B: Market Reality Check Do our bets match the market?

Color should match PMM - shown Black and White here	Question	Frozen Meals	Snack Packs	Healthy Bowls
Retail	*1. Estimated market size and revenue opportunity ($)*	$5.5B	$2.0B	$1.2B
	2. Growth rate for this product/segment	3%	5%	8%
	3. Farella revenue estimate and market share	$360M (6.5%)	$100M (5%)	$50M (4.2%)
	4. Why the customer buys?	Convenience, price, brand familiarity	Healthy snacking, portability	Health, nutrition, trend-driven innovation
	5. Who are the top 3 current competitors?	Bravora, Nestlé, Conagra	Bravora, Kraft Heinz, Mondelez	NüWave, Amy's, Luvo
	6. Top 2 future competitors (names or types)	AI-native disruptors, private label growth	Direct-to-consumer brands, bundling plays	Plant-based innovators, custom diet platforms
	7. Risks shaping demand	Margin pressure, shifting consumer tastes	High SKU churn, packaging cost	Trendy but short cycles, high development cost
	8. Market or buyer dynamics influencing vendor preference or loyalty	Shelf space rotation, retailer negotiations	Impulse purchase dynamics, kid-targeting	Clean label demands, online reviews
	9. Who is the customer buyer (economic or decision maker)	Grocery category manager	Category manager, promotional planner	Wellness category lead
Foodservice	*1. Estimated market size and revenue opportunity ($)*	$2.5B	$1.0B	$800M
	2. Growth rate for this product/segment	2%	4%	6%
	3. Farella revenue estimate and market share	$120M (4.8%)	$40M (4%)	$30M (3.75%)
	4. Why the customer buys	Bulk value, consistency, speed	Portability, compliance, cost control	Health and wellness mandates
	5. Who are the top 3 current competitors?	BoxTop, Sysco, US Foods	BoxTop, Aramark, Compass Group	NüWave, BoxTop, Custom integrators
	6. Top 2 future competitors (names or types)	Ghost kitchens, AI meal prep systems	Vending innovators, school nutrition players	Dietician-driven food platforms, AI personalization
	7. Risks shaping demand	Contract churn, price bidding	Seasonal demand shifts, price sensitivity	Niche menus, training overhead
	8. Market or buyer dynamics influencing vendor preference or loyalty	Volume-based selection, delivery logistics	RFP cycles, institutional loyalty	Customization demand, ingredient sourcing
	9. Who is the customer buyer (economic or decision maker)?	Procurement officer, kitchen ops lead	Foodservice director, vending ops	Institutional wellness lead, chef/ops head

Figure 7.2 MOVE Tool #3B: Market Reality Check Farella Foods Example.

Strategic Response: Complete recipe overhaul, admitted failure publicly, showed transformation transparently.

Result: Stock went from $7 to $300+ by 2020. They won by acknowledging market reality rather than internal rationalization.[5]

Netflix International Reality Check (2016)

Netflix debated international expansion pace. U.S. success suggested replicating the model globally.

Market validation revealed critical differences:

- **Content Preferences**: Local content dominated viewing in most markets
- **Competition**: Strong regional players with local advantages
- **Payment Methods**: Credit card penetration limiting in many markets
- **Infrastructure**: Broadband speeds varying dramatically

Strategic Adjustment: Massive investment in local content, payment partnerships, adaptive streaming technology.

Result: International became majority of subscribers. They succeeded by adapting strategy to market realities rather than forcing U.S. model globally.[6]

Enhancing Your Market Reality Check with AI

After reviewing the complete MRC results, Daniel asked the question on everyone's mind:

"How did we miss Healthy Bowls growing at 8%? Or Bravora moving into premium frozen? Or BoxTop's delivery advantage?"

Michael answered directly: "Because we see our market through our own lens. AI helped us see it through multiple perspectives – customers, competitors, analysts, trends – all at once."

DO's and DON'Ts with Market Reality Check

DO:

- Use multiple data sources but accept uncertainty – perfect data doesn't exist
- Focus on directional insights – is the market growing or shrinking?
- Update continuously as markets move faster
- Act on uncomfortable truths even when they contradict plans
- Connect findings directly to resource decisions

DON'T:

- Wait for perfect data before making decisions
- Ignore evidence that challenges existing strategy
- Treat this as a research exercise – it's a decision tool
- Get paralyzed by analysis – move when direction is clear
- Confuse market research reports with competitive intelligence

The team had used AI throughout the MRC process. Not to replace judgment, but to accelerate intelligence gathering and find patterns humans miss.

The AI-Powered Transformation: What used to take months of consultant research now happens in real-time. Instead of buying static market reports, you get dynamic intelligence. Most importantly, AI enables the continuous validation that makes MRC a living system, not a one-time exercise.

Think about what this means:

- **Your GREEN cells get daily monitoring**: AI tracks every competitive move, patent filing, or customer shift
- **Specific threats get named:** Not "private label competition" but "Trader Joe's launching premium frozen line Q2"
- **Weak signals surface early:** That restaurant chain hiring frozen food experts becomes visible
- **Your team thinks strategically:** Every manager can access CEO-level market intelligence

Why AI Amplifies Market Intelligence

Processes Data Faster: Scans competitive moves, customer reviews, and market trends across thousands of sources while finding patterns invisible to human analysis

Tests Multiple Scenarios: Models how different market changes impact each PMM cell – recession, new competitors, regulatory shifts – with probability weights

Tracks Weak Signals: Identifies emerging threats before they become obvious – patent filings, hiring patterns, partnership announcements

Enables Real-Time Updates: Instead of annual market reports gathering dust, get daily intelligence on GREEN cells, weekly on YELLOW, monthly on BLUE

Companies succeeding with AI-enhanced MRC treat it like a strategic analyst who monitors everything but only alerts on what matters for specific PMM cells. More importantly, they've discovered **AI democratizes strategic thinking**. That high-potential analyzing a YELLOW cell can access the same market intelligence as the CEO. They see patterns across products, markets, capabilities, and competition that functional roles typically miss.

One retail executive explained the transformation: "We used to buy market reports for $50K that were obsolete on delivery. Now our managers use AI to get real-time intelligence for their cells. They're thinking like general managers, not functional heads. The strategic capability building is worth more than the market intelligence."[7]

How to Use AI with Your Market Reality Check

Market Intelligence Enhancement Process:

1 Complete initial MRC using available data
2 Use AI to expand market sizing with comprehensive sources
3 Ask AI to identify competitive patterns and emerging threats
4 Set up monitoring for continuous intelligence updates
5 Update strategic bets as signals emerge – don't wait for quarterly reviews

A European food company used AI to monitor 500+ competitors across their PMM. AI surfaced three critical insights: Asian competitors entering their GREEN cells, customer preferences shifting from taste to sustainability, and regulatory changes that would reshape their market. They adjusted strategy nine months before competitors noticed.

Data Security Note

Use your company's secure AI environment if available. For sensitive data:

- Use enterprise AI platforms with data protection agreements
- Check if your company has approved AI tools with security protocols
- Never use public AI tools for confidential information
- When in doubt, anonymize all company data

Rule of thumb: If you wouldn't share it with a competitor, don't put it in a public AI tool.

AI Prompt+ Guidance

For Market Sizing Validation: ***Prompt:*** "Analyze total addressable market for [frozen meals/healthy snacks/wellness bowls] in [retail/foodservice] channels across [United States]. Include industry reports, government data, and analyst estimates. Reconcile conflicting estimates and explain discrepancies."

- ***What you'll get:*** Multiple market size estimates with source credibility assessment
- ***How to use it:*** Validate whether your market assumptions are realistic

For Competitive Intelligence: ***Prompt:*** "Which specific companies (name them) are best positioned to enter the [frozen meals retail / healthy bowls foodservice] segment in the next 18 months? Consider companies from adjacent industries, restaurant chains going retail, tech companies entering food, or international players. What would their ideal business model look like for this specific cell?"

- ***What you'll get:*** Named companies with specific capabilities that threaten your cell
- ***How to use it:*** Track these specific companies, not generic 'competition'

For Business Model Disruption: ***Prompt:*** "What would the perfect business model look like to disrupt [specific product-market cell]? Consider unit economics, distribution advantages, technology leverage, and customer acquisition. Which three companies have the closest capabilities to execute this model?"

- ***What you'll get:*** Clear view of how disruption might happen and who could do it
- ***How to use it:*** Build defenses against specific models, not general threats

For Customer Behavior Analysis: ***Prompt:*** "Analyze recent customer reviews, social media mentions, and purchase behavior data for [frozen meals/healthy bowls] to identify what factors actually drive purchase decisions. How are these priorities changing?"

- ***What you'll get:*** Real customer voice beyond what they tell you in surveys
- ***How to use it:*** Align innovation priorities with actual purchase drivers

For Scenario Planning: ***Prompt:*** "Model how our Market Reality Check would change under three scenarios: economic recession reduces food spending 10%, private-label quality improves to match brands, or meal kits capture 20% of frozen meal occasions. Which strategic bets remain attractive?"

- ***What you'll get:*** Stress-tested view of which cells stay GREEN under pressure
- ***How to use it:*** Build resilient strategy that works across scenarios

For Gap Analysis: ***Prompt:*** "Compare these internal assumptions [list your PMM scores] with these market indicators [list your MRC findings]. Where are the biggest disconnects between internal confidence and market evidence? Rank gaps by potential impact."

- ***What you'll get:*** Prioritized list of dangerous assumptions requiring attention
- ***How to use it:*** Focus validation efforts on highest-risk bets

How Farella Applied AI to Their Market Reality Check

Their Market Evolution Analysis: "How are purchase drivers evolving differently across Frozen Meals, Snack Packs, and Healthy Bowls categories?"

AI revealed diverging trajectories:

- Frozen Meals: Convenience remains king but clean label becoming table stakes
- Snack Packs: Price and promotion sensitivity increasing – race to bottom
- Healthy Bowls: Instagram-worthiness drives trial, taste drives repeat

"This shapes our innovation immediately," Dr. Raj noted. "Frozen needs clean label fast. Healthy Bowls needs visual appeal."

Their Competitive Pattern Recognition: "What strategic moves by Bravora Foods, NüWave Naturals, and BoxTop Kitchen signal their future direction?"

AI identified telling patterns:

- Bravora: Hiring food scientists and chefs – moving beyond price into quality
- NüWave: Raising Series C funding – capacity expansion coming
- BoxTop: Acquiring route optimization software – doubling down on delivery

"But the real insights came from cell-specific analysis," Michael explained. "We asked AI which companies could disrupt each cell specifically."

Their Cell-Specific Threat Analysis: "Which specific companies could enter Frozen Meals Retail with advantage?"

AI revealed unexpected threats:

- **Trader Joe's**: Testing automated micro-factories for store-made frozen meals
- **Costco**: Developing premium Kirkland frozen meals with restaurant partners
- **Amazon Fresh**: Building frozen meal capabilities through Whole Foods kitchens
- **Regional grocers**: Wegmans, HEB, Publix, all exploring "fresh-frozen" concepts

"**These aren't on our traditional competitor radar**," Daniel realized. "We watch Nestlé and ConAgra while retailers build capabilities to compete directly."

Their Ideal Attacker Analysis: "What would the perfect business model look like to win in Healthy Bowls Retail?"

AI outlined the threat profile:

- Restaurant brand credibility (health halo)
- Subscription-based D2C capability
- Vertical integration from ingredients to freezer
- Social media native marketing
- $15–20 price point acceptance

"**That describes Sweetgreen, Chipotle, or Cava perfectly**," Sarah noted. "They have everything except frozen operations – which they could build or acquire."

Their Customer Journey Mapping: AI analyzed thousands of purchase reviews to map actual behavior:

- Frozen Meal buyers spend eight seconds choosing – packaging critical
- Healthy Bowl buyers read ingredients – transparency wins
- Snack Pack purchases 65% promotional – dangerous dependency

This shaped go-to-market priorities immediately.

Your Move

Right now, your leadership team has probably built strategic plans based on beliefs about your markets. Many beliefs are likely correct. But some could be dangerously wrong. The expensive part is discovering which ones after you've committed resources.

MRC prevents those painful surprises. You know the ones – where you've invested heavily before discovering the market moved differently than expected.

Here's what works:

1. Start with your completed PMM – don't change it
2. Apply market questions to each cell systematically
3. Prioritize **validation effort by cell color** – GREEN cells need deep, continuous validation
4. Use existing intelligence first – you have more than you think
5. Delegate **MRCs to develop strategic thinking** – lift functional leaders to enterprise view
6. Compare internal beliefs vs. external evidence
7. Adjust resource allocation based on gaps
8. Update **continuously with AI** – real-time beats annual reports every time

Your PMM shows where you want to win. MRC shows where you actually can win. The gap between those two insights determines whether your strategy succeeds or fails.

As Daniel told his team: "The MRC didn't change our strategy – it made it smarter. We're still betting on Frozen Meals and Healthy Bowls. But now we know exactly what we're up against and how fast we need to move."

More importantly, the MRC process itself transforms organizational capability. When every leader owns a cell and validates its market reality, you build strategic thinkers at scale. They stop seeing their functional silo and start seeing the integrated business – **products × markets × capabilities × competition**.

The question for every leadership team: "Does external market evidence support your strategic bets, or are you making expensive decisions based on untested assumptions?"

Quick-Action Checklist

- ☐ **Challenge your team:** Which of your GREEN cells would survive if your biggest competitor entered tomorrow?
- ☐ **Compare your top 3 strategic bets** against the market questions – what surprises you?
- ☐ **Pick your biggest revenue cell** and validate its market assumptions – start with what matters most
- ☐ **Ask your sales team:** What market reality are we missing in our strategic plans?

Next: Chapter 8 shows you how to build the capabilities needed to win in your validated cells – because knowing where to compete is only half the battle. You need the right capabilities to actually capture the opportunity.

Notes

1 Based on the author's 25+ years of consulting and client experience.
2 Alan Wolf, "How Best Buy's Hubert Joly Saved the Company from Certain Doom." *Forbes*, June 4, 2019. https://www.forbes.com/sites/alanwolf/2019/06/04/how-best-buys-hubert-joly-saved-the-company-from-certain-doom/.
3 Matthew Goldstein and Tiffany Hsu, "Quibi Is Shutting Down Barely 6 Months after Going Live." *The New York Times*, October 21, 2020. https://www.nytimes.com/2020/10/21/business/quibi-shutting-down.html.
4 Based on the author's 25+ years of consulting and client experience.
5 Bill Taylor. "How Domino's Pizza Reinvented Itself." *Harvard Business Review*, November 28, 2016. https://hbr.org/2016/11/how-dominos-pizza-reinvented-itself.
6 Netflix, Inc., "2016 Letter to Shareholders." January 18, 2017. https://ir.netflix.net/ir-overview/profile/default.aspx.
7 Based on the author's 25+ years of consulting and client experience.

Chapter 8

Build the Capabilities to Win

Invest in What Matters

> "If your biggest competitor hired your best people and licensed your key technologies, how long would it take them to replicate your advantages – and what would be left that's actually defensible?"

Daniel Ross gathered his executive team one week after completing their MRC. The MRC had validated their strategic bets – Frozen Meals and Healthy Bowls as growth engines, specific competitive threats identified, market dynamics confirmed.

Now came the harder question.

"What are we actually building to win in these cells?" Daniel asked, pointing to their PMM on the wall. "We know Frozen Meals Retail is our biggest bet. We know Trader Joe's and regional grocers are coming after us with premium private label. What capabilities give us an edge they can't copy?"

Mark Chen responded confidently. "We've been investing heavily. New production lines. Quality systems. Supply chain improvements."

"Which of those stops Trader Joe's from offering premium frozen at $4.99 versus our $6.00?" Daniel pressed.

Silence.

Dr. Raj Patel spoke up. "Our R&D is strong, but we're built for traditional product development – 18-month cycles, focus groups, stage gates. Meanwhile, NüWave gets from insight to shelf in 12 weeks."

Jennifer Walsh pulled up their capital allocation. "We spent $8M last year on 'strategic capabilities.' But looking closer, $5M went to maintaining legacy systems. Only $3M actually built new advantage."

Sarah Martinez added the market reality. "Even worse, we're investing in yesterday's advantages. Brand heritage and distribution scale matter less when DTC brands can reach consumers directly and retailers launch premium private label."

Daniel stood and drew two circles on the whiteboard: "Current Strengths" and "Future Advantages."

"List our current capabilities," he instructed. The team filled in: brand recognition, manufacturing scale, retail relationships, food safety systems.

"Now, which of these create pricing power in 2028?" Daniel asked. "Which ones can't be replicated by a well-funded competitor in 12 months?"

The uncomfortable truth emerged. Most of their "strategic" capabilities were table stakes – necessary but not differentiating.

"Here's our new rule," Daniel declared. "We don't fund any capability unless it creates an advantage customers will pay premiums for. Period."

DOI: 10.4324/9781003682455-11

The Pattern That Destroys Value

Companies spent over $2T on digital transformation in 2024. Ask their boards: "Which digital investments created advantages customers actually pay more for?" The silence reveals the problem.[1]

Most capability investments create operational competence, not competitive advantage. Companies attend conferences, study best practices, hire consultants. They return with capability roadmaps remarkably similar to competitors'. Then wonder why customers still choose based on price.

Evolution of Competitive Advantage Thinking

Michael Thompson had been researching this evolution for the board presentation. "Understanding how we got here explains why so many capability investments fail," he told the team.

"In the 1950s through 70s," Michael explained, "Harvard economists believed industry structure determined everything. Pick the right industry, profits follow. Individual capabilities didn't matter much."

Mark interrupted. "That's why everyone piled into frozen foods back then – it was a 'good industry.'"

"Exactly. Then Porter flipped the script in the 1980s," Michael continued. "He showed companies could shape their destiny through positioning – cost leadership, differentiation, or focus. But it still emphasized market position over internal capabilities."[2]

"The 1990s brought the resource-based view," Dr. Raj added, warming to the topic. "Suddenly everyone wanted 'core competencies.' Capabilities became the answer to everything."[3]

Jennifer saw the pattern. "And we spent the 2000s building capabilities that looked impressive internally but didn't connect to what customers valued."

"Which brings us to today," Daniel concluded. "Successful companies connect superior capabilities to outcomes customers pay premiums for. Everything else is expensive table stakes."

When Capabilities Don't Create Value

Peloton's Hardware Obsession: Peloton built world-class hardware capabilities:

- Precision engineering and design
- Supply chain for complex electronics
- Premium manufacturing quality
- Retail showroom experience

What customers actually valued:

- Instructor quality and content
- Community and social features
- Convenience of home workouts
- Flexible subscription options

Peloton invested billions in hardware excellence while Mirror focused on content and software. When the market shifted post-COVID, Peloton's hardware capabilities became expensive liabilities.

Result: Stock crashed 95% while lighter business models thrived.[4]

Quibi's Star Power Capability: Quibi assembled unmatched Hollywood talent:

- A-list producers and directors
- Celebrity actors and creators
- Premium production values
- Industry relationships

What mobile viewers wanted:

- Authentic creator content
- Community interaction
- Shareable moments
- Free or low-cost options

Quibi built capabilities for premium TV while users wanted TikTok-style engagement.
Result: Shut down after six months, burning $1.75B.[5]

The New Reality

The half-life of competitive advantage has collapsed:

Digital Capabilities: What took years to build gets replicated in months. A bank spent $50M on mobile features. Within 18 months, every competitor had identical capabilities from white-label providers.
Process Innovations: Best practices spread instantly through LinkedIn and conferences. COVID-driven supply chain "innovations" became industry standard within two years.
Technology Access: AI and cloud platforms democratize advanced capabilities. Retailers' expensive recommendation engines were matched by off-the-shelf solutions.
The harsh truth: Capabilities that can be bought, copied, or outsourced create temporary operational improvements, not sustainable advantage.

The MOVE Solution: Advantage + Future Capabilities Matrix

Advantage-Future Capabilities (AFC) Matrix connects your market-validated opportunities to specific capability investments that create competitive advantages customers will pay for.

The One Question It Answers: "Which capabilities create defensible competitive advantages in our validated market opportunities, and how should we acquire them?"
Critical Insight: Include EVERY cell from your PMM – even BLUE cells. Why? Every cell consumes resources right now. AFC forces you to see where money flows and make conscious decisions about what to change (Figure 8.1).

Financial Reality Check

When you map every PMM cell to its capability investments, shocking patterns emerge:

- BLUE cells often consume 30–40% of capability budgets through "maintenance"
- YELLOW cells get random investments based on functional requests
- GREEN cells – your supposed priorities – sometimes get less than declining segments

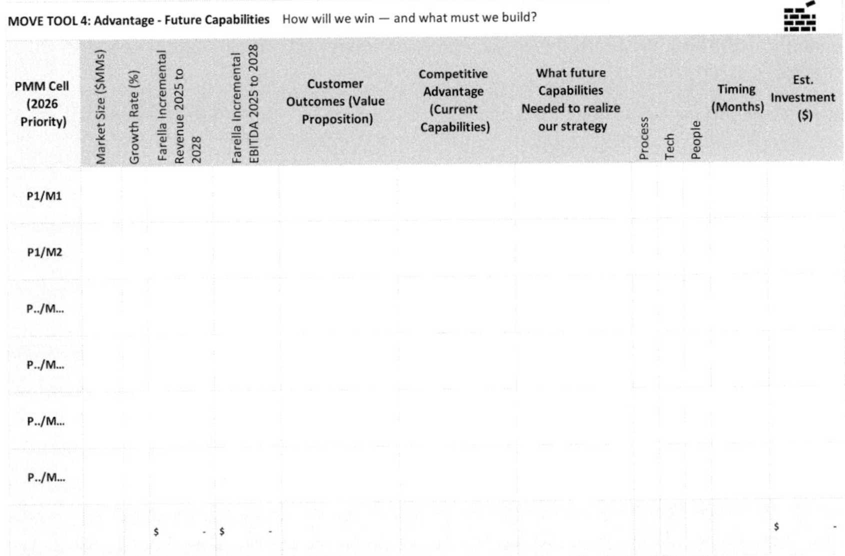

MOVE TOOL 4: Advantage - Future Capabilities How will we win — and what must we build?

PMM Cell (2026 Priority)	Market Size ($MMs)	Growth Rate (%)	Farella Incremental Revenue 2025 to 2028	Farella Incremental EBITDA 2025 to 2028	Customer Outcomes (Value Proposition)	Competitive Advantage (Current Capabilities)	What future Capabilities Needed to realize our strategy	Process	Tech	People	Timing (Months)	Est. Investment ($)
P1/M1												
P1/M2												
P../M...												
P../M...												
P../M...												
P../M...												
			$ -	$ -								$ -

Figure 8.1 MOVE Tool #4: Advantage + Future Capabilities Blank Template.

Until you map it completely, you don't realize you're funding yesterday's business model while starving tomorrow's growth.

How to Build Your AFC

Step 1: Transfer All Market-Validated Opportunities

Start with every cell from your PMM – GREEN, YELLOW, and BLUE. Include market size and growth from your MRC. This grounds capability decisions in market reality.

Step 2: Calculate Incremental Value

For each cell, identify the incremental revenue and EBITDA from your baseline (2025) to your target (2028). This shows what's at stake – the prize for getting capabilities right.

Step 3: Define Customer Value Connection

Specify what customers buy and why they pay premiums. This becomes your north star for capability investments.

Example: Frozen Meals Retail

- What customers buy: Convenient, quality meals at reasonable prices
- Why they pay our premium: Brand trust, consistent quality, broad availability
- Competitive reality: Premium eroding as private label quality improves

Step 4: Map Current and Future Capabilities

Current Capabilities: What advantages do you have today? Be honest about what's truly differentiating vs. table stakes.

Future Capabilities: What new advantages must you build to capture the incremental value? These should directly address competitive threats and customer evolution.

Step 5: Specify Capability Types

Break each capability into three dimensions:

- **Process**: Workflows and methods that deliver value
- **Technology**: Systems and platforms required
- **People**: Skills and expertise needed

This breakdown drives implementation planning and investment allocation.

Step 6: Apply Build/Buy/Partner Logic

Build: When capability creates a unique advantage and you have time. **Buy**: When speed matters more than uniqueness. **Partner**: When you need expertise but not ownership. **Outsource**: When necessary but not strategic.

Step 7: Calculate Investment Requirements

Estimate costs, timelines, and expected returns. Sum total investment across all capabilities. Compare to the total incremental EBITDA. This gives portfolio-level ROIC for your strategic transformation.

Value Proposition vs. Competitive Advantage: Why Your Executives Can't Agree

Picture this scene from a strategy session at a $2B industrial company:

Head of Sales: "Our value proposition is clear – we deliver 99.9% uptime reliability. That's what customers buy."

Head of Product: "No, our value proposition is innovative technology. We have the most advanced predictive analytics in the industry."

Head of Operations: "You're both missing it. Our value proposition is speed – 48-hour service response anywhere in North America."

Head of Marketing: "Actually, our research shows customers value our consultative approach and industry expertise."

Four executives. Four different "value propositions." All talking past each other because they're confusing value proposition with competitive advantage.

Here's the critical distinction

Value Proposition = What customers get (external view)

- The specific benefits customers receive
- The problems you solve for them

- The outcomes they achieve
- What they tell others about why they buy from you

Competitive Advantage = Why they can't get it elsewhere (internal + external view)

- The unique capabilities that deliver the value proposition
- What competitors can't easily replicate
- The moat that protects your market position
- Why customers stay even when competitors offer similar benefits

The confusion happens because:

- Sales focuses on what closes deals (customer-facing benefits)
- Product focuses on what they build (features and technology)
- Operations focuses on what they deliver (service and reliability)
- Marketing focuses on what resonates (messaging and positioning)

Each executive sees their piece of the elephant and thinks it's the whole animal.

External Reality Check: Ask your customers: "What do you actually buy from us?" Their answer is your value proposition. Ask them: "Why don't you switch to competitors?" Their answer points to your competitive advantage.

The two are related but distinct. Your value proposition is what gets customers in the door. Your competitive advantage is what keeps them from leaving.

Global Beverage Company Example: Segment-Specific Distinction

Consider how a global beverage leader's distinction varies by segment:

Enterprise Level

Value Proposition (What customers get):

- Refreshment and consistent quality
- Widely available products
- Affordable beverage options
- Brand customers trust

Competitive Advantage (Why they can't get it elsewhere):

- Unmatched distribution reaching remote locations
- Decades of brand equity and emotional connection
- Proprietary formulations
- Scale economics driving lowest cost position

But drill down by segment and the picture changes:

Convenience Stores Segment:

- Value Prop: Profitable beverages with reliable delivery
- Competitive Advantage: Direct-store-delivery model + merchandising expertise that drives sales

Restaurant Segment:

- Value Prop: Beverage programs that enhance dining experience
- Competitive Advantage: Equipment investment + exclusive partnerships + staff training programs

Vending Segment:

- Value Prop: 24/7 automated beverage access
- Competitive Advantage: Route density making service economically viable where others can't profit

E-commerce Segment:

- Value Prop: Bulk beverages delivered to home
- Competitive Advantage:...None identified. Any retailer can ship beverages equally well

This reveals the critical pattern: The company has different competitive advantages in different segments, even with consistent value propositions. In e-commerce, they have only a value proposition without competitive advantage – making that segment vulnerable to any competitor with delivery capability.

The Strategic Imperative: Product × Market Analysis

Here's what most companies miss: While you need an enterprise-level value proposition and competitive advantage, the real work happens at the product-market intersection. You've already segmented products and markets based on different customer needs and channels. How can you expect one generic capability set to serve all combinations effectively?

Critical Analysis Required for Each Cell:

- What specific value does THIS product deliver to THIS market?
- What capabilities make that value proposition defensible?
- Do we actually have those capabilities or just assume we do?
- What would customers who left us say was missing?
- How does this connect back to our MRC findings and Vision?

The Linked Logic Test: Vision → "We will win through X" → PMM → "In these specific product-market cells" → MRC → "Against these specific competitors" → AFC → "With these specific capabilities" → Value Proposition → "Delivering this specific value" → Competitive Advantage → "That others can't match because..."

If any link breaks, your strategy breaks.

From Strategy to Functional Alignment:

Once leadership aligns on VP and CA by cell, functional clarity follows:

Sales knows exactly what to emphasize:

- Frozen Meals Retail: "Brand trust and consistent quality" (until innovation acceleration kicks in)
- Healthy Bowls Retail: "Fastest trending flavors with clean labels"
- Not generic "we're a quality food company"

Marketing campaigns become targeted:

- Different messages for different cells
- Budget allocated based on cell priority (GREEN vs. BLUE)
- No more one-size-fits-all brand campaigns

Operations investments align:

- Innovation acceleration for GREEN cells
- Maintenance only for BLUE cells
- No more "peanut butter" spreading of capital

Customer Validation Essential: Talk to great customers: "Why do you stay with us?" Talk to lost customers: "Why did you leave?" Map their answers to your VP/CA assumptions by cell. The gaps reveal where your strategy meets reality.

The Leadership Lesson: Stop asking "What's our value proposition?" in isolation. Start asking "What's our value proposition AND what makes it defensible?"

Your executives aren't wrong – they're each seeing different segments where different capabilities create advantage. The CEO's job is to ensure:

1 Clear value proposition that customers understand
2 Distinct competitive advantages by segment
3 Investment priorities based on where advantages are strongest
4 Exit strategies for segments where you have no real advantage
5 Functional alignment once VP/CA is clear by cell

Without this distinction, you'll invest in capabilities that deliver value propositions competitors can easily match – expensive parity instead of profitable advantage.

Putting AFC Into Practice: The Farella Journey

Daniel and his team assembled their AFC matrix, pulling forward every insight from their strategic journey.

"Remember," Daniel emphasized, "each row represents a PMM cell – all six of them. We're seeing where every dollar of capability investment goes, not just our favorites."

GREEN Cells: Highest Priority

Frozen Meals: Retail (Future GREEN)

- Market Reality: \$5.5B market, 3% growth, but margin pressure from private label
- Incremental Opportunity: \$51M revenue, \$6M EBITDA by 2028
- Customer Value: Convenience, value, brand trust
- Current Advantage: Efficient cold chain, brand legacy (eroding)
- Future Capabilities Needed:
    - **Innovation acceleration** (12 → 6 month cycles)
    - **Premium positioning** through clean label
    - **Cold chain efficiency** to protect margins
- Investment: \$1.0M over 18 months
- Build/Buy: Build an innovation process, buy clean-label expertise

"This is our biggest bet," Mark noted. "But the investment seems light for the challenge."

Jennifer explained: "We're leveraging existing assets – brand and distribution. The $1M focuses on what changes the game: speed and clean label to fight private label premiumization."

Healthy Bowls: Retail (Emerging GREEN)

- Market Reality: $1.2B market, 8% growth, competitive but fragmented
- Incremental Opportunity: $7M revenue, $1M EBITDA by 2028
- Customer Value: Health focus, high protein, clean label
- Current Advantage: Some health SKUs, but lagging innovation
- Future Capabilities Needed:
    - **Nutritional R&D** leadership
    - **Wellness branding** authenticity
    - **Strategic partnerships** with health influencers
- Investment: $850K over six months
- Build/Buy: Build R&D, partner for branding

Sarah's eyes lit up. "This is where we can leapfrog NüWave. They're constrained by fresh complexity. Our shelf-stable advantage plus breakthrough nutrition could win."

YELLOW Cells: Selective Investment

Frozen Meals: Foodservice (Stable YELLOW)

- Market Reality: $2.5B market, 2% growth, commodity dynamics
- Incremental Opportunity: $17M revenue, $1.5M EBITDA
- Customer Value: Institutional reliability, ease of prep
- Current Advantage: Established channels and logistics
- Future Capabilities Needed:
    - **Menu integration** systems
    - **Logistics upgrades** to match BoxTop
- Investment: $1.2M over 12 months
- Build/Buy: Partner for systems, upgrade logistics

"BoxTop is killing us on delivery reliability," Mark admitted. "This investment just keeps us competitive."

BLUE Cells: Minimize Investment

Snack Packs: Retail (Declining BLUE)

- Market Reality: $2B market, 5% growth but brutal margins
- Incremental Opportunity: $14M revenue, $4.5M EBITDA
- Customer Value: Portability, variety, portion control
- Current Advantage: Multi-pack operations (commodity)
- Future Capabilities Needed:
    - **SKU flexibility** only
    - **Minimal** innovation

- Investment: $950K maintenance
- Build/Buy: Optimize existing only

"I hate putting any money here," Daniel said, "but we need the cash flow for now."

Strategic Discoveries

The complete AFC revealed stunning misalignment:

"Look at historical spending," Jennifer pointed to her analysis. "Last three years, we invested $15M in capabilities. But $9M went to Snack Packs and Foodservice – our BLUE and YELLOW cells. Meanwhile, Healthy Bowls – our highest growth opportunity – got almost nothing."

Total Strategic Investment Required: $5.55M over 18–24 months. **Expected Incremental EBITDA**: $15M by 2028. **Portfolio ROIC**: 270% over three years

"Let me break this down," Jennifer explained, seeing some puzzled faces. "We're investing $5.55M total across all capabilities. By 2028, those capabilities should generate an additional $15M in EBITDA annually – that's pure profit improvement above our current $60M baseline."

"So we nearly triple our money?" asked Tom Stevens from the board.

"Actually, it's better than that," Jennifer continued. "The 270% return is simplified. Think of it this way: we spend $5.55M once to build capabilities. But that $15M in additional EBITDA comes back every year after 2028. It's like buying an asset for $5.55M that pays you $15M annually."

Dr. Raj wanted more detail. "What about time value of money? Implementation risk?"

Jennifer pulled up her detailed analysis. "Great questions. For this strategic view, I'm showing simple returns to keep focus on relative priorities. But for board approval, we'll run full NPV analysis with:

- Discount rates reflecting our cost of capital
- Probability adjustments for execution risk
- Sensitivity analysis on market growth assumptions
- Competitive response scenarios

Even with conservative assumptions – 12% discount rate, 70% execution success – the NPV exceeds $35M."

"But here's what matters most," Daniel interjected. "Look at the return differences between cells. **Healthy Bowls Retail: $850K investment for $1M EBITDA – over 117% annual return. Compare that to Snack Packs Foodservice: $750K investment for $1M EBITDA – barely 40% return after accounting for risk.**"

The board member leaned forward. "So this isn't just about total returns. It's about seeing which specific bets create value versus destroy it."

"Exactly," Jennifer confirmed. "Without this cell-by-cell view, we'd keep funding Snack Packs because 'it's 20% of revenue.' Now we see it's destroying value while Healthy Bowls – just 4% of revenue today – offers our highest returns."

Mark Chen had an operational insight: "This also shows timing. Frozen Meals Retail needs 18 months for capability building. Healthy Bowls needs just six months. We could capture Healthy Bowls returns faster while building for the bigger Frozen Meals opportunity."

"One final point," Jennifer added. "**This ROIC assumes we execute all cells. But what if we dropped all BLUE cells and doubled down on GREEN? The focused portfolio might deliver 400%+ returns by concentrating resources where we have real advantage.**"

Daniel brought the discussion back to execution reality. "This AFC isn't just analysis – it's the starting point for our execution roadmap. Each capability becomes a project with real timelines and budgets."

He pointed to the AFC matrix. "When the board asks 'How will you execute your strategy?' this is the answer. Not vague initiatives but specific projects:

- Innovation acceleration for Frozen Meals: $1M, starting Q1, 18-month completion
- Nutritional R&D for Healthy Bowls: $850K, starting immediately, six-month sprint
- Menu integration systems: $1.2M, partner selection Q2, 12-month rollout

Each has an owner, budget, timeline, and clear connection to EBITDA improvement."

"This is what I've been missing in strategy presentations," Tom Stevens noted. "Usually we get vision and goals. This shows exactly how you'll get there – which capabilities, what cost, when they deliver."

Michael Thompson added: "And because each capability ties to specific PMM cells, we can track whether our investments actually deliver the competitive advantages we're betting on. If Healthy Bowls R&D doesn't accelerate innovation to eight-week cycles, we know quickly and can adjust."

"The execution sequencing matters too," Mark observed. "We're starting with Healthy Bowls capabilities – 6-month timeline, highest ROIC. Those quick wins fund the longer Frozen Meals transformation. It's self-financing strategy."

Why This Time Is Different

Tom Stevens, the board member, raised the elephant in the room. "We've funded capability initiatives before. Digital transformation, operational excellence, innovation labs. Why should we believe this delivers results?"

Daniel had been waiting for this. "Because those initiatives failed from unclear, unvalidated thinking. Someone said 'we need digital' without connecting it to specific competitive advantages in specific cells. MOVE prevents that. Every capability here ties to:

- A validated market opportunity from our MRC
- A specific competitive threat we must address
- Clear customer value that drives premium pricing
- Measurable EBITDA improvement

We're not funding buzzwords. We're building specific advantages to capture specific opportunities."

The Talent Reality

"Let's talk about the harder truth," Daniel continued. "Some of these capabilities require different leadership. Our current team built a successful traditional food company. But speed-to-market innovation? Wellness partnerships? That might need new talent."

The room tensed. This was the conversation everyone avoided.

"Healthy Bowls needs someone who thinks in 8-week cycles, not 18-month stage gates," Sarah said carefully. "That might not be our current R&D structure."

Dr. Raj nodded slowly. "I've built traditional R&D excellence. But you're right – this needs a different mindset. Maybe I oversee platform capabilities while we bring in someone who's done rapid innovation."

"This AFC doesn't just drive capital allocation," Michael observed. "It shapes organization structure and succession planning. We need leaders who match our future, not our past."

Competitive Advantage Has a Shorter Half-Life

"But what happens when competitors copy our innovation acceleration?" Mark asked. "These moats have less water than they used to."

"Exactly why we need a living strategy system," Daniel replied. "Static advantages die fast. But if we're constantly using MOVE tools – updating MRC quarterly, adjusting AFC annually – we see when advantages erode and where new ones must be built. **It's proactive defense, not reactive scrambling.**"

Jennifer built on this: "Think of capabilities as a portfolio. Some create temporary advantage – we milk them while building the next. Others compound – innovation acceleration makes our next capabilities faster to build. **We're not seeking permanent moats but sustainable capability evolution.**"

The Capital Allocation Reality

"Let's address the political elephant," Daniel said bluntly. "This AFC means some executives get investment, others don't. Snack Packs leadership won't be happy watching resources flow to Frozen and Healthy."

He looked around the table. "But CEO responsibility is **disproportionate capital allocation – deliberately concentrated where advantage can be built**. If you're wed to your function over our enterprise strategy, you're on the wrong team."

"The data makes it easier," Jennifer added. "When Snack Packs shows 40% ROIC versus Healthy Bowls at 117%, the conversation changes from politics to mathematics. **Executives need to get on board with where the company is going, not protect their silo.**"

Mark, who ran operations across all products, showed the right mindset: "I'd rather run operations for two winning categories than three where one is dying. Concentrate resources where we can win."

Cross-Functional Leadership Requirements

"One final point," Daniel said. "These capabilities don't fit in functional boxes. Innovation acceleration cuts across R&D, operations, and marketing. Wellness partnerships span business development and brand."

He pulled up the organizational implication. "This AFC surfaces 2–3 major cross-functional initiatives:

- Innovation acceleration platform (Raj plus Sarah plus Mark)
- Wellness ecosystem development (Sarah plus new hire)
- Supply chain speed transformation (Mark plus Raj)

Each needs a senior leader who can drive across silos. That's how strategy becomes execution – clear initiatives with clear owners who have CEO backing to break through functional walls."

Daniel summarized: "So when someone asks about our strategy, we don't just say 'focus on Frozen and Healthy.' We show them this AFC – exactly which capabilities we're building, why they create advantage, what they cost, when they deliver, and how they connect to financial outcomes. Strategy becomes executable projects, not PowerPoint promises."

Daniel pulled up the AFC matrix (Figure 8.2). "Every investment ties to a specific cell with validated market growth, identified customer value, and clear competitive gaps. We're not funding departments – we're funding advantages."

The Capability Debates

The real value emerged in the debates about future capabilities.

For Frozen Meals Retail, Dr. Raj pushed for advanced R&D: "We need molecular gastronomy capabilities, novel ingredients, breakthrough nutrition science."

Sarah disagreed. "Consumers don't want science experiments. They want clean labels they understand, delivered fast. Speed beats perfection."

Michael Thompson brought market perspective: "The MRC showed Trader Joe's winning with simple, quality ingredients at sharp prices. Our advantage isn't complexity – it's doing simple better and faster."

They settled on innovation acceleration and clean label focus – capabilities that addressed the actual competitive threat.

For Healthy Bowls, the debate centered on partnerships.

"Why partner for wellness branding?" Mark questioned. "We should build our own authentic story."

Sarah had learned from past mistakes. "Because authenticity takes years to build and seconds to destroy. Partner with established wellness brands who've already earned trust. We bring the food expertise, they bring the health credibility."

Capability Integration

Dr. Raj raised a critical point: "These capabilities cut across cells. Nutritional R&D helps both Frozen Meals and Healthy Bowls. How do we avoid silos?"

Daniel drew connections on the board. "That's the power of seeing all cells together. We build shared capabilities that leverage across the portfolio."

Shared Capability Platforms:

- **Innovation acceleration**: Serves all retail cells
- **Clean label expertise**: Enables premium positioning across products
- **Digital marketing**: Supports both Frozen and Healthy positioning

"Instead of six separate capability plans," Michael noted, "we have three platforms that create advantage across multiple cells."

MOVE TOOL 4: Advantage - Future Capabilities How will we win — and what must we build?

PMM Cell (2026 Priority)	Market Size ($MMs)	Growth Rate (%)	Farella Incremental Revenue 2025 to 2028	Farella Incremental EBITDA 2025 to 2028	Customer Outcomes (Value Proposition)	Competitive Advantage (Current Capabilities)	What future Capabilities Needed to realize our strategy	Process	Tech	People	Timing (Months)	Est. Investment ($)
Frozen Meals – Retail	$ 5,000	6	$ 30	$ 5.00	Convenience, value meals, brand trust	Efficient cold chain, brand legacy	Meal innovation center, Cold chain expansion	✓	✓	✓	6	$ 1,000,000
Snack Packs – Retail	$ 2,000	5	$ 20	$ 3.50	Portability, snacking variety, portion control	Multi-pack operations, snack brand assets	Retail segmentation, Portion design, SKU agility	✓		✓	5	$ 950,000
Healthy Bowls – Retail	$ 1,200	8	$ 15	$ 2.50	Health focus, high protein, clean label	Some health SKUs, lagging innovation	Nutritional R&D, Wellness branding, Partnerships	✓	✓	✓	7	$ 850,000
Frozen Meals – Foodservice	$ 2,000	4	$ 15	$ 2.00	Institutional reliability, ease of prep	Foodservice channels, logistics	Institutional menu integration, Logistics upgrades	✓	✓	✓	4	$ 1,200,000
Snack Packs – Foodservice	$ 1,000	3	$ 10	$ 1.00	Bulk snack delivery, cost control	Basic channel partnerships	B2B snack pack R&D, Distribution integration	✓		✓	5	$ 750,000
Healthy Bowls – Foodservice	$ 800	5	$ 10	$ 1.00	Diet-specific offerings, innovation	Limited health-foodservice overlap	Functional R&D, DTC testbeds, New co-packers	✓	✓	✓	6	$ 800,000
			$ 100	$ 15.00								$ 5,550,000

Figure 8.2 MOVE Tool #4: Advantage + Future Capabilities Farella Foods Example.

Success Stories from Focused Capabilities

Chobani's Protein Platform While yogurt competitors fought on price, Chobani built capabilities around one advantage: authentic, high-protein Greek yogurt.

- Customer Value: Better nutrition, authentic taste, simple ingredients
- Capability Focus: Straining process, supply chain for quality milk, authentic branding
- Competitive Result: Commanded 30–50% price premiums, created new category
- Outcome: From startup to $1.5B in five years[6]

Trader Joe's Private-Label Revolution Instead of competing with brands on marketing spend, Trader Joe's built unique sourcing capabilities:

- Customer Value: Interesting products at sharp prices
- Capability Focus: Direct supplier relationships, rapid testing, curated selection
- Competitive Result: 80% private label with premium perception
- Outcome: Highest revenue per square foot in grocery[7]

These companies didn't build every capability – they built the ones that created customer outcomes competitors couldn't match.

Enhancing Your AFC with AI

After completing their initial AFC, Farella used AI to sharpen their capability strategy.

"AI didn't replace our thinking," Michael explained. "It challenged our assumptions and revealed patterns we missed."

How Farella Applied AI to AFC

Capability Benchmarking: "What specific capabilities enabled food companies to accelerate innovation from 18 to 6 months?"

AI analyzed hundreds of examples, revealing:

- Rapid prototyping labs (not just R&D kitchens)
- Direct-to-consumer testing channels
- Modular formulation platforms
- Cross-functional innovation teams

"We were thinking traditional R&D expansion," Dr. Raj admitted. "AI showed us it's about process redesign, not just more scientists. **That insight alone saved us $2M in misdirected hiring.**"

Investment Optimization: "Compare build vs. partner approaches for wellness branding in food. What determines success?"

AI's analysis was sobering:

- Build success rate: 20% (requires five plus years)
- Partner success rate: 65% (when aligned properly)
- Key success factor: Partner credibility in target community

This validated Sarah's instinct to partner rather than build wellness credentials from scratch. **"AI turned our gut feeling into data-driven strategy,"** she noted.

Competitive Threat Modeling: "Which capabilities would Trader Joe's need to replicate our Healthy Bowls advantage?"

AI identified the gap:

- Trader Joe's has sourcing and price advantages
- Lacks: nutritional R&D depth, health positioning, speed in trending categories
- Time to build: 18–24 months with focused investment

"**That's our window**," Daniel realized. "**18 months to establish leadership before they can respond.** AI didn't tell us what to do – it showed us how much time we have to do it."

The team saw AI's true value: not replacing strategic thinking but accelerating it. Every capability decision now had data, patterns, and competitive intelligence that would have taken months to gather manually.

Data Security Note

Use your company's secure AI environment when possible. For sensitive capability planning:

- Use enterprise AI platforms with security protocols
- Never share specific investment amounts or strategic priorities in public tools
- Anonymize company information when using external AI
- Treat capability strategies as board-level confidential

Remember: Your capability plans reveal competitive strategy. Protect them accordingly.

AI Prompts for Capability Building

For Cross-Industry Learning: ***Prompt:*** "What capabilities enabled food companies to reduce innovation cycles from 18 to 6 months while maintaining quality? Include specific process, technology, and organizational changes."

- ***What you'll get:*** Concrete examples of innovation acceleration
- ***How to use it:*** Identify which approaches fit your context

For Build vs. Buy Decisions: ***Prompt:*** "Compare success rates for building versus acquiring [specific capability] in the food industry. What factors predict success versus failure?"

- ***What you'll get:*** Data-driven guidance on acquisition strategy
- ***How to use it:*** Make informed build/buy/partner decisions

For Competitive Gaps: ***Prompt:*** "What capabilities would [specific competitor] need to replicate [your advantage]? Estimate time and investment required based on their current position."

- ***What you'll get:*** Realistic view of your competitive moat
- ***How to use it:*** Prioritize capabilities hardest to replicate

For Investment Validation: ***Prompt:*** "Analyze ROI patterns for [specific capability] investments in CPG companies. What level of investment typically yields meaningful competitive advantage?"

- ***What you'll get:*** Benchmarks for investment sizing
- ***How to use it:*** Validate your investment levels against outcomes

Your Move

Most companies build capabilities because competitors have them. They invest millions to achieve competitive parity – the expensive privilege of competing on price.

AFC forces a different question: Which capabilities create advantages customers will pay premiums for?

When you map every PMM cell to required capabilities, shocking patterns emerge. You'll likely discover you're overinvesting in declining segments while starving growth opportunities. You're building impressive competencies that deliver commodity value.

Three Questions Before Your Next Capability Investment:

1 Can you name three specific customers who will pay 20% more because of this capability?
2 If competitors copy this capability (and they will), what advantage remains?
3 Does this capability directly address a validated competitive threat from your MRC?

If you can't answer with specific evidence, you're about to fund another best practice that creates no competitive advantage.

As Daniel told his board: "We're not building capabilities to match industry standards. We're building specific advantages in specific cells where we've validated customer willingness to pay premiums. Every dollar ties to a validated market opportunity and competitive gap."

The result: $5.55M in targeted investments to capture $15M in incremental EBITDA – **270% ROIC because every capability creates advantage, not just competence**.

Quick-Action Checklist

- □ **Map current capability spending** to your PMM cells – what percentage supports GREEN priorities?
- □ **Identify one capability** that creates real pricing power – what makes it defensible?
- □ **Calculate portfolio ROIC** on capability investments – total investment vs. incremental EBITDA
- □ **Challenge your team**: Which "strategic" capabilities could competitors copy in 12 months?

Next: Chapter 9 shows you how to measure whether your capability investments deliver the intended advantages – because building capabilities is only valuable if they create the customer outcomes and competitive moats you planned.

Notes

1 "IDC FutureScape: Worldwide Digital Transformation 2024 Predictions." IDC, October 2023. https://www.idc.com/research/viewtoc.jsp?containerId=US49726223.
2 Michael E. Porter, ***Competitive Strategy: Techniques for Analyzing Industries and Competitors*** (New York: Free Press, 1980).
3 C.K. Prahalad and Gary Hamel, "The Core Competence of the Corporation." *Harvard Business Review* 68, no. 3 (May-June 1990): 79–91.
4 Peloton Interactive, Inc., "Form 10-K Annual Report." Securities and Exchange Commission, September 23, 2022. https://investor.onepeloton.com/sec-filings.
5 Matthew Goldstein and Tiffany Hsu, "Quibi Is Shutting Down Barely 6 Months After Going Live." *The New York Times*, October 21, 2020.
6 Based on the author's 25+ years of consulting and client experience.
7 "Trader Joe's: A Case Study in Management Excellence." Stanford Graduate School of Business Case Study, 2013.

Chapter 9

Measure What Moves the Needle

Strategic Numbers

"How many KPIs are on your dashboard right now, and which three actually predict whether you'll hit your strategic objectives? Can you even tell?"

Daniel Ross stood before his executive team six months after launching their transformation initiatives. The conference room walls displayed their quarterly business review – slide after slide of metrics, charts, and performance indicators.

"We're tracking 87 KPIs across the enterprise," Jennifer Walsh reported, clicking through financial slides. "On-time delivery improved 4%. Customer complaints down 8%. Manufacturing efficiency up 3%."

Mark Chen added operational metrics. "Production variance is within tolerance. Inventory turns increased. Labor productivity up 2.3%."

Daniel interrupted. "That's all interesting. But we promised to transform Farella [fictional example] from a commodity food company to a focused category leader with 9.2% EBITDA margins. Which of these 87 metrics tells us if we're on track?"

The room fell silent. The truth was uncomfortable – they were measuring everything except what mattered for their strategic transformation.

"We just spent an hour proving we're busy, not that we're winning," Daniel continued. "We're drowning in operational data but have no strategic insight."

Jennifer pulled up their main dashboard. "Look at this – we track daily production variance but only review innovation cycle times quarterly. We measure yesterday's manufacturing efficiency but not tomorrow's competitive advantage."

"We've built a measurement system that impresses rather than improves," Daniel admitted. "We're done with that."

Michael Thompson suggested radical simplification. "What if we identified just 8 indicators that actually predict strategic success? Measures that tell us if we're building competitive advantage, not just keeping the lights on."

"Show me," Daniel said.

Michael sketched on the whiteboard. "Think about explaining our business to a new investor. You wouldn't show 87 KPIs. You'd say: 'Here's what we're building, here's how we know if we're winning, and here's what needs fixing.'"

The room shifted. They'd been measuring activity, not advantage.

"But wait," Sarah Martinez connected the dots. "We just spent months building strategy with MOVE tools. Our Strategic Assumptions showed market shifts. Vision defined our focus. Product-Market Matrix identified our bets. Market Reality Check validated them. Advantage+ Future Capabilities showed what we need to build. Why isn't our measurement system built from these same insights?"

The room went quiet. She was right. They'd built strategy outside-in but measurement inside-out.

DOI: 10.4324/9781003682455-12

The Universal Measurement Trap
Every company falls into the same trap. They track what's easy instead of what matters.
The Evolution of Strategic Measurement

Understanding measurement evolution helps explain why most systems fail to drive strategy.

Financial-Only Era (1950s–1980s): Companies measured success through P&L statements. If revenue grew and costs dropped, strategy worked. Simple when competitive advantages lasted decades.

Balanced Scorecard Revolution (1990s): Kaplan and Norton revealed that financial metrics were autopsy reports. By the time financial results showed problems, competitive damage was done. They added customer, process, and learning perspectives for a "balanced" view.[1]

KPI Explosion (2000s): Technology made everything measurable. Companies went from tracking 20 metrics to 200. Dashboards became overwhelming. Executives spent more time debating measurements than making decisions.

The Death of "Key" – When Everything Became Critical

The word "key" once meant vital, essential, the critical few. By 2010, the average Fortune 500 company tracked 200+ "Key" Performance Indicators. When everything is key, nothing is.

The pattern was predictable. Each function demanded representation. Sales added "key" metrics. Marketing insisted theirs were "critical." Operations couldn't be left out. IT needed "strategic" measures. HR required "essential" indicators.

The absurdity became clear when companies started asking executives which of their "key" metrics actually mattered. Most struggled to name more than a handful that truly predicted strategic success.

One CPG executive confessed: "We had 147 KPIs marked as 'critical to monitor.' Our monthly review took three days. We spent more time debating why metrics were yellow than making them green."[2]

The proliferation destroyed focus. Dashboards became political documents – every function got their metrics to avoid feeling excluded. Strategy suffocated under operational noise.

Real-Time Everything (2010s–Present): Digital transformation promised instant insight. Companies built war rooms with live dashboards. But data velocity didn't equal insight quality. Most real-time metrics measured operational noise, not strategic signal.

Strategic Indicators (Now): Leading companies dramatically simplify. They identify 6–12 indicators that predict strategic success. Everything else becomes supporting data, not board-level distraction.

Michael Thompson had studied this evolution. "Every era added complexity," he told the team. "We kept the old metrics and added new ones. Nobody wanted to be the one to say no."

When Measurement Goes Wrong

Wells Fargo's Metric Meltdown

Wells Fargo became the cautionary tale of measurement gone wrong. Their strategic goal: deepen customer relationships through cross-selling.

Their measurement seemed logical:

- Track products per customer
- Set aggressive targets
- Monitor daily progress
- Reward achievement

But they measured activity, not value. Employees opened 3.5 million unauthorized accounts to hit targets. Metrics showed "success" while destroying trust.

The lesson: Wrong metrics optimize for disaster. They measured account quantity, not relationship quality. They tracked what was easy to game, not what created sustainable value.

Result: $3B in fines, CEO resignation, permanent reputation damage.[3]

Peloton's Pandemic Dashboard Disaster

Peloton became the modern cautionary tale of measuring the wrong revolution. During 2020–2021, their dashboards showed pure success:

- Subscriber growth: 472% increase
- Bike delivery wait times: 10+ weeks (indicating "strong demand")
- Class attendance: Record highs
- Customer engagement: 20+ workouts monthly

What they didn't measure:

- Gym reopening impact on retention
- Subscriber acquisition cost trending unsustainable
- Used bike market proliferation
- Competitive connected fitness explosion
- True lifetime value with normalized behavior

Their dashboards showed green lights based on pandemic anomalies while the real business model crumbled. Stock price fell 95% from its peak as reality emerged.

CEO John Foley later admitted: "We measured growth assuming the new normal would persist. Our metrics showed success while our actual strategic position deteriorated."[4]

When Measurement Systems Fail

Most measurement systems prove you're busy. They don't prove you're winning. They create control theater while your position erodes.

Universal symptoms:

- Monthly reviews that consume days but change nothing
- Dashboards where everything is perpetually "on track"
- Variance explanations blaming "market conditions"
- Metrics that mysteriously improve before board meetings
- Color-coded scorecards with 50+ indicators

Jennifer had seen this pattern at three companies. "We spend millions on analytics platforms. Executives feel informed watching numbers update. But ask which metrics predict strategic success – silence."

The Hidden Cost

Research shows executives spend 23% of their time in measurement meetings. That's one full day per week looking backward instead of building forward.[5]

But dig deeper into the real costs:

Time Destruction

The measurement meeting cycle consumes massive executive time. Between weekly dashboards, monthly reviews, and quarterly deep dives, leaders spend days analyzing history instead of building the future. The real cost isn't just time – it's the opportunity cost of what doesn't get done while executives debate variances.

Decision Paralysis

Microsoft's 2024 Work Trend Index found that data overload increased decision time by 40%. Leaders spent more time debating metric definitions than solving problems. One pharmaceutical CEO tracked the waste: "We spent 200 hours annually arguing about forecast accuracy calculations. Meanwhile, competitors launched new products."[6]

Strategic Blindness

The real cost? While you perfect dashboards, competitors eat your lunch. Companies tracking 50+ KPIs move like molasses compared to those tracking 15 that matter.

A retail executive captured it perfectly: "We had beautiful dashboards showing everything green. Six months later, a digital competitor had taken 20% market share. Our 200 KPIs missed the only trend that mattered – customer migration to mobile."

Critical signals hide behind operational metrics showing "green."

The MOVE Solution: Strategic Numbers Dashboard

Strategic numbers flip measurement on its head. Instead of tracking everything, you track only what predicts success.

The One Question It Answers: "Which 6–10 indicators will tell us months in advance whether our strategy is working or failing?"

This isn't another balanced scorecard with 30+ metrics. It's radical focus – only measures that predict strategic success for YOUR specific strategy make the cut.

This is enterprise strategy measurement, not functional scorecards. Every business unit can have their operational metrics. But at the enterprise level, you need unity and focus. Eight numbers everyone understands, not 200 nobody remembers.

Why This Tool Creates Breakthrough Value

Traditional dashboards are autopsies. Strategic numbers are early warning systems.

Most dashboards include every metric so no function feels left out. Strategic numbers don't care about politics – if a metric doesn't predict strategic success, it's out.

The power? Your strategic numbers come straight from your MOVE journey:

- Strategic Assumptions identified trends to monitor
- Vision defined what success looks like
- PMM showed which cells must deliver

MOVE TOOL 5: Strategic Numbers Dashboard	Are we on track — and how will we know early?						
Category	Indicator	Metric	Actual (2025)	Target (2026)	Gap	Data Source	Frequency
Financial							
Customer							
Process/Technology							
People							

Figure 9.1 MOVE Tool #5: Strategic Numbers Dashboard Blank Template.

- MRC validated growth rates and competitive dynamics
- AFC highlighted capabilities that need to perform (Figure 9.1)

Leading vs. Lagging Revolution

By the time your financial metrics show problems, the game is over. Revenue is the final score, not the play-by-play.

The critical shift:

- Lagging: Market share → Leading: Innovation cycle speed
- Lagging: Customer satisfaction → Leading: Retention rate trends
- Lagging: Revenue growth → Leading: New product adoption
- Lagging: Employee turnover → Leading: Engagement scores
- Lagging: EBITDA margin → Leading: Value-add mix changes

The best leading indicators share three traits:

1 They move before results move
2 You can actually do something about them
3 They obviously connect to winning

How to Build Your Strategic Numbers Dashboard

Building your Strategic Numbers Dashboard completes the MOVE logic chain. This one-page tool becomes your early warning system – measuring whether the strategy you built is actually working.

Step 1: Connect Back to Your MOVE Journey

Pull out your other four MOVE tools. Your strategic numbers emerge directly from what you've already built:

- Strategic Assumptions revealed the external trends to monitor
- Vision + Driving Force defined what winning looks like

- Product-Market Matrix sets specific financial targets by year
- Market Reality Check validated which bets to pursue
- Advantage+ Future Capabilities showed what you must build

Your strategic numbers measure progress on all of these – creating one integrated system.

Step 2: Identify 6–8 Leading Indicators

For each category below, find one to two indicators that predict whether your strategy is working:

Financial Indicators: Connect to your PMM targets

- Revenue quality (growth from strategic cells)
- Margin trajectory (toward your Vision goal)

Customer Indicators: Validate your market bets

- Retention in strategic categories
- Adoption of new innovations

Process Indicators: Track capability building

- Innovation speed vs. competitors
- Operational excellence metrics

People Indicators: Measure organizational readiness

- Leadership bench in critical roles
- Engagement in key functions

Step 3: Set Targets and Accountability

For each indicator:

- Set targets that represent strategic progress (not incremental improvement)
- Assign one owner who connects their metric to overall success
- Define monthly or quarterly measurement (not daily noise)
- Document data sources and calculation methods

Step 4: Create Your One-Page Dashboard

Like all MOVE tools, strategic numbers fit on one page. Simple format:

- Eight indicators maximum
- Current performance vs. target
- Trend direction
- Owner accountability
- Direct link to strategy

Remember: You build this once, then refine it. Don't keep rebuilding – sharpen your use of the tool.

Putting It Into Practice: Farella's Strategic Numbers

Daniel's team spent two weeks building their Strategic Numbers Dashboard. They went from 87 confused metrics to 8 that actually matter.

"Here's what we'll track and why each predicts our strategic success," Michael explained. "But notice something critical – while we start with financial targets because that's how we keep score, the indicators we can actually influence are people and processes."

Daniel nodded. **"We don't directly control revenue. We control whether our people are engaged, whether our processes deliver value to customers, and whether we're building capabilities. Do those right, customers pay us."**

Financial Category (two indicators)

Yes, they tracked financial outcomes – but as results, not drivers:

Revenue Growth vs. Budget

- 2025 Actual: $700M
- 2026 Target: $735M (+5%)
- Why it matters: Shows if focus strategy drives growth
- Leading indicator: Growth concentrated in Frozen/Healthy

EBITDA Improvement

- 2025 Actual: $60M (8.6%)
- 2026 Target: $65M (8.8%)
- Why it matters: Validates margin improvement thesis
- Leading indicator: Mix shift to higher-margin cells

"Notice we're not tracking revenue by itself," Jennifer explained. "We're tracking quality of growth – is it coming from our strategic focus areas?"

Customer Category (two indicators)

Customer Satisfaction Index

- 2025 Actual: 74
- 2026 Target: 85+
- Why it matters: Predicts whether innovation resonates
- Leading indicator: Satisfaction in Frozen/Healthy specifically

Customer Retention Rate

- 2025 Actual: 81%
- 2026 Target: 90%+
- Why it matters: Shows if we're building advantage or just trading
- Leading indicator: Retention in strategic categories

Sarah saw the connection: "If we're truly building advantage through innovation, customers should stay with us even when private label attacks on price."

Process/Technology Category (two indicators)

Product Innovation Cycle Completion

- 2025 Actual: 60% on-time
- 2026 Target: 90%+
- Why it matters: Speed is our weapon against private label
- Leading indicator: Frozen/Healthy launches specifically

Supply Chain Efficiency

- 2025 Actual: 82% on-time delivery
- 2026 Target: 95%+
- Why it matters: Can't beat BoxTop without operational excellence
- Leading indicator: Performance in key retail accounts

"These aren't generic operational metrics," Mark emphasized. "They directly connect to our competitive strategy – speed and reliability where it matters most. When we nail these processes, customers get value. When customers get value, we get paid."

People Category (two indicators)

Leadership Bench Strength

- 2025 Actual: 52% ready now
- 2026 Target: 70%
- Why it matters: Transformation needs different leaders
- Leading indicator: Percentage of key roles with identified successors ready to step up

"We measure how many critical positions have someone ready to take over tomorrow," explained Jennifer. "52% means barely half our key roles have prepared successors. That's a transformation killer."

Employee Engagement Score

- 2025 Actual: 68%
- 2026 Target: 80%
- Why it matters: Engaged employees drive innovation
- Leading indicator: Engagement in R&D and marketing

Dr. Raj connected to their AFC work (Figure 9.2):

> We identified capability gaps. These people metrics tell us if we're building the talent to fill them. Because at the end of the day, it's people who innovate, people who serve customers, people who execute. Get the right people doing the right things, everything else follows.

The Power of Simplification

"We went from 87 KPIs to 8 strategic indicators," Daniel summarized. "But look what's NOT here:"

- No vanity metrics
- No operational minutiae

MOVE TOOL 5: Strategic Numbers Dashboard Are we on track — and how will we know early?

Category	Indicator	Metric	Actual (2025)	Target (2026)	Gap	Data Source	Frequency
Financial	Revenue	YOY growth vs. budget	700	**735**	-35	Finance	Quarterly
	EBITDA	YOY EBITDA $	60	**75**	-15	Finance	Quarterly
Customer	Customer Satisfaction Index (CSI)	Avg. satisfaction rating (survey)	0.74	**0.85**	-0.11	Feedback	Quarterly
	Customer Retention Rate	% retained from PY	0.81	**0.9**	-0.09	CRM	Quarterly
Process/Technology	Product Innovation Cycle Completion	% of projects completed on-time	60%	**90%**	-30%	PM Tool	Quarterly
	Supply Chain Efficiency Ratio	% on-time delivery	82%	**95%**	-13%	Ops System	Monthly
People	Leadership Bench Strength	% of leaders ready for promotion	52%	**70%**	-18%	HR	Quarterly
	Employee Engagement Score	% of employees actively engaged	68%	**80%**	-12%	HR Survey	Bi-Annually

Figure 9.2 MOVE Tool #5: Strategic Numbers Dashboard Farella Foods Example.

- No functional silos
- Just eight numbers that predict strategic success

More importantly, six of the eight focused on what they could actually control – people and processes that create customer value. Financial results would follow.

The first quarter revealed insights their old system missed:

- Revenue grew 4% but only 1% from strategic categories (problem)
- Innovation cycles improved 20% but only in Snacks (wrong focus)
- Leadership bench strength increased but not in critical roles (misalignment)

"Our old dashboard would show green lights everywhere," Daniel observed. "This one shows where we're actually at risk."

Board Reporting Revolution

The next quarterly review transformed. Instead of 47 slides, Daniel presented one page with eight numbers.

"This is our strategic health," he began. "Two financial outcomes that show if we're winning. Six people and process indicators we directly control to make those outcomes happen."

The conversation changed:

- From "Why is revenue up?" to "Are the right people in the right roles?"
- From "Good efficiency gains" to "Are our processes creating customer value?"
- From reviewing history to managing what drives the future

Jennifer noted: "First time we actually understand what we control versus what we hope for. We manage people and processes. Customers decide if we get paid."

One board member pushed back: "Only eight metrics? What about all our other measures?"

"Those still exist for operational management," Daniel clarified. "But for enterprise strategy – for knowing if Farella will win or lose – these eight tell us everything. Ask Corporate Finance how much time we waste creating reports nobody uses. We're done with that."

The board got it. The logic chain from people to process to customer to financial was finally visible. These weren't random metrics – they showed exactly how value gets created.

Success Stories: The Power of Focus

Amazon's Customer Obsession Through Metrics

Amazon tracks its performance against roughly 500 measurable goals, and nearly 80% of those have to do with customer objectives. Jeff Bezos built a "culture of metrics" but with a crucial difference – the vast majority focus on customer outcomes, not internal operations.

For example, one of Amazon's metrics shows that even a minuscule 0.1-second delay in a web-page loading can translate into a 1% drop in customer activity. This granular focus on customer experience metrics drove every decision.[7]

Amazon tracks Net Promoter Scores, customer satisfaction ratings, and delivery performance with extraordinary detail. These metrics influence decisions at every level, creating an organization where customer feedback directly shapes business strategy.

The lesson: Even with hundreds of metrics, Amazon maintains focus by ensuring 80% connect directly to customer value. It's not the number of metrics that matters – it's what they measure.

Southwest Airlines' Three Numbers

While competitors tracked hundreds of metrics, Southwest focused on three:

- Turnaround time (drives asset utilization)
- Customer complaints per 10,000 (predicts loyalty)
- Cost per available seat mile (validates efficiency)

This radical simplification forced clarity. Either planes turned fast, customers were happy, and costs stayed low – or something was strategically wrong.

Result: Decades of profitable growth while competitors struggled.[8]

Toyota's Manufacturing Excellence

While competitors track hundreds of manufacturing variables, Toyota's Production System famously focuses on a handful of critical measures:

- Time-to-market (22 months for Tundra vs. industry's 30–40 months)
- Lead time from materials to finished vehicle
- Just-in-time inventory levels
- First-time quality rates

Toyota averages 24 months from design freeze to production, regularly reaches 15 months, and has achieved instances as low as 10 months. This speed comes from measuring what matters – cycle time and quality – not tracking every possible metric.[9]

The lesson extends beyond manufacturing. Whether it's customer obsession at Amazon or operational excellence at Toyota, companies that focus their metrics on strategic outcomes outperform those measuring everything.

Enhancing Your Strategic Numbers with AI

"Traditional dashboards are like driving using only your rearview mirror," Daniel told his team. "AI turns them into GPS – showing what's ahead, not just what's behind."

The Real-Time Revolution

The game-changer isn't just AI – it's AI processing strategic signals as they happen. Traditional monthly reviews meant problems festered for weeks. AI-enhanced dashboards spot issues in days, sometimes hours.

Consider DoorDash's strategic transformation. While competitors reviewed monthly delivery metrics, DoorDash's AI monitored real-time signals:

- Social sentiment shifts predicted market share changes six weeks early
- Driver availability patterns showed capacity constraints before they impacted service
- Order complexity trends revealed changing consumer preferences instantly

This speed advantage lets them adjust 10x faster than competitors using traditional dashboards. When COVID shifted demand patterns, their AI detected changes in 48 hours. Competitors took weeks to see the same trends in monthly reports.[10]

Speed as Strategic Weapon

For Farella, real-time AI monitoring revealed:

- Competitor promotional patterns before they impacted sales
- Supply chain disruptions while still manageable
- Innovation excitement declining during development, not after launch

"We went from autopsies to prevention," Michael explained. "AI tells us what's about to break, not what already broke."

Pattern Recognition Across Indicators

AI continuously analyzes relationships between indicators that humans miss. At Farella, AI spotted that R&D hiring patterns predicted innovation cycle completion by two to four months. When hiring slowed, innovation suffered quarters later.

"This let us intervene before problems appeared in our metrics," Dr. Raj explained. "We fixed talent pipeline issues before innovation stalled."

Anomaly Detection Before Impact

Traditional dashboards show problems after they occur. AI-enhanced dashboards spot anomalies while manageable.

Farella's AI flagged unusual patterns:

- Customer retention strong overall but weakening in key retail accounts
- Innovation cycles meeting targets but quality scores declining
- Employee engagement high but turnover increasing in critical roles

"Without AI pattern recognition, these would show up months later as missed targets," Michael noted.

Predictive Power in Practice

Six months later, their AI-enhanced dashboard caught three problems before they bit:

Innovation Alert: Product development hit deadlines but customer testing showed weak enthusiasm. AI predicted satisfaction would drop in six months.

Competitive Signal: Patent filings and LinkedIn hiring showed Bravora preparing premium frozen launch. Normal competitive intelligence would miss this until launch day.

Talent Risk: Engagement scores looked fine but AI spotted early resignation patterns in R&D. Predicted 15% knowledge loss coming.

Daniel's team took pre-emptive action:

- Restructured innovation process for quality, not just speed
- Accelerated premium frozen development before Bravora's entry
- Launched retention program for critical R&D talent

"AI didn't replace our judgment," Daniel reflected. "It gave us time to use it."

Data Security Note

Use your company's secure AI environment when available. For sensitive strategic indicators:

- Use enterprise AI platforms with data protection
- Never share strategic metrics in public AI tools
- Anonymize all company data when using external AI
- Treat indicator data as board-confidential

Remember: Your strategic indicators reveal competitive strategy. Protect them accordingly.

AI Prompts for Strategic Indicators

Use these prompts in your secure AI environment to enhance your strategic numbers:

For Pattern Recognition: Prompt: "Analyze correlations between these indicators over 24 months: [revenue growth %, retention rate, innovation cycle time, etc.]. Which indicators predict others? What lag times exist?"

- What you'll get: Hidden relationships and predictive patterns
- How to use it: Focus on leading indicators with the strongest predictive power

For Anomaly Detection: Prompt: "Review these indicator trends and identify statistical anomalies or emerging patterns that signal strategic risks or opportunities. Include confidence levels."

- What you'll get: Early warning signals before they impact results
- How to use it: Investigate anomalies before they become problems

For Target Validation: Prompt: "Given our strategic objectives and current performance, what indicator targets represent meaningful progress while remaining achievable? Model interdependencies."

- What you'll get: Realistic targets based on systemic relationships
- How to use it: Set stretch targets that motivate without demoralizing

For Competitive Benchmarking: Prompt: "Based on public data, estimate strategic indicator performance for food companies successfully fighting private label. What patterns predict success?"

- What you'll get: External validation of your indicator choices
- How to use it: Confirm you're measuring what matters for competitive advantage

For Dashboard Design: Prompt: "Given these 8 strategic indicators [list them], design a one-page dashboard layout that shows current vs. target, trends, and accountability. Prioritize visual clarity."

- What you'll get: Clean dashboard format focusing on what matters
- How to use it: Create a template your team will actually use

For Scenario Planning: Prompt: "If these indicators trend as projected [share projections], what strategic risks and opportunities emerge? Model three scenarios with probabilities."

- What you'll get: Early warning of strategic pivots needed
- How to use it: Prepare contingency plans before problems hit

The companies that win don't have prettier dashboards. They have better radar.

Making Strategic Numbers Work

DO:

- Focus on leading indicators you control (people and processes)
- Link every metric directly to customer value creation
- Assign one owner per metric with clear accountability
- Keep to eight to ten indicators maximum for enterprise strategy
- Measure monthly or quarterly for strategic insight

DON'T:

- Confuse enterprise strategy metrics with operational dashboards
- Add metrics to make functions feel included
- Track daily variations that create noise not signal
- Use lagging financial indicators as primary measures
- Keep rebuilding from scratch instead of refining

Your Move

Your dashboards are lying to you. Not with bad data, but by focusing on outcomes you don't control instead of the drivers you do.

Here's the truth every executive knows but rarely admits: You don't manage revenue. You manage people who serve customers through processes that create value. When those work, revenue follows.

Strategic numbers aren't about tracking financial results better. They're about measuring whether your people are engaged, your processes deliver value, and you're building the capabilities to win. Get those right, and customers pay you.

The Linked Logic Completes

Strategic numbers complete the MOVE system – the final link that makes strategy real. Look at what you built:

Move 1: Strategic Assumptions spotted trends others missed.
Move 2: Vision + Driving Force chose where to play and how to win.

Move 3A: Product-Market Matrix made the money real. Specific targets by year.
Move 3B: Market Reality Check pressure-tested your bets against actual markets.
Move 4: Advantage+ Future Capabilities showed exactly what you need to build.
Move 5: Strategic numbers tells you if it's working. Your early warning system.

Five tools. Five pages. One system that actually works.

As Daniel told his team: "We're not measuring better. We're measuring what matters. These eight numbers tell us months before everyone else whether we're winning or losing."

Remember: Farella went from 87 metrics to 8. Not 80. Not 18. Eight numbers that actually predict success.

Quick-Action Checklist

- ☐ Count your current KPIs – if over 20, you're probably measuring activity not strategy
- ☐ Identify which metrics actually predicted your last strategic success or failure
- ☐ Ask your team: "If we could only track 8 numbers, which would tell us if we're winning?"
- ☐ Test the link: Do your indicators connect directly to your Vision and Product-Market Matrix targets?

You've now built a complete strategy system. **Five tools, five pages, one integrated logic chain.**

Strategic Assumptions spotted opportunities. Vision chose where to play. PMM and MRC made bets and validated them. AFC identified what to build. Strategic numbers measure if it's working.

The strategy is built. Time to make it happen.

Notes

1 Robert S. Kaplan and David P. Norton, "The Balanced Scorecard – Measures That Drive Performance." *Harvard Business Review* 70, no. 1 (January-February 1992): 71–79.
2 Based on the author's 25+ years of consulting and client experience.
3 "Wells Fargo Account Fraud Scandal." U.S. Senate Committee on Banking, Housing, and Urban Affairs, September 2016. https://www.banking.senate.gov/newsroom/majority/shelby-statement-at-hearing-on-wells-fargo.
4 Peloton Interactive, Inc., "Peloton Reports Fiscal Year 2022 Third Quarter Results." Press Release, May 10, 2022. https://investor.onepeloton.com/news-releases/.
5 Leslie A. Perlow, Constance Noonan Hadley, and Eunice Eun. "Stop the Meeting Madness." *Harvard Business Review* 95, no. 4 (July-August 2017): 62–69.
6 Peter Gordon Roetzel, "Information Overload in the Information Age: A Review of the Literature from Business Administration, Business Psychology, and Related Disciplines with a Bibliometric Approach and Framework Development." *Business Research* 12 (2019): 479–522.
7 Scott Galloway, *The Four: The Hidden DNA of Amazon, Apple, Facebook, and Google* (New York: Portfolio, 2017).
8 Jody Hoffer Gittell, *The Southwest Airlines Way* (New York: McGraw-Hill, 2003).
9 Jeffrey K. Liker, *The Toyota Way: 14 Management Principles from the World's Greatest Manufacturer* (New York: McGraw-Hill, 2004).
10 "DoorDash S-1 Registration Statement." Securities and Exchange Commission, November 13, 2020. https://www.sec.gov/Archives/edgar/data/1792789/000119312520292381/d752207ds1.htm.

Part III

STRATEGY TO ACTION

Execute and Adjust

You Have Five Strategic Pages. Now What?

Part II gave you five one-page tools that create strategic clarity:

- Strategic Assumptions: what's changing in your world
- Vision + Driving Force: where you're going and how you'll win
- Product-Market Matrix + Market Reality Check: your bets validated against competition
- Advantage + Future Capabilities: what you'll build to win
- Strategic Numbers: the metrics that matter

Five pages. Complete strategy. Everyone aligned.

The Real Question: Monday Morning

Strategic clarity is powerful. But it's not enough.

Right now, in companies everywhere, brilliant strategies are dying slow deaths. Not because they're wrong. Because they never translate into different choices about:

- Which projects get funded vs. killed
- How resources actually flow
- What rhythm keeps strategy alive

The gap between strategy and execution isn't about intelligence or effort. It's about translation. You need tools that turn strategic choices into funded projects and maintained momentum.

Why Good Strategies Stop at the Boardroom Door

I've watched this pattern hundreds of times. A leadership team spends days crafting strategy. They achieve real clarity about where to play and how to win. Everyone leaves energized. Then three months later, nothing has actually changed.

You know the symptoms. Fifty-seven initiatives all labeled "strategic priority." Resource allocation that looks exactly like last year despite a completely different strategy. Dashboards with 47 metrics where everything glows green while market share drops red. Annual planning cycles trying to catch quarterly market shifts.

One consumer goods company I worked with discovered something shocking. After creating brilliant strategy, they mapped their project portfolio against it. Of 52 initiatives consuming $30M annually, exactly seven connected to their stated strategy. The rest were zombies – projects that made sense once but now just consumed resources.

DOI: 10.4324/9781003682455-13

Another pattern: resource inertia. A financial services firm pivoted to digital-first strategy. Six months later? Their digital team still had 12 people while their branch operations had 200. Same budgets, same org chart, different strategy. The strategy said "digital wins." The resource allocation said "branches forever."

Then there's measurement theater. Companies create these gorgeous dashboards – 50, 60, sometimes 100+ metrics. Every division green. Stock price red. Why? They're measuring activity, not strategy. They track what's easy to count, not what predicts winning. By the time lagging indicators flash warning, competitors have already won.

A Different Approach to Execution

What if execution wasn't separate from strategy? What if the same clarity and simplicity that makes MOVE's strategy tools work could transform how you execute? What if AI could help you spot patterns in your project portfolio and flag when initiatives drift from strategy?

That's exactly what Part III delivers. Not more complexity. Not elaborate project management systems. Just two practical tools that translate strategic choices into action – and help you adjust when reality teaches you something new.

These tools respect your time and intelligence. They assume you know your business. They provide structure without prescription, clarity without rigidity. And with AI as your thinking partner, you can process more signals, spot misalignment faster, and adjust before small gaps become big problems.

Part III: Strategy to Action

The next two chapters give you the execution tools that make strategy real:

Chapter 10: Execute: Turn Strategy into Signature Initiatives

You probably have dozens of initiatives competing for resources. This tool helps you see which ones actually advance your strategy and which ones just consume time and money.

The Strategic Project Portfolio works differently than traditional prioritization. Instead of complex scoring models that take weeks to complete, you'll use a simple framework that maps every initiative against your five strategic pages. In about two hours, you can:

- Score each project against your actual strategic choices
- Identify which initiatives directly build competitive advantage
- Spot the zombies that consume resources without strategic impact
- Reorganize survivors into three to four signature programs with critical mass

Most leadership teams discover they can free up 30–40% of their resources just by stopping things that don't connect to strategy. That's not about working harder – it's about working on what matters with enough resources to actually win.

Chapter 11: Keep the Beat: Establish a Quarterly Cadence

Strategy isn't a document you create once a year. It's a discipline you practice every quarter. But nobody needs another reporting meeting where everyone reads slides to each other.

The MOVE Quarterly Business Review (QBR) is different. It's a two-hour decision engine that replaces ten hours of unproductive meetings. You'll learn a specific format that:

- Reviews strategic progress, not just operational metrics
- Catches problems while they're still small enough to fix

- Adjusts quickly when reality doesn't match assumptions
- Maintains momentum without creating bureaucracy

The QBR format respects that executives are busy. It focuses on decisions, not presentations. On adjustments, not admiration. Most teams find it actually energizes them rather than draining them – because they're solving real strategic issues, not performing theater.

What Success Looks Like

When companies implement these execution tools, things shift fast.

That technology company that found 33 disconnected initiatives? They didn't just kill them. They redirected $12M to double down on three signature programs that actually built their stated advantage. Eighteen months later, they'd taken market leadership in two new categories.

The food manufacturer who consolidated 23 capability projects into 4? Same people, same budget. But instead of peanut butter spread across everything, they achieved critical mass. Their innovation cycle dropped from 18 months to 8. Speed became their advantage.

My favorite transformation: a healthcare division that dreaded their monthly three-hour "strategic" reviews. Mostly PowerPoint theater. They switched to two-hour quarterly sessions focused on decisions, not presentations. Six months later, they'd made more strategic progress than in the previous two years. Not by meeting more, but by meeting better.

None of these companies added complexity. They subtracted it. They didn't hire armies of consultants. They used simple tools their own teams could run.

Your Choice Point

You've built strategic clarity with five powerful pages. That alone puts you ahead of most organizations still drowning in PowerPoint.

But clarity without execution is just expensive thinking. And execution without adjustment is just stubborn hoping. Part III shows you how to translate clarity into funded projects and sustained rhythm – while staying agile enough to adjust as you learn. Not through complex systems that require armies of consultants. Through simple tools that your team can use immediately, enhanced by AI when you need deeper pattern recognition.

Your strategy is clear. Your choices are visible. Now let's make them real – and keep them relevant.

Turn the page. It's time to execute and adjust.

Chapter 10

Execute

Turn Strategy into Signature Initiatives

"If your biggest competitor is putting 70% of resources behind one breakthrough initiative while you're spreading 3% across 31 projects, who do you think customers will notice?"

Daniel Ross stared at the quarterly review dashboard. Something wasn't adding up. They'd built a clear strategy through MOVE – Strategic Assumptions identified wellness trends, Vision focused on winning through taste and speed, PMM showed GREEN bets in Frozen and Healthy, AFC defined capabilities to build, Strategic Numbers tracked progress.

Yet the dashboard showed 47 active projects labeled "strategic," consuming $45M annually. And that was just counting major initiatives – dozens of sub-projects lurked beneath each one.

"Michael," Daniel called to his VP Strategy. "Pull together every project we're running. Every single one. I need to see them all in one place."

Michael Thompson looked up from his laptop. For years, he'd been buried in PowerPoint decks, creating presentations about strategy rather than driving it. This felt different – actionable.

"Give me the weekend," Michael said. "I'll compile everything – every project that someone has labeled strategic, not counting all the sub-projects."

Monday morning revealed the truth. The conference room walls were covered with project sheets – 47 initiatives ranging from critical cold chain upgrades to someone's pet project for workspace redesign.

"This is what strategic drift looks like," Daniel said quietly. "We know exactly where we need to go. We've built the roadmap. But look at where we're actually spending resources."

Sarah Martinez, normally quick with creative solutions, was unusually quiet. She saw her own marketing projects scattered across the wall – many disconnected from commercial reality, just as Ross had suspected when he arrived.

"We're not lacking strategy," Jennifer Walsh observed, her CFO skepticism showing. "We're lacking the discipline to execute it."

Over the past few months, the executive team at Farella Foods [fictional example] had invested serious time building the full MOVE system. Their Strategic Assumptions identified wellness and convenience as unstoppable trends. Vision focused on winning through taste, simplicity, and speed. Product-Market Matrix identified GREEN bets in Retail Frozen Meals and Healthy Bowls. Advantage+ Future Capabilities defined what they needed to build – category innovation, consumer marketing, and operational speed. Strategic Numbers tracked whether they were winning.

They had clarity.

But what became clear next was sobering: while the strategy was tight, their execution engine was still scattered.

When they held up the current project portfolio against their newly defined PMM and AFC, the disconnect hit hard. Most projects weren't supporting the strategy. They were remnants of the

DOI: 10.4324/9781003682455-14

old Farella – when they tried to be everything to everyone. Legacy innovation projects for Snack Packs that were bleeding cash. Foodservice expansions that diluted focus. Pet projects from every function.

"Look at this," Jennifer Walsh pointed to the screen. "We're spending $3M on a new dessert line when our Healthy Bowls are underfunded by $5M."

It wasn't incompetence. It was strategic drift.

The numbers confirmed it: millions in annual project budgets, top performers tied up in initiatives that didn't connect to their GREEN bets. Nearly 80% of executive time consumed by work that didn't align with "Focus to Win."

Daniel paused. "We don't have an execution problem. We have a focus problem. We're busy, not strategic."

Michael Thompson had prepared for this moment. "What if we consolidated everything into three signature initiatives that directly build what our AFC said we need?"

What followed wasn't just portfolio management – it was strategic surgery.

The Pattern of Project Proliferation

The project proliferation problem began innocently enough. In the 1990s, companies discovered that organizing work into "projects" made things more visible and accountable than traditional functional silos. Project management became a profession. PMOs were born. Certifications emerged.[1]

But somewhere along the way, everything became a project. Customer satisfaction improvement became a project. Cost reduction became a project. Culture change became a project. Each department wanted their own strategic initiative to show they were contributing to success.

The logic seemed reasonable: if project management is good, and strategy is important, then having lots of strategic projects must be better. This spawned the era of initiative explosion – companies running 15–20, even 30 strategic initiatives, with many more projects buried under each one. A single "Digital Transformation Initiative" might contain 40 projects. "Customer Excellence" could hide another 25.

Why Traditional Portfolio Management Fails

Traditional portfolio management tried to solve this with sophisticated scoring models, resource optimization algorithms, and complex governance structures. But these approaches missed the fundamental problem: they managed projects, not strategy.

Consider how most companies handle their portfolio:

- Annual planning cycles that lock in projects for 12 months
- Democratic scoring where every function gets representation
- Complex stage-gates that slow decision making
- Resource allocation based on last year plus adjustments

The result? Companies excel at managing dozens of projects efficiently while their strategy suffocates under the weight of unfocused execution.

"We became world-class at running projects that didn't matter," one Fortune 500 executive admitted. "Our PMO won awards while our market share evaporated."[2]

The proliferation happens gradually. A new CEO arrives with fresh ideas – launch innovation labs. Market conditions shift – add digital acceleration. Competitors make moves – create customer experience programs. Each response makes sense in isolation. Together, they create strategic chaos.

Hidden Cost of Being Busy

The cost goes beyond failed projects. Organizations struggle to kill initiatives because leaders keep layering on new ones without removing old ones. It's addition without subtraction – strategic hoarding disguised as strategic thinking.

Consider the contrast:

- Mondelez focused on Power Brands while competitors managed hundreds of SKUs[3]
- Trader Joe's carries 4,000 items while typical grocers stock 50,000[4]
- In-N-Out Burger has four menu items while McDonald's has over 100[5]

We know how those stories play out. **Companies that try to do everything achieve nothing memorable. Companies that focus on a few big bets create categories.**

The Power of Focused Execution

When companies commit to focus, the results speak for themselves:

Chobani's Three-Initiative Revolution: When Hamdi Ulukaya bought a defunct yogurt plant, he didn't try to make 50 products. He focused on three initiatives: Perfect the Product (authentic Greek yogurt), Win Premium Shelf Space (not compete on price), and Build Word-of-Mouth (no traditional advertising).

Result: From zero to $1B in five years, taking 20% of the U.S. yogurt market.[6]

Liquid Death's Focused Disruption: While beverage giants managed hundreds of SKUs across dozens of categories, Liquid Death focused on one thing: making water cool. Three initiatives: Killer Branding (death to plastic bottles), Rock Concert Distribution (venues and tattoo parlors), and Social Rebellion (content that big brands can't touch).

Result: $700M valuation in three years selling water.[7]

These companies understood what Farella was about to learn: concentration beats diversification in strategy execution.

Meanwhile, Farella's competitors were accelerating. NüWave launched products in 12 weeks while Farella took 18 months. Bravora undercut prices by 30% through operational focus. BoxTop guaranteed 99.5% delivery while Farella struggled at 94%.

The speed difference wasn't about working harder. It was about focus. Competitors concentrated resources on what mattered. Farella spread resources across everything.

When Michael compiled Farella's projects, the truth was stark. You're running 47 major projects labeled "strategic." After scoring them against your strategy, only 16 actually supported your GREEN bets in Frozen and Healthy. The other 31? Legacy projects, IT maintenance, and departmental wish lists.

Every department had protected their pet projects. The Workforce Plugin Maintenance that scored 24? Still consuming $2M annually. Meanwhile, your PMM said to dominate Retail Frozen Meals and scale Healthy Bowls, but critical capabilities like Cold Chain Expansion were competing for resources with zombie projects.

NüWave Naturals doesn't have this problem. They killed everything except three initiatives. They put 70% of resources behind plant-based innovation. You're splitting resources across 47 major projects. They're concentrating on three. Guess who's winning.

The MOVE Solution: Strategic Project Portfolio

SPP takes your Future Capabilities from the AFC Matrix and consolidates them into two to three signature initiatives that everyone understands and resources flow to them naturally.

The One Question It Answers: "How do we turn the capabilities we must build into signature initiatives that everyone understands and resources flow to naturally?"

This isn't about project management. It's about strategic concentration – putting enough resources behind your biggest bets to actually win.

The Direct Connection to Your MOVE Journey

Your SPP is the bridge between strategy and execution:

- **SA** revealed trends you must respond to
- **VDF** defined where you'll win
- **PMM** identified specific bets to place
- **MRC** validated those bets
- **AFC** showed what you must build
- **SN** measure if it's working
- **Now SPP turns capabilities into funded projects**

Without this tool, you have strategy documents and good intentions. With it, you have focused execution that builds competitive advantage.

Why This Creates Breakthrough Value

From Capabilities to Projects: The Future Capabilities in your AFC Matrix aren't abstract concepts – they're your project list. Each capability you must build becomes a project. The SPP consolidates these into signature initiatives that create competitive advantage.

From Scattered to Concentrated Resources: Organizations focusing on two to three signature initiatives achieve 60% better strategic success rates. They put 70% of resources behind their biggest bets instead of spreading 3% across 30 projects.[8]

From Internal Complexity to Market Clarity: The T-Shirt Test reveals whether you have real strategy or internal theater. Your signature initiatives should be so clear that employees would proudly wear them on a T-shirt. If people would be embarrassed to wear it, customers won't understand it (Figure 10.1).

MOVE Tool 6A: Strategic Project Portfolio What few bets will move the numbers?

Projects	Strategic Objective	Owner	Start Date	End Date	Expected ROI	Outcome (2028)	Current or New	Decision	Initiative	Score
P1										
P2										
P3										
P4										
P5										
P6										
P7										
P8										
P9										
P10										
P11										
P12										
P13										
P14										
P15										
P16										
P17										
P18										
PN....										

Figure 10.1 MOVE TOOL #6: Strategic Project Portfolio Blank Template.

How to Build Your Strategic Project Portfolio

Step 1: Gather All Projects: Future and Current

List every project:

- Future Projects: Each Future Capability from your AFC Matrix becomes a project
- Current Projects: All existing initiatives already underway

Don't filter yet – visibility is power. You'll often discover 30–50 projects when you include everything. The shock of seeing them all listed is part of the cure.

Step 2: Evaluate Against Strategic Criteria

Score each project using weighted criteria that connect to your MOVE strategy:

Strategic Project Scoring Criteria

Criteria Weight Description

- Vision Alignment 10 Direct support of "Focus to Win" strategy
- PMM Support 10 Builds advantage in GREEN cells (Frozen/Healthy Retail)
- Capability Building 8 Creates capabilities from AFC Matrix
- Competitive Response 6 Strengthens position vs. Bravora/NüWave
- Timing 6 Critical now vs. can wait
- Current Advantage 8 Leverages existing strengths

Score each project 1–10 for each criterion. Multiply by weight. Total score determines priority.

What to Do with Low Scores: Projects scoring in the bottom 20% are telling you something – they don't support your Vision, don't build GREEN cell advantages, and don't create future capabilities. The scoring reveals they're misaligned with your strategy. Reallocate their resources to initiatives that drive your future, not maintain your past.

Step 3: Consolidate into three to four Signature Initiatives

Group your highest-scoring projects into themes that make strategic sense. Look at your projects and ask: "What story would make every employee understand why these projects matter?"

The best consolidation often comes from your business fundamentals:

RCP: Revenue, Competitiveness, Profit

- Revenue: all projects that drive growth in target segments
- Competitiveness: all projects that differentiate from private label
- Profit: all projects that improve margins and efficiency

PMC: Product, Market, Competitiveness

- Product: all projects making better food faster
- Market: all projects winning in Retail
- Competitiveness: all projects creating speed advantage

Real Examples: The Good and The Bad

Clear and Memorable:

- Chipotle: "Food with Integrity"[9]
- Sweetgreen: "Connecting People to Real Food"[10]
- Oatly: "Post-Milk Generation"[11]
- Beyond Meat: "The Future of Protein"[12]

Corporate Word Salad:

- "Delivering Quality First Programme"
- "Strategic Excellence Initiative"
- "Digital Business Enhancement"
- "Holistic Customer Experience Journey"

T-Shirt Test: Your signature initiatives should be so clear that employees would proudly wear them on a T-shirt at a food industry conference. If people would be embarrassed to wear it, retailers won't understand it.

Step 4: Create one-Page Project Plans

The market is flooded with sophisticated project management tools – Monday.com, Asana, Smartsheet, MS Project. Companies invest millions in these platforms, creating beautiful dashboards that track every milestone, dependency, and resource allocation.

But here's what often happens: You ask a project owner, "How does this project directly create the business value our strategy requires?" The response? A pause, followed by pulling up colorful Gantt charts showing activities, not outcomes.

"We implemented a world-class project management system," one CEO told us. "Every project had green status lights. Every milestone was tracked. We celebrated our 'execution excellence.' Six months later, we missed our strategic targets. We'd optimized activity tracking while our strategy struggled."[13]

The tools aren't the problem. The disconnect between project activity and strategic value is. Your project dashboards might show 100% on-time milestone completion while delivering little of the competitive advantage your strategy demands.

That's why each project needs a simple, one-page plan that any project owner can explain without opening their laptop:

Simple One-Page Project Template

WHAT Project Statement (one sentence that everyone understands)
WHY Business Value: Maximum three objectives showing impact on Revenue, Cost, or Profit
HOW Key Activities: Ten maximum that deliver the objectives
HOW MUCH: Investment Required – Budget, people, capability requirements
WHO: Single accountable owner, regions, functions, dependencies
WHEN: Start/finish dates, quarterly milestones
WHAT IF: Top three risks with mitigation strategies

This template works in Excel, MS Project, or on a napkin. The tool doesn't matter. What matters is that every project owner can answer: "How does my project build the specific capability our strategy requires?" Without checking their dashboard. Without consulting the PMO. From memory, with conviction.

If they can't, you're funding activity theater, not strategic execution.

Step 5: Establish Exception-Based Reporting

During Farella's Q3 Executive Review, they introduced a radical change to portfolio reviews. No more walking through every project. No more death by PowerPoint. Just focus on what needs attention.

"New rule," Daniel announced. "We only discuss RED or YELLOW indicators. If it's GREEN, it's working. Don't waste time telling us what's already succeeding."

The dashboard tracked four dimensions for each project:

- **Time**: On schedule or delayed?
- **Cost $**: Within budget or overrun?
- **Cost Hours**: Resource allocation on track?
- **Performance**: Delivering business objectives? (Figure 10.2)

The reporting rhythm depends on project nature:

- Innovation projects: Monthly (fast-changing, need quick pivots)
- Infrastructure builds: Quarterly (longer cycles, stable milestones)
- Quick wins: Bi-weekly (rapid execution, tight timelines)

The key is matching reporting frequency to meaningful progress intervals. Weekly updates on a two-year infrastructure project waste time. Quarterly updates on rapid innovation miss critical pivot points.

Project leads were instructed to answer only three questions for any RED or YELLOW status:

1. **What's causing the problem?**
2. **What specific corrective action is underway?**
3. **What do you need from leadership to unblock it?**

The first review under this system was revelatory. The Retail Pack Redesign showed YELLOW on Time. Sarah Martinez explained in 30 seconds: "Design finalized but supplier samples delayed. Need procurement to expedite. Action already initiated."

"Done," Mark Chen responded. "I'll call them today."

The Frozen Pizza Reformulation was RED on Performance. Dr. Raj was direct: "Taste tests failed. Reformulating. Need two more weeks and $50K for accelerated testing."

Project Name	Product / Market	Owner	T	C$	C.hr	P	Key Updates	Critical Actions	Prob. of Success (EBITDA)	2026 Total Sales Impact ($MM)	2026 Total EBITDA Impact ($MM)	Annual EBITDA Impact ($MM)
Retail Pack Redesign	Tomato Sauces / NA	LS	Green	Yellow	Green	Red	Design finalized; samples approved	Secure production line slot; update retailers	High	3.2	0.75	1.1
Frozen Pizza Reformulation	Frozen Meals / EU	AK	Yellow	Red	Red	Yellow	Delayed due to ingredient shipment	Negotiate alt. supplier; update formulations	Medium	2.8	0.35	0.6
Olive Oil Expansion	Premium / Asia	RP	Green	Green	Yellow	Green	Packaging testing complete	Finalize distribution partners	High	1.5	0.55	0.75
Direct-to-Consumer Launch	All Products / DTC	MH	Red	Red	Yellow	Red	E-comm site delayed; low engagement	Relaunch plan; update SEO and ads	Low	1.2	-0.15	0.1
Pasta Shape Automation	Dry Pasta / Global	TS	Green	Green	Green	Green	New line ready; testing underway	Train ops team; finalize QA checklist	High	4	1.15	1.4

Figure 10.2 MOVE Tool #6: Strategic Project Portfolio Exception Reporting Farella Foods Example (sub-projects of strategic initiatives).

"Approved," Daniel said. "Next."

In 45 minutes, they'd reviewed the entire portfolio. Compare that to their old three-hour marathons where every project manager presented slides regardless of status.

"This isn't reporting theater," Jennifer Walsh observed. "It's actually managing the business."

The impact was immediate:

- Executive time on portfolio reviews dropped 75%
- Issues got resolved in days, not weeks
- Project managers focused on delivery, not PowerPoint
- Senior leaders spent time removing barriers, not listening to success stories

As Michael Thompson noted: "We went from admiring problems to solving them. GREEN means go. YELLOW means caution. RED means act now. Everything else is noise."

The dashboard became a living tool – updated weekly, reviewed monthly, acted on immediately. No narratives about successful projects. No long explanations. Just exceptions that need executive attention.

This is what strategic portfolio management looks like: senior time focused on removing barriers, not reviewing successes. Accountability for results, not activity. Speed through focus, not process.

Farella's Strategic Consolidation

Monday morning. The war room walls displayed all 47 major projects. The executive team assembled for what would become a pivotal session.

"Let's start with reality," Michael Thompson began. "We found 47 major projects across the company labeled as strategic. That's not counting the dozens of sub-projects under each one."

He pulled up the framework:

Strategic Project Scoring Criteria

- **Drives Major Goals and Vision** (Weight: 10): Direct connection to your Vision from Chapter 5
- **Aligns with Priority Product-Market Cells** (Weight: 10): Supports GREEN bets from your PMM
- **Maximizes Key Capability Development** (Weight: 8): Builds Future Capabilities from your Advantage+Future Capabilities Matrix
- **Maximizes Global Competitiveness** (Weight: 6): Creates differentiation versus competitors
- **Timing and Urgency** (Weight: 6): Market window or competitive pressure
- **Enhances Current Competitive Advantage** (Weight: 8): Strengthens existing core positions

Score each project on a scale of one to ten for each criterion. Multiply by weight. Total score determines priority.

"No politics. No protecting favorites," Daniel emphasized. "Just brutal honesty about what supports our strategy."

Mark Chen shifted uncomfortably. His operational expertise told him several projects were necessary for daily operations. But necessity didn't mean strategic.

"Even our ERP maintenance?" Mark asked, already knowing the answer.

"Especially that," Jennifer Walsh interjected, surprising everyone. The CFO typically protected every investment. "I've been skeptical of spending without guaranteed ROI. But maintaining yesterday's systems while competitors build tomorrow's advantages? That's the worst ROI of all."

The scoring began. Three hours of honest assessment. Some revelations:

Dr. Raj Patel watched his pet R&D projects get scored: "That autonomous packaging line I've been pushing? It scored 36. It's technically brilliant but doesn't build any capability from our AFC. It's theater, not strategy."

Sarah Martinez faced her own reality: "Half my marketing initiatives are disconnected from commercial outcomes. This influencer program for GenZ? We don't even have products they want. Score: 24."

"Look at the pattern," Michael summarized:

High Scorers (60–88 points): 14 projects directly tied to AFC capabilities – APPROVED

Mid Scorers (40–59 points): 20 projects with partial strategic value – DELAYED

Low Scorers (24–39 points): 13 projects that were pure legacy – KILLED

"We're approving only the 14 high-scoring projects and focusing them into three signature initiatives," Daniel announced. "Everything else is either killed or delayed. That's $20M and 50 people redirected to what matters."

The freed resources changed everything. Instead of 50 people spread across 47 projects, they concentrated talent on three initiatives. Instead of $45M funding everything, they focused $35M on strategic priorities. Speed comes from focus, not frantic activity (Figure 10.3).

Mark Chen winced but didn't protest. His legacy processes couldn't save projects that didn't build future capabilities.

Jennifer ran quick numbers: "Killing these eight projects frees up $12M and roughly 50 FTEs. That's real resources for real strategy."

What Emerged Were Three Signature Initiatives that Would Transform Farella

Initiative 1: Win in Growth Segments

Objective: Accelerate profitable growth in Retail Frozen, Healthy Bowls, and strategic Foodservice segments.

This consolidated seven high-scoring projects that directly supported their PMM GREEN bets:

MOVE Tool 6A: Strategic Project Portfolio What few bets will move the numbers?

Projects	Strategic Objective	Owner	Start Date	End Date	Expected ROI	Outcome (2028)	Current or New	Decision	Initiative	Score
Meal Innovation Center	Develop new meals to drive premium growth	VP Product	2025-09-01	2026-04-01	High	$10M Rev	New	**Approve**	**Premium Rev**	**48**
Cold Chain Expansion	Improve cold supply chain reliability	VP Ops	2025-11-12	2026-05-01	Medium	$10M Rev	New	**Approve**	**Margin Exp**	**48**
Retail Segmentation Engine	Enable customer targeting by format (Retail)	VP Mkting	2025-11-09	2026-04-01	High	$10M Rev	New	**Approve**	**Premium Rev**	**48**
Portion Design Platform	Design portions to match health trends	VP Product	2025-10-01	2026-03-31	Med	$5M Rev	New	**Approve**	**Premium Rev**	**48**
SKU Agility Upgrade	Increase response speed to demand shifts	VP Product	2025-07-29	2026-02-02	High	$10M Rev	New	**Approve**	**Operational Speec**	**48**
Nutritional R&D Center	Develop health-focused food solutions	Head of R&D	2025-07-29	2026-03-21	Medium	$10M Rev	New	**Approve**	**Premium Rev**	**48**
Wellness Branding Rollout	Establish leadership in wellness	VP Mkting	2025-07-11	2026-01-11	Medium	$10M Rev	New	**Approve**	**Operational Speec**	**48**
Logistics Integration Program	Streamline logistics for margin lift	VP Ops	2025-10-13	2026-06-18	High	$10M Eff	New	**Approve**	**Margin Exp**	**48**
DTC Testbeds Setup	Accelerate testing of new health SKUs	VP Product	2025-10-01	2026-04-01	Medium	$5M Rev	New	**Kill**	**N/A**	**24**
New Co-Packer Onboarding	Add flexibility for new formats	VP Ops	2025-10-10	2026-04-01	Medium	$5M Rev	New	**Approve**	**Margin Exp**	**48**
Legacy ERP Maintenance	Maintain stability of existing ERP	CIO	2025-07-01	2026-01-31	Low	$2M Soft Met	Current	**Delay**	**Digital Core**	**24**
Outdated SKU Refresh	Update packaging on legacy SKUs	VP Product	2025-11-27	2026-03-31	Low	$1M Cost	Current	**Kill**	**Frozen Meals**	**24**
Food Safety Audit Compliance	Update compliance processes	VP Ops	2025-08-01	2026-04-27	Low	$0M	Current	**Kill**	**Margin Exp**	**24**
DTC Portal Upgrade	Improve DTC site UX	VP Mkting	2025-10-12	2026-03-01	Medium	$2M Rev	Current	**Delay**	**N/A**	**24**
Digital Loyalty Pilot	Test new points-based program	VP Mkting	2025-09-01	2026-03-01	Low	$2M Rev	Current	**Delay**	**N/A**	**24**
Sustainability Report Automation	Auto-generate annual ESG metrics	IT Lead	2025-09-11	2026-02-01	Low	$1M Cost	Current	**Kill**	**Digital Core**	**24**
Frozen Line Retooling	Update equipment for frozen plant	VP Ops	2025-10-01	2026-04-01	Medium	$3M Cost	Current	**Approve**	**Frozen Meals**	**36**
Workflow Plugin Maintenance	Maintain legacy internal plugins	IT Lead	2025-09-16	2026-04-26	Low	$0M	Current	**Kill**	**Digital Core**	**24**
Old Retail Promo Portal	Retire outdated promotional system	VP Sales	2025-08-22	2026-02-24	Low	$0M	Current	**Kill**	**Retail Format**	**24**

Figure 10.3 MOVE Tool #6: Strategic Project Portfolio Farella Foods Example.

Projects Include:

- Retail Segmentation Engine (88): Enable customer micro-targeting
- Nutritional R&D Center (88): Develop health-focused innovations
- Quick Service Customization (60): Streamline QSR partnerships
- Trade Show Expansion (60): Grow presence in food space
- DTC Testbeds Setup (48): Accelerate new product testing
- New Co-Packer Onboarding (48): Scale production quickly
- Strategic Partnerships Program (48): Build ecosystem advantages

PMM Cells Supported: Retail Frozen ($30M), Retail Healthy Bowls ($15M), Retail Snack Packs ($20M). **Revenue Target:** $50M incremental by 2028. **EBITDA Target:** $7.5M incremental by 2028. **Owner:** Dr. Raj Patel (R&D → Chief Innovation Officer).

"This is how we beat NüWave and private label," Raj explained. "We concentrate innovation in the categories that matter – Frozen and Healthy – while they spread thin across everything."

Initiative 2: Restore Operational Discipline

Objective: Strengthen margins through supply chain excellence, cost optimization, and complexity reduction.

This pulled together four critical projects for margin restoration:

Projects Include:

- Cold Chain Expansion (88): Improve cold supply chain reliability
- SKU Agility Upgrade (88): Increase response speed to demand shifts
- Portion Design Platform (88): Design portions to match health trends
- Wellness Branding Rollout (88): Establish leadership in wellness segment

PMM Cells Supported: Foodservice Frozen ($15M), Foodservice Snack Packs ($10M), operational excellence across all cells. **Revenue Target:** $40M incremental by 2028. **EBITDA Target:** $6M incremental by 2028. **Owner:** Mark Chen (COO).

"Every point of margin matters when you're at 8.6% EBITDA," Mark said. "This initiative gets us back to double digits by fixing the basics – supply chain, SKU count, and operational waste."

Initiative 3: Build Future-Ready Capabilities

Objective: Create strategic capabilities for sustained competitive advantage and market responsiveness.

This brought together three essential capability-building projects:

Projects Include:

- Dedicated B2B Center (60): Develop dedicated foodservice solutions
- ColdDTC Portal Launch (60): Enable direct-to-consumer frozen delivery
- Sustainability Impact Automation (60): Automate green analytics and ESG metrics

PMM Cells Supported: Foodservice Healthy Bowls ($10M), plus enablement across all cells. **Revenue Target:** $10M incremental by 2028. **EBITDA Target:** $1.5M incremental by 2028. **Owner:** Michael Thompson (VP Strategy → Chief Transformation Officer)

"These aren't sexy projects, but they're the capabilities that let us compete in 2028," Michael explained. "B2B expertise for foodservice, DTC for testing, and sustainability because every RFP now demands it."

Daniel summarized the math: "Three initiatives. $100M incremental revenue. $15M incremental EBITDA. Every dollar traceable back to our six GREEN PMM cells. That's how strategy becomes execution."

The room felt different: For the first time in years, Farella had focus. Not 31 scattered projects but three initiatives that would transform their business:

1. **Win in Growth Segments**: $50M revenue from Retail excellence
2. **Restore Operational Discipline**: $40M revenue with margin improvement
3. **Build Future-Ready Capabilities**: $10M revenue from new channels

Total: $100M incremental revenue, $15M incremental EBITDA by 2028, fully aligned with their PMM GREEN bets.

"You know what this means?" Sarah Martinez said, her marketing instincts finally aligned with commercial reality. "We can actually explain our strategy in one sentence. That's something NüWave can't do with their 47 SKU launches."

Mark Chen, who'd started the day protecting legacy processes, saw it differently now: "Bravora might have cost advantages, but they're trying to win everywhere. We're concentrating resources where we can actually win."

Even Jennifer Walsh, the skeptical CFO, was convinced: "For the first time, I can draw a straight line from investment to return. These aren't hope-based projects. They're strategy-based investments."

Making Strategic Portfolio Work

DO:

- Consolidate related projects into three memorable signature initiatives
- Give each initiative a single owner with real authority
- Apply the T-shirt test – if you wouldn't wear it, don't fund it
- Cut the bottom 20% of projects immediately
- Track by exception – focus only on problems

DON'T:

- Let departments keep pet projects outside the portfolio
- Use generic names like "Excellence Initiative"
- Assign initiatives to committees or co-owners
- Keep zombie projects alive because they're "almost done"
- Create new projects without killing old ones

Enhanced with AI

After consolidating into three initiatives, Farella's team used AI to optimize execution. But Jennifer raised the security concern immediately.

"We can't upload our strategic plans to ChatGPT," she said firmly.

Daniel agreed. "We'll use our enterprise AI platform – ringfenced, no training on our data, everything stays internal."

They used AI to pressure-test their portfolio:

Portfolio Reality Check: "Here are 31 current projects and our 3 new initiatives. Which current projects could be folded into the new initiatives? Which should be killed? Which capabilities from our AFC have no projects?"
Sequencing Strategy: "Our Initiative 1 has 5 projects. What's the optimal sequence to build capabilities fastest? What dependencies exist? What could we parallel process?"
Competitive Gaming: "If Bravora and NüWave see our three initiatives, what counter-moves would they likely make? How should we adjust?"

The insights changed their execution plan:

1 **Accelerate Healthy Bowls**: AI spotted that whoever owns the wellness position in frozen will dominate the category for a decade
2 **Kill more SKUs faster**: Analysis showed 60% of SKUs could go without revenue impact, not the 40% they planned
3 **Partner for GenAI**: Building proprietary AI would take too long; partner for tech, own the food application

"AI didn't play politics," Jennifer noted. "It just showed us what would win."

The strategic portfolio was set. Three initiatives. Clear ownership. Direct line from capabilities to market victory. But more importantly, Farella now had what their competitors lacked – focus.

While NüWave scattered resources across 47 SKU launches trying to catch every trend, Farella concentrated on building three transformative capabilities. While Bravora tried to dominate every channel and category through cost, Farella picked their battles. While BoxTop competed on operational perfection everywhere, Farella focused operational excellence where it mattered most.

"This is how David beats Goliath in CPG," Daniel concluded. "Not by doing everything, but by doing the right things with overwhelming force."

Data Security Note

Use your company's secure AI environment if available. For sensitive data:

- Use enterprise AI platforms with data protection agreements
- Check if your company has approved AI tools with security protocols
- Never use public AI tools for confidential strategic information
- When in doubt, anonymize all company data

Rule of thumb: If you wouldn't share it with a competitor, don't put it in a public AI tool.

AI Prompts for Strategic Portfolio

For Portfolio Optimization: "Our Win in Growth Segments initiative has 5 projects and $15M budget. Model 3 different ways to sequence projects that build capabilities fastest. Show time-to-market and competitive risk for each option."

For Resource Reality: "Our top 50 people are spread across 31 projects. Which people working on low-priority projects have skills critical for our three signature initiatives? What's the revenue acceleration if we move them?"
For Competitive Intelligence: "Track recent M&A, new products, and hiring in frozen meals and healthy bowls. Which competitors are building similar capabilities? What's their likely time-to-market?"
For Risk Mitigation: "Our three initiatives assume we can innovate faster than private label. What are the top 5 risks to this assumption? What early warning signals should we monitor?"
For Capability Gaps: "Compare our AFC Matrix future capabilities to our three initiatives. Which capabilities have no projects building them? What's the competitive risk of these gaps?"
For Initiative Interdependencies: "Analyze our three signature initiatives for hidden dependencies and synergies. Where could accelerating one initiative speed up another? Where might they compete for resources?"

Your Move

Your competitors are winning because they're doing less, better. While you're managing 31 projects, they're putting 70% of resources behind three initiatives that matter.

SPP forces brutal focus. Kill the bottom 20%. Consolidate the rest into signature initiatives everyone understands. Put real resources behind your biggest bets.

The bridge from strategy to execution isn't built with more projects. It's built by doing fewer things with overwhelming force.

"Focus to Win" isn't just Farella's strategy – it's the only strategy that works.

Quick-Action Checklist

- ☐ Count your current "strategic" projects – if it's over ten, you don't have strategy
- ☐ Apply the T-shirt test to your initiatives – would employees wear them proudly?
- ☐ Identify which projects consume resources but don't build AFC capabilities
- ☐ Kill the bottom 20% by next week – no exceptions

Next: Chapter 11 shows you how to establish the quarterly rhythm that keeps your signature initiatives on track while adapting faster than markets change.

Notes

1 Project Management Institute, "A Guide to the Project Management Body of Knowledge (PMBOK Guide)." 6th ed. (Newtown Square, PA: Project Management Institute, 2017).
2 Based on the author's 25+ years of consulting and client experience.
3 Mondelez International. "2023 Annual Report." Accessed January 2025. https://ir.mondelezinternational.com/annual-reports.
4 Trader Joe's. "About Trader Joe's." Accessed January 2025. https://www.traderjoes.com/about.
5 In-N-Out Burger. "Menu." Accessed January 2025. https://www.in-n-out.com/menu.
6 David Gelles, "How Hamdi Ulukaya Built Chobani into a $1 Billion Empire." *The New York Times*, June 14, 2013.
7 "Liquid Death Valued at $700 Million." *Bloomberg*, January 2022.
8 Based on the author's 25+ years of consulting and client experience.
9 Chipotle Mexican Grill, "Food with Integrity." Accessed January 2025. https://www.chipotle.com/food-with-integrity.
10 Sweetgreen, "Our Mission." Accessed January 2025. https://www.sweetgreen.com/mission.
11 Oatly, "The Oatly Way." Accessed January 2025. https://www.oatly.com/en-us/the-oatly-way.
12 Beyond Meat, "Our Mission." Accessed January 2025. https://www.beyondmeat.com/en-US/mission.
13 Based on the author's 25+ years of consulting and client experience.

Chapter 11

Keep the Beat

Establish a Quarterly Cadence

Daniel Ross stared at the conference room whiteboard. The Farella Foods [fictional example] Q2 business review was just a week away, and this one mattered. The board meeting followed immediately after, and his board had zero patience for explanations about "market headwinds" or "temporary setbacks." They wanted to know if the Focus to Win strategy was working.

Historically, these reviews had been marathons: two full days, seventeen presentations, over 300 slides documenting every operational detail. Each executive brought their version of reality, polished for protection rather than progress.

"We're about to turn strategic clarity into elaborate presentations," Daniel told his team during the QBR prep call.

They had built the complete MOVE system. Strategic Assumptions revealed wellness and convenience megatrends. Vision focused on winning through taste, simplicity, and speed. The Product-Market Matrix showed GREEN bets in Retail Frozen and Healthy Bowls. AFC identified capabilities to build. The Strategic Portfolio consolidated to three initiatives. Strategic Numbers tracked eight indicators.

But old habits die hard. Sarah Martinez had already prepared 41 slides on brand performance. Mark Chen built operational dashboards showing every production metric. Jennifer Walsh planned to walk through the complete P&L line by line.

Daniel cut in. "Stop. We're not here to document Q2. We're here to fix Q3."

The room quieted.

He turned to Sarah. "What's the root cause of our revenue miss in Frozen Meals?"

"Well… private label gained share, and we had some promotional timing issues – "

"That's not a root cause. That's a symptom. Why did private label beat us? Why did our promotions fail? What are we doing differently next quarter?"

Silence.

Daniel continued, "We have Strategic Numbers showing exactly where we're winning and losing. We have GREEN bets that define our future. But if you can't explain why we missed and what's changing in two pages, you don't understand it well enough to fix it."

Jennifer raised her hand. "But the board expects comprehensive updates. Risk matrices, compliance reports, detailed variance analysis – "

"The board expects us to win," Daniel said firmly. "They want evidence we understand our gaps and are fixing them. Everything else is secondary."

He pulled up a simple template on his laptop.

"Starting now, every QBR follows this format: Page one identifies root causes. Page two commits to next quarter actions. If it doesn't connect to our Strategic Numbers or GREEN bets, it doesn't make the meeting."

DOI: 10.4324/9781003682455-15

Michael Thompson had been watching this exchange carefully. For years, he'd been buried in PowerPoint decks, creating presentations about strategy rather than driving it. This felt different – actionable.

"Daniel's right," Michael said. "I've been preparing quarterly reviews for a decade. We document everything except the two things that matter: why we missed and what we're doing about it."

Sarah looked at her 41 slides. "So all this brand performance data..."

"Send it in an email if someone needs it," Daniel replied. "But in this room, we focus on solving problems."

"Why just two pages?" Mark asked. "Seems arbitrary."

"It's not about the pages," Daniel explained. "It's about the discipline. **Two pages force you to identify what truly matters.** You can't hide behind data. You can't bury the lead. Every P&L owner – from division heads down to product managers – can create their own two pages. It rolls up clean, without interpretation layers. I get direct insight into what's actually happening, not someone's version of someone else's story."

Jennifer saw it immediately. "So instead of seventeen presentations interpreting data, we get **clear root causes straight from the people who own the numbers**."

"Exactly. Two pages of truth beats 200 slides of interpretation every time."

The shift wasn't easy. Quarterly business reviews had been elaborate productions since the 1980s, when major corporations institutionalized them as strategic checkpoints. Back then, information was scarce. Real-time data didn't exist. Gathering quarterly performance required serious effort. Reviews were how leadership teams gained visibility.

Under demanding CEOs, these sessions had teeth. Leaders who couldn't explain performance gaps and provide concrete fixes faced consequences. Reviews drove decisions, not just documented data.

Today, everyone has dashboards. Analytics flow continuously. Yet companies still run QBRs like it's 1985 – elaborate presentations consuming weeks of preparation for meetings where nothing gets decided.

I'd seen this pattern firsthand. A CEO of a major CPG company had invited me to observe his quarterly business review in Miami. Eight division presidents would present their results and action plans. Each got 45 minutes to present, 15 minutes for Q&A.[1]

"Challenge them," the CEO told me. "I need an outside perspective."

I watched eight polished presentations – all different formats, all avoiding the hard questions. Veterans breezed through expecting no pushback. Newer leaders over-prepared with defensive detail.

After each presentation, I asked the same question: **"What's the root cause of your biggest P&L gap, and what specific action will fix it next quarter?"**

Most stumbled. They offered surface explanations: "Competition took share." "Pricing pressure increased." "Retail dynamics shifted."

But those aren't root causes. They're excuses.

I'd seen the same pattern in Nordic companies known for their consensus culture. One executive described their quarterly reviews: "We meet four times to discuss what everyone already knows. By the time we reach consensus on the problem, the market has moved on."[2]

During our debrief, the CEO saw it clearly. His leaders had spent weeks preparing presentations that didn't answer the only question that mattered: **Why did we miss and what are we doing about it?**

"My board meeting is next week," he said. "I need solutions, not stories."

That Miami experience shaped my thinking about quarterly reviews. Companies need a different approach – one that forces root cause analysis and drives immediate action.

Daniel was implementing exactly that approach at Farella. Like that CEO in Miami, he recognized his team was spending more time preparing presentations than solving problems. The difference? Daniel wasn't going to wait for a consultant to point it out.

The Two-Page QBR would replace comprehensive presentations with focused analysis that drives strategic action.

"Let me show you how this works," Daniel said, projecting a simple framework on the screen.

"Page one forces root cause analysis. Every business operates on one truth: Revenue minus Cost equals Profit. When something goes wrong, it hits one of these three. Your job is to identify which one and why."

Mark Chen leaned forward. "But root causes can be complex. Multiple factors – "

"Pick the primary one," Daniel interrupted. "The one that, if fixed, would have the biggest impact. This isn't academic analysis. It's practical problem-solving."

Jennifer Walsh was already calculating. "So if our Frozen Meals revenue is down $10M, and costs are up $3M..."

"Your profit gap is $13M," Daniel finished. "Now tell me why. And don't say 'competition.' Tell me the operational reality. What specifically caused customers to choose private label over us?"

How to Build Your Two-Page QBR

The Two-Page QBR answers two questions:

- **Page 1:** Why did we miss? (RCA)
- **Page 2:** What will we do? (NQA)

Step 1: Identify Performance Gaps

Compare actual results to forecast for each strategic initiative. Focus only on **significant variances** – typically 10% or more. Calculate the R-C=P impact of each gap.

Don't document everything that happened. **Identify what matters.**

Step 2: Root Cause Analysis (Page 1)

For each major gap:

- List three possible causes
- Gather evidence to support or eliminate each cause
- Select the most probable root cause based on data
- Quantify the impact on Revenue, Cost, or Profit

Many executives know techniques like the **five Whys** to dig deeper from symptom to cause.[3] Use whatever method works – the key is getting past surface explanations to operational reality.

The test: Can you explain in one sentence why you missed and what drove it?

Step 3: Define Corrective Actions (Page 2)

For each root cause:

- Create specific actions that fix the root cause (not the symptom)
- Assign **one owner** – no committees
- Set completion within **90 days** – longer actions won't impact next quarter
- Estimate realistic success probability

Critical discipline: You'll identify many possible actions. Pick only the vital few that will actually close the gap. More actions mean less focus.

If your action doesn't directly address the root cause, it's activity, not strategy.

Step 4: Run the QBR Meeting

- Start with **silent reading** of the two pages
- Discuss and validate root causes
- Commit to corrective actions
- **No presentations, no slides** – just focused discussion

The entire meeting should take **90 minutes or less.**

Step 5: Monthly Business Reviews (MBRs)

When market pace accelerates, many executives add **monthly mini-QBRs** using the same two-page format. Why wait a full quarter if you know the root cause now?

30-minute monthly check-ins prevent quarterly surprises and enable faster course correction. Same format, faster rhythm.

The framework was elegantly simple. Companies like Amazon had proven that focused analysis beats comprehensive documentation. Their six-page narratives and "dive deep" sessions drove more decisions in 30 minutes than most companies made in day-long reviews.[4]

Microsoft's transformation under Satya Nadella followed similar principles. They eliminated comprehensive presentations, focusing instead on three questions: What surprised us? Why did it happen? What are we changing? This cultural shift contributed to their successful cloud transformation.[5]

Meanwhile, companies that clung to elaborate quarterly presentations struggled. Nokia's 100-slide reviews from 2007 to 2010 became legendary for missing the smartphone shift entirely. Teams spent more time perfecting slides than understanding market changes.[6]

The message was clear: focused analysis beats comprehensive documentation. And Daniel was about to prove it at Farella.

"Here's how we'll build our Two-Page QBR," Daniel continued, walking through the process.

Building Farella's First Two-Page QBR

"Let's work through this together," Daniel said. "We'll start with our three signature initiatives."

Michael pulled up the performance data:

Initiative 1: Win in Growth Segments

- Revenue: $115M actual vs $125.5M forecast
- Cost: $108M actual vs $104.5M forecast
- Profit: $7M actual vs $21M forecast

"Ugly," Mark muttered.

"Honest," Daniel corrected. "Now let's get to root causes."

Sarah had done her homework. "I've identified three possible causes for the revenue miss: ineffective promotional strategy, delayed product launches, and sales force allocation issues."

"Walk us through your analysis," Daniel encouraged.

"Promotional timing wasn't the issue – we hit all our planned windows. Product launches were on schedule. But when I dug into sales force activity..." Sarah paused, pulling up data. "Our reps spent 78% of their time protecting base business instead of hunting new opportunities in growth segments."

Dr. Raj nodded. "That explains why our Healthy Bowls aren't getting shelf space. The sales team prioritizes what they know – Frozen Meals – over what we need to grow."

"So the root cause is sales force allocation," Jennifer summarized. "Not competition, not pricing. Our own behavior."

"Exactly," Daniel said. "Now what's the fix?"

Mark jumped in. "Dedicated growth segment hunters. Separate from base business protection."

"How many?" Jennifer pressed. "What's the cost?"

"Three dedicated reps," Sarah calculated quickly. "Maybe $450K fully loaded. But if they capture even 10% of the opportunity, that's $5M revenue."

Daniel smiled. This was strategic problem-solving, not performance theater.

They continued through each initiative and market segment. The team discovered patterns they'd missed in traditional reviews.

Sarah pulled up the data for Frozen Meals. "Look at this – we thought private label was killing us on price. But the root cause data shows **we lost customers when we changed our recipe** to reduce sodium. They didn't switch for price. They switched because we changed what they loved."

"That's a **$10M lesson**," Jennifer noted. "We spent months analyzing competitive pricing when the answer was in our own kitchen."

Mark Chen had his own revelation with operations. "I've been blaming our suppliers for cost overruns in Healthy Bowls. But look at the data – **we're single-sourced on quinoa**. When they raised prices 20%, we had no options. That's not a supplier problem. That's a sourcing strategy problem."

Dr. Raj connected the dots. "This is what we've been missing. Every quarter we'd present what happened – sales declined, costs increased, competition intensified. But we never asked **why at this level of detail**. We never connected specific causes to specific fixes."

"Wait," Daniel interrupted. "We're only looking at negative variances. What about Harold?"

The team looked puzzled.

"I once sat in a QBR where this top sales guy Harold never said a word the entire session," Daniel explained. "I asked the CEO what was up. He said 'Harold beat his numbers again so we just leave him alone.' But that's exactly wrong. We need to understand **why Harold wins** – maybe his methods, his customers, his territory. **Positive variance teaches as much as negative.**"[7]

Michael pulled up the data. "Actually, our Foodservice Frozen Meals beat forecast by 15%. We didn't even analyze it."

"Exactly," Daniel said. "Figure out why. Maybe there's something we can scale."

The team worked through each major variance, building their RCA systematically (Figure 11.1).

"Look at these patterns," Michael observed. "Frozen Meals missed because of customer defection, not competitive pricing. Snack Packs bled money on trade promotions, not product costs. Healthy Bowls suffered from ingredient sourcing, not market demand."

Jennifer was already calculating impacts. "If we fix just these three root causes, we recover **$17M in profit next quarter**."

"Now you're thinking like operators, not reporters," Daniel said. "Page two is where we commit to specific actions."

The team built out their commitments, but Daniel pushed for discipline.

"We've identified twelve possible actions," Sarah said, reviewing her list. "Dedicated sales reps, new promotional strategy, recipe reversal, packaging updates – "

"Stop," Daniel interrupted. "That's exactly the trap. **We can't do twelve things well. Pick three that will actually move the needle.**"

"But they're all important," Sarah protested.

"Important isn't the same as vital," Jennifer countered. "What's the ONE action that would recover the most revenue?"

Sarah studied the data. "The dedicated growth segment hunters. If we redirect sales focus, we recover 50% of the gap."

"Good. What else?" Daniel pressed.

MOVE TOOL 7A: Root Cause Analysis Why are we missing — what's the real cause?

Metric	Frozen Meals	Snack Packs	Healthy Bowls	Qtr. Totals
Forecasted from PMM				
•R	$ 125.5	$ 36.5	$ 21.0	**183.0**
•C	$ 104.5	$ 27.3	$ 16.8	**148.5**
•P	$ 21.0	$ 9.3	$ 4.3	**34.5**
Actual				
•R	$ 115.0	$ 32.0	$ 23.0	**170.0**
•C	$ 108.0	$ 29.0	$ 15.5	**152.5**
•P	$ 7.0	$ 3.0	$ 7.5	**17.5**
GAP: + or –				
•R	$ (10.5)	$ (4.5)	$ 2.0	**$ (13.0)**
•C	$ 3.5	$ 1.8	$ (1.3)	**4.0**
•P	$ (14.0)	$ (6.3)	$ 3.3	**$ (17.0)**
Top 3 Possible Causes of + and – Gaps (Focus on R,C)	Inadequate forecasting model	Inaccurate pricing by channel	Improved consumer brand awareness	
	Delayed cold chain maintenance	Excessive trade promotions	Ingredient sourcing delays resolved	
	Inefficient production line scheduling	Unaligned pack sizes with new formats	Increased wellness program promotions	
Confirmed or Most Likely Cause of + or – Gap	Inefficient production line scheduling	Excessive trade promotions	Increased wellness program promotions	
	Reschedule plant production runs	Revise channel pricing models	Double down on retail promotions	
Action to Remove Cause for next quarter impact	Accelerate cold chain upgrade	Rationalize promotional calendar	Secure long-term supplier contracts	

Figure 11.1 MOVE Tool #7A: Root Cause Analysis Revenue – Cost = Profit

Mark jumped in. "For my cold chain issues, I've got five possible fixes. But honestly? **Accelerating the technology upgrade from Q4 to Q3** stops the bleeding fastest. Same budget, just timing."

"What about the trade promotion mess in Snack Packs?" Jennifer asked.

"Kill them," Sarah said bluntly. "I know that sounds radical, but the data is clear. Every dollar in trade promotion returns seventy cents. We're literally paying for volume."

"What's the customer impact?" Dr. Raj asked.

"Short-term volume drop of 20%," Sarah admitted. "But profit improves immediately. We can reinvest in product innovation instead of buying unprofitable sales."

Daniel nodded. "Now you're making real choices. Not everything that's broken needs fixing. Fix what matters most."

They worked through each action, ensuring clarity (Figure 11.2).

"Notice what we're NOT doing," Daniel emphasized. "We're not fixing everything. We're not forming committees. We're picking the **vital few actions** that address root causes with highest impact."

Sarah studied the plan. "This is radically different. Each action has one owner, clear timing, specific impact."

"And realistic probability," Jennifer added. "We're not promising 100% success. We're being honest about execution risk."

Mark Chen, who'd initially resisted the simplified approach, saw the power. "In our old reviews, we'd have discussed my cold chain issues for 30 minutes without deciding anything. Here, it's clear: upgrade the tech, accelerate the timeline, measure the impact."

Dr. Raj was already thinking ahead. "If we run QBRs this way every quarter, we'll start seeing patterns. Which fixes work, which don't, what root causes keep recurring."

"That's the real power," Michael agreed. "Not just fixing this quarter, but learning what drives our business."

MOVE TOOL 7B: Next Quarter Action Items What must we do now?

PRODUCT	Next Qtr. REVENUE ($)	+/-Gap	Next Qtr. COST ($)	+/-Gap	Next Qtr. PROFIT ($)	+/-Gap	Key Actions to Close Gaps	Owner	Timing Action with Impact R, C, P	Prob. of achieving next qtr.
Frozen Meals	$ 115	$ (10.5)	$ 108	$ 3.5	$ 7	$ (14.0)	Reschedule plant production runs, accelerate cold chain upgrade	VP Ops	R impact Q3, P impact Q4	75% R, 70% P
Snack Packs	$ 32	$ (4.5)	$ 29	$ 1.8	$ 3	$ (6.3)	Revise channel pricing models, rationalize promotional calendar	VP Marketing	C impact Q3, R impact early Q4	70% C, 65% R
Healthy Bowls	$ 23	$ 2.0	$ 16	$ (1.3)	$ 8	$ 3.3	Double down on retail promotions, secure long-term supplier contracts	VP Marketing	R impact mid Q3, C impact Q4	60% R, 75% C
Total Gap Previous Quarter		$ (13.0)		$ 4.0		$ (17.0)	**Additional Actions / Comments**			

Figure 11.2 MOVE Tool #7B: Next Quarter Action Items Farella Foods Example.

The meeting that would have consumed two days took 90 minutes. More importantly, it produced clear decisions rather than comprehensive documentation.

As the team dispersed, Jennifer pulled Daniel aside. "The board will love this clarity. But what about all the other reporting they expect?"

"Send whatever compliance requires," Daniel replied. "But in the boardroom, lead with these two pages. Show them we understand our business and we're fixing what's broken."

The next week proved Daniel right. The board meeting that usually ran four hours finished in two. Board members spent more time discussing strategic options than questioning historical numbers.

"Finally," one board member commented, "a management team that diagnoses problems instead of documenting them."

The clarity of the Two-Page QBR had transformed how Farella operated. But three months into using the new format, they discovered something even more powerful – AI could help them spot patterns humans missed entirely.

The AI Advantage in Root Cause Analysis

Jennifer Walsh was struggling to understand why foodservice margins had eroded despite stable pricing.

"I've analyzed everything," she said during prep. "Volume is up, pricing held, but margins dropped **200 basis points**."

Michael suggested using their secure AI platform. "Let's see if AI can spot patterns we're missing."

Jennifer crafted the prompt carefully: "Analyze our foodservice transaction data for Q2. Compare order patterns, product mix, delivery costs, and customer segments. **What explains our 200 basis point margin erosion?**"

The AI surfaced insights humans had missed:

- **Small orders increased 40%**, driving up per-unit delivery costs
- Customers shifted from high-margin frozen to low-margin fresh
- New accounts ordered trial sizes with promotional pricing
- Tuesday/Thursday delivery clustering created overtime costs

"Those aren't guesses," Jennifer noted. "That's **pattern recognition across thousands of orders** we couldn't analyze manually."

The team then asked AI to model fixes:

- **Minimum order requirements** would improve margins 150 basis points
- **Delivery charge restructuring** could recover another 50 basis points
- **Route optimization** for clustered days would save $200K quarterly

"AI didn't replace our thinking," Daniel observed. "It **enhanced our ability to find root causes**."

Data Security Note

For QBR analysis with AI:

- Use only approved enterprise AI platforms
- Never input full P&L data into public tools
- Anonymize customer and pricing information
- Treat AI prompts as board-level confidential

Remember: Your QBR data reveals competitive strategy. Protect it accordingly.

The integration of AI into their QBR process became standard practice. Not to replace human judgment, but to surface patterns and test hypotheses faster than manual analysis allowed.

Companies across industries were discovering similar advantages. Adobe used AI-enhanced QBRs during their Creative Cloud transition to identify customer resistance patterns and adjust pricing strategies quarterly.[8] Spotify deployed similar approaches for market expansion, using AI to spot early warning signals in new geographic launches.[9]

The pattern was consistent: companies that combined human strategic thinking with AI pattern recognition made better decisions faster.

Tracking Patterns That Matter

After six quarters of running Two-Page QBRs, Farella discovered something powerful: **the patterns revealed strategic shifts**.

"Look at this," Michael showed Daniel during their planning session. "Every quarter, our 'small order problem' in Foodservice gets worse. Started at 20% of orders, now it's 40%."

"That's not just an operational issue," Daniel realized. "That's telling us the market is fragmenting. Our Strategic Assumptions about consolidation might be wrong."

Jennifer added her insight. "And see this pattern? Every time we raise prices, we don't lose customers immediately. The defection happens **two quarters later**. Traditional QBRs would miss that lag."

This was the hidden power of systematic root cause analysis. **When you track real causes over time, you spot strategic shifts early.** It connects directly back to your PMM and Strategic Assumptions:

- **Recurring root causes** signal structural problems requiring capability investment
- **New root causes** indicate market shifts that might invalidate your assumptions
- **Successful patterns** from positive variances show what to double down on
- **Seasonal patterns** help separate noise from real strategic signals

"We're not just fixing quarters anymore," Daniel observed. "We're getting **early warning signals** about whether our strategy still fits the market."

But implementing any new QBR approach – with or without AI – requires discipline. Here's what Farella learned about making it work.

Making Two-Page QBR Work

DO:

- Force honest root cause analysis (especially internal causes)
- Make actions specific with single owners and deadlines
- Calculate realistic success probabilities
- Focus discussion on decisions, not data display
- Track previous quarter's commitments

DON'T:

- Allow presentations beyond two pages
- Accept vague root causes like "market conditions"
- Commit to actions without clear owners
- Let the discussion drift into operational details
- Tolerate excuses disguised as explanations

AI Prompts for Strategic QBR Analysis

For Root Cause Discovery: "Analyze our Q2 performance data showing $30M revenue shortfall in Frozen Meals. Compare sales patterns, customer behavior, promotional effectiveness, and competitive activity. What are the three most probable root causes based on the data?"

For Action Modeling: "Given root causes of sales bandwidth constraints and customer churn from recipe changes, model 5 different corrective action combinations. Show expected Q3 impact, implementation requirements, and success probability based on our capabilities."

For Pattern Recognition: "Review our last 8 QBRs. Which root causes appear repeatedly? Which corrective actions actually delivered promised results? What patterns predict success versus failure?"

For Competitive Intelligence: "Based on public earnings calls and industry reports, how are food companies successfully addressing private label pressure? What actions show measurable impact within 90 days?"

For Predictive Alerts: "Analyze our current performance trajectory and market conditions. Which metrics are likely to miss targets next quarter? What early warning signals should we monitor?"

Your Move

Every quarter, companies face the same choice: spend weeks creating presentations that document history, or spend hours identifying root causes and driving corrective actions.

The Two-Page QBR isn't just a format change – it's a **mindset shift** from reporting to managing, from documentation to decision-making, from looking backward to driving forward.

Daniel transformed Farella's quarterly reviews from elaborate productions into strategic weapons. While competitors still run marathon presentation sessions, Farella identifies and fixes problems in **90 minutes**.

The math is compelling: **85% less prep time, 70% faster decisions, 40% better performance prediction.**[10] But the real value comes from organizational learning – when you systematically identify root causes and track corrective actions, you understand what truly drives your business.

The strategic bonus: QBR patterns become your early warning system. When root causes shift, when new patterns emerge, when positive variances reveal unexpected opportunities – you're seeing strategic changes before they show up in annual results.

Quick-Action Checklist

- □ **Calculate hours spent preparing your last QBR** – if over 40, consider whether you're creating presentations or value
- □ **Pick one division to pilot Two-Page QBR next quarter** – ideally with your strongest leader who will embrace the change
- □ **Ask each executive: "What's the root cause of your biggest gap?"** – their clarity reveals how well you're all managing strategically
- □ **Consider monthly mini-QBRs** if your market moves faster than quarterly cycles allow

Next: Part IV shows how MOVE works when everything changes – from Tuesday morning crises to bold strategic moves to making acquisitions actually deliver value.

Notes

1. Based on the author's 25+ years of consulting and client experience.
2. Based on the author's 25+ years of consulting and client experience.
3. Taiichi Ohno, *Toyota Production System: Beyond Large-Scale Production* (Portland, OR: Productivity Press, 1988).
4. Jeff Bezos, "2017 Letter to Shareholders." Amazon, April 18, 2018. https://www.aboutamazon.com/news/company-news/2017-letter-to-shareholders.
5. Satya Nadella, *Hit Refresh: The Quest to Rediscover Microsoft's Soul and Imagine a Better Future for Everyone* (New York: HarperBusiness, 2017).
6. Yves Doz and Mikko Kosonen. "Nokia's Strategic Inflection Point." INSEAD Case Study, 2011.
7. Based on the author's 25+ years of consulting and client experience.
8. "Adobe's Digital Transformation." Harvard Business School Case Study, 2020.
9. "Spotify Technology S.A. Annual Report 2023." Spotify Investors, March 2024.
10. Based on the author's 25+ years of consulting and client experience.

Part IV

High-Stakes Situations

How Strategy Shows Up When It Matters Most

You've built your MOVE system. Strategic Assumptions guide your thinking. Your PMM shows where to play. Capabilities are being built. Projects are focused. Numbers tell the truth. Quarterly reviews drive action.

But business doesn't follow quarterly schedules.

A competitor announces a game-changing move on a random Tuesday. An acquisition opportunity appears with a two-week decision window. The board demands a bold strategic shift. Your budget process threatens to undo your strategic focus.

These are the situations that test leaders. The moments where strategy either guides you forward or leaves you guessing.

Part IV transforms MOVE from a planning system into a **response system**. The same tools that built your strategy become precision instruments for high-stakes situations every CEO faces:

- **Chapter 12: 'BUSTED':** When Tuesday changes everything – use MOVE tools for rapid strategic response
- **Chapter 13: BOLD MOVES:** When quiet means danger – structured provocation breaks you free
- **Chapter 14: BETTER:** Make acquisitions actually pay off post-transaction by integrating MOVE from day one
- **Chapter 15: BUDGET:** Align capital with competitive moves, not organizational politics
- **Chapter 16: BOARD READY:** In your first 100 days – move up with strategic credibility
- **Chapter 17: MOVE WHAT MATTERS:** One system, everywhere you go – MOVE travels with you

Each situation shows how executives use MOVE tools in concentrated bursts to solve specific challenges leaders face or create. Not annual planning exercises – **targeted applications when the stakes are highest**.

Daniel Ross discovered this six months into Farella's [fictional example] transformation. When their largest competitor announced a shocking acquisition, he didn't panic. He pulled out the PMM, ran scenarios through Strategic Assumptions, and had three strategic options ready in 48 hours.

"The tools work even better under pressure," he told his team. "When you don't have time for elaborate analysis, MOVE forces clarity."

Your competitors scramble when disruption hits. You'll be ready with tools that turn chaos into opportunity.

Turn the page. Master MOVE in the moments that matter most.

DOI: 10.4324/9781003682455-16

Chapter 12

'BUSTED'

When Tuesday Changes Everything

Tuesday, 6:14 AM. The call no executive wants.

"Tim, we're locked out. Everything. Ransomware hit us overnight." The voice wasn't panicked – it was worse. It was resigned. This mid-market manufacturer's entire operation had stopped. Production lines frozen. Customer shipments halted. Twenty-two hundred employees with nothing to do.[1]

"How long?" I asked.

"IT says two weeks minimum to rebuild from backups. If the backups work."

His leadership team had sprung into crisis mode. IT recovery activated. Legal engaged. PR drafting statements. All the right operational moves. But something was missing.

"I don't need IT recovery plans," he said. "Those are running. I need strategic options for when we emerge. Because when we do, everything will be different."

He was right. Crisis doesn't just disrupt operations – it reshapes markets. The real question: How do you turn what just happened into strategic advantage?

The Problem: External Shocks Are Now Normal

Tuesday morning disruptions aren't exceptions anymore – they're business as usual. Your competitor gets acquired. New regulations drop. Technology hits a tipping point. Currency crashes. The shock already hit – now what?

Most companies stay in operational response mode. Crisis management. Damage control. All necessary but not sufficient. While you're managing today's crisis operationally, someone else is thinking strategically. By the time you've weathered the storm, they own the new landscape.

Here's what happens in most companies:

- Operations takes over completely
- All thinking goes defensive
- Strategic questions wait for "after the crisis"
- Opportunities expire while committees meet

But the biggest failure? Treating each crisis as isolated. Smart companies recognize that crises reveal patterns. They expose weaknesses. They accelerate trends. Every shock teaches something if you're paying attention strategically, not just operationally.

The MOVE Solution: Turn Shock into Strategy

Your MOVE foundation becomes your crisis navigation system. You're not starting from zero – you have strategic infrastructure.

DOI: 10.4324/9781003682455-17

Your Strategic Assumptions already mapped the external landscape. The shock that just hit? There were breadcrumbs in your assumptions – you just missed their urgency.

Now trace back:

- Which assumption just accelerated from five years to five months?
- What constant we thought permanent just broke?
- Which competitor move we flagged as "possible" just became real?

The framework for rapid response:

- **TRENDS**: What patterns were already emerging?
- **TRIGGER**: What specific event just occurred?
- **IMPLICATIONS**: What should we do now?
  - Risk Mitigation: Protect what matters
  - Opportunity Capture: Build new advantage

External shocks cluster into four patterns. Each requires different thinking.

Type 1: Growth Acceleration

Your biggest competitor exits. New regulation opens markets. Technology makes the impossible feasible. The market suddenly tilts your way.

But beware false signals. COVID taught brutal lessons. E-commerce saw five years of growth in five months and hired accordingly. Then reality returned. Growth didn't just slow – it went negative. Winners questioned whether spikes were sustainable acceleration or borrowed growth.[2]

Example: Italian Fashion House's Digital Leap

When COVID locked down Milan, this traditional fashion house faced disaster. No fashion weeks. No showrooms. No buyers visiting.[3]

Using the framework:

- **TREND**: Fashion digitalization accelerating
- **TRIGGER**: Physical fashion weeks cancelled
- **IMPLICATIONS**:
  - Risk Mitigation: Virtual showrooms, maintain relationships
  - Opportunity Capture: Blend heritage with digital, reach global audiences

They built virtual ateliers showing craftsmen working. Created AR experiences. Turned Italian heritage into digital differentiator.

Results: Reached 10X more buyers than physical shows. Orders up 40%. What started as crisis response became permanent model.

Type 2: Competition & Disruption

Major acquisition creates a giant. New entrant brings different rules. Technology disrupts your value chain. The game suddenly has new rules.

Example: Brazilian Retailer's Amazon Response

When Amazon entered Brazil, most retailers panicked. One major chain chose offense over defense.[4]

Framework application:

- **TREND**: E-commerce platforms reshaping retail
- **TRIGGER**: Amazon launches with massive investment
- **IMPLICATIONS**:
    - Risk Mitigation: Protect profitable categories, strengthen local ties
    - Opportunity Capture: Focus on experience Amazon can't deliver

They pivoted to experiential retail. Stores became community hubs. Used Brazilian roots as advantage – local payment methods Amazon didn't understand, relationships algorithms couldn't replicate.

Result: Instead of losing share, they grew. Amazon became their customer acquisition tool.

Type 3: New Bets & Exploration

Adjacent market opens. Technology hits viability. Customer shifts reveal needs. The impossible becomes possible.

Example: Japanese Manufacturer's Digital Twin Revolution

COVID prevented on-site equipment maintenance. Technicians couldn't travel. Machines would fail without prevention.[5]

Crisis response:

- **TREND**: Digital twin technology maturing
- **TRIGGER**: Travel restrictions prevent maintenance
- **IMPLICATIONS**:
    - Risk Mitigation: Train local partners, extend warranties
    - Opportunity Capture: Build digital twin platform, transform service model

Built digital twins of equipment. Enabled predictive maintenance. Turned service from cost to subscription.

What started as crisis response became highest-margin business. Competitors still trying to return to travel-based service while they own the future.

Type 4: Profit Protection

Tariffs hit. Currency crashes. Supply chain breaks. Input costs spike. Revenue holds but profits evaporate.

Example: Mexican Manufacturer's Peso Crisis

When peso crashed 40%, this exporter should have celebrated – cheaper exports mean advantage. But imported component costs spiked, wiping out gains.[6]

Strategic response:

- **TREND**: Currency volatility permanent fixture
- **TRIGGER**: 40% devaluation overnight
- **IMPLICATIONS**:
    - Risk Mitigation: Hedge exposures, renegotiate contracts
    - Opportunity Capture: Redesign for local inputs, make volatility a differentiator

Redesigned products for 80% local content. Offered customers currency protection. Competitors couldn't match – still dependent on imports.

Three years later, margins exceeded pre-crisis levels. The peso crisis made them stronger.

After Crisis Hits: Your Playbook

1. **Get Clear on** Reality: What specifically changed? Who's impacted? What's broken? What's the real deadline?

   Don't jump to solutions. First understand the new reality.
2. **Deploy the Framework:** Gather key thinkers – not necessarily senior team. You want strategic minds.

   Work TRENDS-TRIGGER-IMPLICATIONS. Confirm what trend this represents. Generate both risks AND opportunities. Push beyond obvious responses.
3. **Convert to Options:** Identify three to five strategic options. Not tactics – moves that change position. Each should be:

   - Specific enough to execute
   - Different enough to matter
   - Bold enough to create advantage

4. **Decide and Deploy:** Pick your path. Assign a believer. Set aggressive milestones. Then execute fully. Half-hearted execution of bold strategy fails every time.

Completing the Ransomware Story

That afternoon, we assembled his leadership team. Seven executives fueled by adrenaline and bad coffee.

"What has this event taught you about your business that you didn't know yesterday?"

The CFO: "Our backup systems are decorative. Useless in reality."

Head of Sales: "Three customers offered help. Twelve threatened to switch. We were wrong about who's loyal."

We worked on the framework:

- **TREND**: Cyber attacks on manufacturers up 300% annually[7]
- **TRIGGER**: Ransomware with two-week downtime
- **IMPLICATIONS**:
  - Risk Mitigation: Communication plan, manual workarounds, legal protection
  - Opportunity Capture: Accelerate cloud migration, restructure while down, build cyber resilience as differentiator

The conversation shifted from recovery to transformation. Could they do three-year cloud migration in three months while rebuilding? Could they restructure operations using crisis as cover?

By Friday's board meeting, they presented transformation:

1. Compress cloud migration to 90 days
2. Turn crisis communication into competitive advantage
3. Build then sell cyber resilience to peers
4. Eliminate all single points of failure

Six months later: New cloud infrastructure. Industry-leading transparency. Growing consulting practice. Revenue up 15%.

"The ransomware was horrible," the CEO said. "It was also the best thing that happened to us. We stopped asking 'how do we recover?' and started asking 'how do we emerge stronger?'"

Using AI to Amplify Response

AI accelerates crisis response when used right. Give it your framework first, then ask it to expand.

For Growth Acceleration: "Here's our TRENDS-TRIGGER-IMPLICATIONS for competitor exit. Test our thinking. What scenarios are we missing? Generate three additional response options we haven't considered."
For Competitive Disruption: "Amazon entered our market. Here's our framework [insert]. What risks are we underestimating? What opportunities beyond partner/defend/attack?"
For New Exploration: "GenAI now viable for our industry. Our implications [insert]. What adjacent opportunities exist? Model success probabilities."
For Profit Protection: "40% currency hit. Our analysis [insert]. Stress-test scenarios. Generate strategies that create advantage, not just damage control."

AI doesn't replace judgment. It expands options. Use it to see around corners your experience hasn't encountered.

Note: Keep proprietary data out of prompts. Focus on patterns and possibilities.

Your Move: From Crisis to Advantage

In crisis, first movers usually win. But moving fast without thinking creates chaos. The framework lets you think and move simultaneously.

While competitors form committees, you're generating options. While they analyze, you're testing. While they decide, you're executing. By the time they finish analysis, you're in market.

Clear options also calm panicked organizations. When people see paths forward – not just problems – fear transforms to focus. Energy channels toward solutions.

Every shock creates market gaps. New needs emerge. Weaknesses get exposed. Assumptions shatter. But these opportunities expire fast. Move first or fight for scraps.

The framework works because you're not building new strategy. You're adjusting existing strategy based on new reality. Your MOVE foundation makes this possible.

Tuesday will bring the next shock. When it does, you'll have a system for turning disruption into advantage. Not perfect strategy – fast strategy that improves your position while others scramble.

Strategic Tension Question: "When the unexpected hits Tuesday, do you have a system for strategic options by Friday – or do you just manage the crisis and hope?"

Notes

1 Based on author's 25+ years consulting and client experience.
2 "E-commerce During COVID-19." UNCTAD Report, October 2021. https://unctad.org/news/how-covid-19-triggered-digital-and-e-commerce-turning-point.
3 Camera Nazionale della Moda Italiana, "Milan Fashion Week Goes Digital." Press Release, June 2020. https://www.cameramoda.it/en/news/1656/milan-fashion-week-goes-digital/.
4 "Amazon Launches in Brazil with Full Marketplace." Reuters, October 18, 2019. https://www.reuters.com/article/us-amazon-com-brazil-idUSKBN1WX1YV.
5 "Digital Twin Market in Manufacturing." MarketsandMarkets Research Report, 2023. https://www.marketsandmarkets.com/Market-Reports/digital-twin-market-225269522.html.
6 "Mexican Peso Crisis and Manufacturing Impact." Bank of Mexico Economic Report, 2020. https://www.banxico.org.mx/publications-and-press/banco-de-mexico-reports/index-en.html.
7 "Manufacturing Industry Ransomware Report 2023." Cybersecurity and Infrastructure Security Agency (CISA), 2023. https://www.cisa.gov/topics/cybersecurity-best-practices/ransomware.

Chapter 13

BOLD MOVES

When Quiet Means Danger

The European logistics CEO looked exhausted despite the successful planning session. Every initiative made sense. Every projection felt achievable. The board would approve without question.

"That's exactly the problem," he told me. "We just planned to be 10% better at what we already do. Meanwhile, Amazon's reimagining logistics entirely."[1]

His company had gotten so good at incremental improvement, they'd forgotten how to think transformatively. Success had made them safe. Safe had made them vulnerable.

"My best people save their crazy ideas for startups they're secretly planning," he admitted. "In our meetings, they propose tweaks. At home, they design revolutions."

The Problem: Your Best Thinking Stays Hidden

Here's what frustrates CEOs: They shouldn't need special sessions to generate transformative thinking. That's what executive teams are for. When the CEO has to force dangerous questions, something's broken.

Most executives know they should be thinking bigger. They see the same signals you see. They have the same concerns about competitive threats. But they've learned to wait for permission rather than bring forward ideas that might seem "too bold."

Large organizations develop antibodies against bold thinking:

- "We tried that before"
- "The board won't approve"
- "Our customers won't accept it"
- "That's not how our industry works"
- "Let's study it more"

These phrases seem reasonable. That's what makes them deadly. Your next breakthrough dies in someone's throat, choked by cultural conditioning.

When things are quiet, when every plan feels safe, when nobody's proposing anything that makes you nervous – you're already behind. The absence of bold thinking is the biggest risk of all.

Consider what happens when companies ignore this warning. Blockbuster had multiple chances to buy Netflix for $50M in 2000. Their executives thought the DVD-by-mail model wasn't worth disrupting their profitable store network. They chose quiet over transformation. We know how that ended.[2]

The Wake-Up Call

That afternoon, I worked with the logistics team using five questions. Each question follows the same framework – take your existing trends and add a dangerous lens.

DOI: 10.4324/9781003682455-18

The CEO had been clear with me beforehand: "My team should be bringing these ideas without needing a special session. This is their wake-up call."

We started with: "What would end our current model?"

Nervous laughter. Then silence. Then the head of operations spoke: "Autonomous vehicles eliminate our drivers. AI routing eliminates our planners. Software eats our entire business."

The CEO leaned forward. "Good. Now what do we do about it?"

The room transformed. For the first time in years, they weren't defending – they were attacking. Their own business model. Their own assumptions. Their own limits.

The BOLD MOVES Framework

You already have trends from your Strategic Assumptions. The BOLD MOVES framework adds provocative questions to push beyond safe thinking. Here's how it works:

1 Take your TRENDS (from existing strategy work)
2 Add a BOLD MOVES QUESTION
3 Surface IMPLICATIONS

- Organic: What could we build/change ourselves?
- Inorganic: What could we acquire/partner for?

4 Calculate IMPACT (Revenue and EBITDA for each)
5 Assess RISKS (for the critical few worth pursuing)

The goal: Find two to three moves that could transform your position. Not a laundry list – the critical few that matter.

The Five Questions

Question 1: What Would End Our Current Business Model?

Every business model eventually faces disruption. The question is whether you'll see it coming and do something about it.

Take your trends. Add this lens. What could make your business irrelevant? Then ask: Could we do it first?

Real Example: Microsoft faced this question with Skype and Teams. They'd acquired Skype for $8.5B in 2011, and it was generating significant revenue. But they saw communication shifting to integrated collaboration platforms. Rather than protect Skype, Microsoft launched Teams in 2017 and actively pushed users to migrate. They even stopped inviting Skype for Business employees to company meetings to force organizational focus on Teams. By 2025, Skype will be completely shut down. Microsoft chose to cannibalize their own $8.5B acquisition rather than let competitors do it for them.[3]

Question 2: What Would 10X Improvement Look Like?

You can optimize to 20% better. You can't optimize to 10X. Different magnitude requires different thinking.

Take your trends. Imagine 10X value, speed, or efficiency. What would have to change fundamentally?

Real Example: SpaceX asked this question about space launch costs. Traditional aerospace focused on incremental improvements – making rockets 10–20% more efficient. Elon Musk asked: What if we made launches 10X cheaper? The answer: reusable rockets. Everyone said it was impossible. The Falcon 9 now lands itself and flies again, reducing launch costs by more than 90%. They didn't optimize the old model – they reimagined it entirely.[4]

Question 3: Do We Have a Hidden Billion-Dollar Business?

Most companies have unicorns buried in their org chart. A capability. A platform. A division that could be worth $1B standalone.

Review your assets through the lens of current trends. What's constraining that value?

Real Example: Microsoft had a hidden giant in Xbox Game Pass. For years, it was just another subscription service competing with PlayStation. Then they asked: What if this became the "Netflix of gaming"? They pivoted from selling consoles to building a platform that works on any device – phones, tablets, TVs, competing consoles. Game Pass now has 33 million subscribers and is projected to generate over $5B annually by 2025. The billion-dollar business was hiding inside their gaming division all along.[5]

Question 4: If We Started Fresh Today, What Would We Build?

Zero legacy. Zero constraints. Just your knowledge and the trends. What's different? What wouldn't exist?

Real Example: When Brian Chesky returned to lead Airbnb post-pandemic, he asked this exact question. If Airbnb started today, would it have 2 million listing categories? Would hosts manage everything themselves? The answer was no. They simplified to just four categories (rooms, homes, unique stays, experiences) and launched Airbnb Rooms to return to their core – affordable stays in someone's home. They eliminated the complexity that had accumulated over years. Revenue jumped 18% as they returned to what made them revolutionary.[6]

Question 5: What's Our Moonshot?

What seems impossible today but might not be tomorrow given the trends? What would transform everything if you could pull it off?

Real Example: Moderna's moonshot was using mRNA technology for vaccines – something most pharma companies thought was decades away from commercialization. They'd been working on it since 2010, losing money every year. When COVID hit, their "impossible" bet became reality. They went from never having a commercial product to delivering 807 million vaccine doses and generating $18.5B in revenue in 2021. Their moonshot saved lives and transformed the company from a research startup to a pharmaceutical giant.[7]

How It Actually Works

Here's what happened with the logistics company:

Their trends (from existing strategy work):

- Autonomous vehicles advancing rapidly
- Driver shortage accelerating
- Customers demanding predictive visibility

The question: What would end our current model?

Implications they surfaced:

- Organic: Build autonomous fleet operations ourselves
  - Impact: Protect revenue and improve margins
  - Risk: Technology timeline, regulatory uncertainty
- Inorganic: Partner with or acquire self-driving capabilities
  - Impact: New revenue streams and competitive positioning
  - Risk: Integration complexity, capital requirements

Two hours. Three transformative ideas. Not because I told them what to think – because the questions unlocked what they already knew but hadn't said.

When I followed up months later, they were pursuing clear bets in predictive logistics and autonomous partnerships with real dollars behind them. The session had shifted their thinking from defensive to offensive.

Making It Stick

Don't run a special "innovation session." Use one question in your regular leadership meetings. Make dangerous thinking normal.

The key is integration, not isolation. When bold moves become part of your regular strategic rhythm, they stop being scary and start being standard. Pick one question per quarter. Spend 30 minutes in your regular leadership meeting. Make it as routine as reviewing financial results.

Bring in different people based on the question. If you're asking about hidden unicorns, include the head of that division. If you're exploring moonshots, bring in your technical experts. It's also good development for high-potentials to see how transformative thinking works.

Common Pitfalls to Avoid

Treating This Like Brainstorming: These questions require homework, not just creativity. When someone says "AI will transform everything," ask for specifics. Which processes? What technology? What's the real impact?

Everything Must Be a Moonshot: Microsoft Teams wasn't a moonshot – it was a logical evolution from Skype. The best bold moves often seem obvious in retrospect. They're bold because you act on them, not because they're crazy.

Waiting for Crisis: Companies often wait until they're in trouble to ask these questions. By then, options are limited and resources are constrained. Ask them when you're strong.

After working through a question with your team, use AI to go deeper:

"Given these trends [list them] and this strategic move [describe it], what analogous transformations have succeeded in other industries?"

"What early signals would indicate this trend is accelerating?"

"Which companies globally are best positioned to lead this change?"

Note: Keep confidential data out of AI prompts. Focus on patterns and external benchmarks.

The Real Test

Your executives should be bringing you uncomfortable ideas regularly. They should propose killing products that still make money. They should suggest strategies that scare them.

If they're not, these questions are your diagnostic tool. Use them to shake things up.

But here's the real test: After using these questions once, does your team start bringing transformative ideas without prompting? If not, you have a culture problem, not a strategy problem.

Smart executives will get the wake-up call. They'll realize that in a world where Netflix cannibalizes its own DVD business, where SpaceX makes rockets reusable, where Microsoft transforms gaming subscriptions – playing it safe is the riskiest strategy of all.

When Quiet Means Danger

The pattern is consistent across industries. Companies that seem untouchable become vulnerable the moment they stop questioning their own model. The quiet periods – when everyone agrees, when strategies feel safe, when bold ideas stop flowing – those are the danger zones.

Your best thinkers have transformative ideas. The question is whether your culture lets them voice those ideas or forces them to save them for their next opportunity. If you're not hearing ideas that make you uncomfortable, that challenge fundamental assumptions, that risk current revenue for future position – then your organization has already chosen decline over disruption.

When things are quiet, that's exactly when to act. Quiet means your best thinkers are saving their radical ideas for somewhere else. Quiet means disruption is building where you're not looking.

The time to ask dangerous questions is when you're strong enough to act on the answers. And if your team isn't asking these questions on their own, that's the most dangerous signal of all.

Is your team bringing you ideas that could transform the business – or are you still waiting in the quiet?

Notes

1 Based on the author's 25+ years of consulting and client experience.

2 Richard A. Gershon, "Netflix: A Case Study in the New Digital Economy." *Media Management and Economics Research in a Transmedia Environment*, edited by Alan B. Albarran (New York: Routledge, 2013), 205–220.

3 Tom Warren, "Microsoft Teams is Officially Replacing Skype for Business." *The Verge*, July 31, 2017. https://www.theverge.com/2017/7/31/16069726/microsoft-teams-replacing-skype-for-business.

4 Andrew Jones, "SpaceX's Reusable Falcon 9 Rocket Has Fundamentally Changed the Economics of Space." *Quartz*, March 30, 2021. https://qz.com/1990218/spacexs-reusable-falcon-9-rocket-has-changed-the-economics-of-space.

5 Tom Warren, "Microsoft's Xbox Game Pass Subscribers Reached 33 Million." *The Verge*, January 25, 2024. https://www.theverge.com/2024/1/25/24049634/microsoft-xbox-game-pass-subscribers-34-million.

6 Airbnb, Inc., "Airbnb Reports First Quarter 2023 Results." Press Release, May 9, 2023. https://news.airbnb.com/airbnb-first-quarter-2023-financial-results/.

7 Moderna, Inc., "Moderna Reports Fourth Quarter and Fiscal Year 2021 Financial Results." Press Release, February 24, 2022. https://investors.modernatx.com/news/news-details/2022/Moderna-Reports-Fourth-Quarter-and-Fiscal-Year-2021-Financial-Results/default.aspx.

Chapter 14

BETTER

Make Acquisitions Actually Pay Off Post-Transaction

Your business case projected 20% EBITDA improvement. What if the real opportunity is 25% or more by combining strategic thinking, not just operations?

A $400M manufacturing company had just closed an $80M acquisition of a long-established regional competitor. The bankers projected synergies – mostly headcount reduction and system consolidation. Classic playbook: cut costs, integrate systems, achieve 20% EBITDA improvement.[1]

"What are we missing?" the CEO asked me. "We're integrating everything except their strategic insights and experience."

The Missed Opportunity

Let's be honest – most acquisitions destroy value. Not because the deal was wrong, but because the integration is backward. Companies focus on combining systems, cutting costs, eliminating redundancies. They miss the real prize: combining strategic intelligence.

You didn't just buy assets and customers. You bought executives who know things you don't. They competed against you successfully. They understand why certain customers chose them over you. They see market opportunities from a different angle.

Here's what most teams miss: Those acquired executives aren't just new employees. They hold insights that could transform your combined business. But traditional integration buries this intelligence under process harmonization and reporting structures.

The pattern is consistent. Month 1: Everyone's excited about "best of both companies." Month 3: Corporate processes dominate. Month 6: Key talent starts leaving. Month 12: You hit your cost synergies but miss the real opportunity.

The MOVE +1 Approach

Here's what we did differently with that $400M manufacturing company. They already had their MOVE tools in place.

What they hadn't done was enhance these tools with what they'd just bought.

The company you just acquired IS an inorganic implication of your strategy. They succeeded where you struggled. They saw opportunities you missed. Now they're yours. Make that intelligence visible.

Strategic Assumptions +1: We laid out the acquiring company's existing assumptions. Then the acquired executives presented theirs. No judgment, no debate – just "here's how we each see the world."

DOI: 10.4324/9781003682455-19

The differences told the story:

- We saw consolidation around large players
- They saw fragmentation into regional specialists
- We focused on operational efficiency
- They focused on customer responsiveness

Both views were right – for different segments. The combined view revealed opportunities that added 5% to EBITDA beyond the business case. Same market, different lenses, new opportunities.

Vision Enhancement: The acquiring company's vision focused on scale and efficiency. Vision rarely changes completely, but it can be enhanced.

The acquired company brought a different perspective on customer service and flexibility.

Through dialogue, we enhanced the vision to capture both strengths. This unlocked a strategy neither could execute alone.

PMM +1: This is where the real action happens. We mapped both companies' matrices side by side:

- They were strong where we were weak
- We dominated segments they'd abandoned
- Our biggest battles were in cells neither was winning

The combined PMM showed specific cells where we could now win together. That's where the 5% EBITDA improvement lives – revenue growth from cells you couldn't capture alone.

Capabilities That Compound: The AFC work revealed capabilities that multiply:

- Our scale + their flexibility = serve new segments profitably
- Our systems + their local knowledge = premium positioning
- Our capital + their innovation = faster product development

The acquiring company already had their strategic projects list. The +1 thinking revealed which projects to accelerate, which new ones to add, and which to stop because the acquired team had already tried and failed.

They presented the MOVE +1 thinking with a clear rationale. The numbers and logic spoke for themselves.

The Results Speak

Original business case: 20% EBITDA improvement through cost synergies. Actual result: 28% EBITDA improvement.

That's 8% points beyond the business case. Not from cutting more costs. From revenue opportunities neither company could capture alone. Combined revenue grew 40% in two years. ROIC exceeded projections by 8% points.

The board asked why every acquisition doesn't work this way.

Simple: Most companies integrate operations. We enhanced strategic thinking.

Why This Works

The acquired executives see your business differently than you do. They competed against you. They know your weaknesses. They understand why customers chose them.

The acquired team brings:

- Different customer relationships
- Different market assumptions
- Different capability strengths
- Different competitive insights

But traditional integration treats them as employees to be integrated, not strategists to be heard.

Acquired executives see competitive patterns, customer behaviors, and market opportunities from a completely different vantage point. They know which of your strategies frustrated them most. They understand which customer segments you're serving poorly.

Let's be honest – many CEOs worry about giving acquired executives too much influence too soon. They want to establish control first. But that's exactly when you lose the strategic intelligence you paid for. The best insights come in the first 90 days, before corporate antibodies kick in.

Here's what I've learned: Using MOVE tools post-acquisition can beat the business case by 5% or more on EBITDA. In my experience, this light approach has delivered meaningful results.[2]

Why? Because the business case only captures what bankers can model – cost cuts and obvious revenue synergies. It doesn't capture what happens when different perspectives combine to see opportunities neither saw before.

Making It Work

Don't limit this to your usual leadership team. Bring in people with specific knowledge for the question at hand. It's also a good development opportunity for high-potential directors to see how transformative thinking works.

Here's how to run the MOVE +1 enhancement:

Surface the Intelligence Bring together your strategy team and the top three to five executives from the acquired company. You already have your MOVE tools. Now enhance them.

Run two one-day sessions. Day 1: Build the +1 enhancements. Let each side present their view of the market. Document the differences – these are your opportunities.

Between sessions: Let it soak. Gather data to validate what emerged. With AI, you can quickly analyze patterns and size opportunities.

Day 2: Return with proof. What seemed interesting becomes actionable with numbers attached.

Enhance Each Tool Work through your MOVE tools systematically:

- SA: What insights do they bring?
- Vision: How can their perspective enhance (not replace) yours?
- PMM: Which cells can you win together?
- Capabilities: What combinations create advantage?
- Strategic Projects: What accelerates, what's new, what stops?

Your CFO might say "We already modeled the synergies."

Here's the distinction: They modeled cost cuts. They haven't looked through a PMM with new thinking in the room. That's where the additional 5% lives.

Quantify the +1 Value: Be specific about the EBITDA impact:

- New market cells = revenue growth

- Combined capabilities = competitive advantage
- Better strategic projects = higher ROI

Example: "We can serve the Southwest region by combining your local presence with our manufacturing capacity – worth $20M in year one."

Present the MOVE +1 Results: Show the board:

- Your original strategy
- The +1 enhancements
- The incremental value (that extra 5%+)
- Who does what to capture it

You're not questioning the deal. You're finding value with the people who know the market best – your new partners who were recently your competition.

The Real Shift

Here's what's fundamentally different: Stop thinking of acquired executives as resources to be integrated. Think of them as strategists who enhance your view of the market.

They're not just bringing customers and capabilities. They're bringing intelligence about:

- Why customers choose differently
- Where markets are really heading
- Which capabilities actually matter
- How to win segments you've struggled in

When you surface this through structured tools, not random conversations, you consistently beat the business case.

Here's what else happens: When acquired executives help shape strategy, they stay. When they're just told to execute your strategy, they leave. Think about the math – keeping one key executive who knows why customers choose them is worth more than any retention bonus.

Let's be clear – integration teams are essential. There's a long list of operational tasks that must happen. This is different. It's a parallel track focused on strategic value while the integration team handles operations. Two days of strategic thinking while 200 integration tasks proceed. Different people, different purpose, both necessary.

This assumes the right conditions. The acquired executives need to want to contribute, not just wait for their earnout. They need to see a future worth building. You'll know quickly – in the first session, engagement becomes apparent. When they lean in, you get the 5%. When they don't, you get compliance but no insight.

Think about the competitive intelligence you're sitting on. These executives know:

- Which of your salespeople they feared most
- Which of your products kept them up at night
- Which customers they thought they could take
- Why they won when they won

That intelligence, surfaced through structured tools, is worth more than any cost synergy.

Your Next Acquisition

Next time you're evaluating a deal, ask: What strategic intelligence are we buying? How will their perspective enhance our strategy? What could we achieve together that neither can alone?

Budget time in month one for combined strategy sessions. Use structured tools to surface insights. Track strategic value creation separately from cost synergies.

Tell your board: "We're going to try to beat the business case by combining strategic thinking, not just operations." Then track it monthly. Show them if new market combinations and strategic insights build incremental EBITDA.

The math could be compelling. On a $1B revenue business, 5% additional EBITDA improvement is $50M annually. At a 10× multiple, that's $500M in enterprise value.[3] Worth exploring on every acquisition.

The Bottom Line

The best acquisitions don't just achieve the business case – they often exceed it through strategic intelligence combination.

Using MOVE tools with the combined leadership team in the first 90 days can generate 5% or more additional EBITDA improvement. Not from cost cuts already modeled. From revenue opportunities and strategic combinations neither company could see alone.

Your next acquisition might have this 5% opportunity. Two days of structured strategic thinking in month one could surface it. Track it separately. Report it to the board. See what happens.

The executives you're acquiring know things that could transform your business. They see opportunities you miss. They understand the capabilities you need. But only if you treat them as strategic partners from day one.

Strategic integration can beat operational integration. It's how good deals might become great ones. It's how 20% projected returns could become 25% or more.

Next acquisition, why not block the time? Run the tools. Look for the extra value. Turn integration from just a cost exercise into a potential value creation engine.

Two days. Only upside. Worth trying.

Notes

1 Based on the author's 25+ years of consulting and client experience.
2 Based on the author's 25+ years of consulting and client experience.
3 Damodaran, Aswath. "The Value of Synergy." Stern School of Business, October 2005. http://pages.stern.nyu.edu/~adamodar/pdfiles/papers/synergy.pdf.

Chapter 15

BUDGET

Align Capital with Competitive Moves

Your budget reveals your real strategy – regardless of what your PowerPoints say.

Daniel had been through plenty of budgeting cycles in his career – but none like the one now facing him at Farella Foods [fictional example].

It was late June. Business performance was steady. Retail partners were mostly happy. But Daniel had a growing discomfort. Something felt misaligned. His executive team had spent the last nine months building out their strategy – clear assumptions, a focused PMM, a few signature initiatives – and yet none of that strategic logic was reflected in how money was being allocated.

The Disconnect

Finance had already kicked off the budgeting season with the usual top-down guidance: target a 10% revenue lift, adjust for inflation, freeze non-critical hiring, and cap travel and discretionary spending. The rest, predictably, would be a tug-of-war between departments.

"I'm looking at budget drafts that don't match the bets we agreed on," Daniel told his CFO. "We said Product 3 was an Explore play – but it's getting more dollars than Product 1, which we all agreed is our core profit driver."

The CFO didn't disagree. "It's how the templates are built. Each VP justifies their own piece. The system doesn't force alignment."

Daniel shook his head. "That's the problem. We've upgraded our strategy, but we're still budgeting like we did five years ago – by department, not by strategic priority."

Let's be honest – we're operating on different assumptions. Strategy assumes we'll fund our biggest opportunities. Budgeting assumes we'll protect departmental territories. These assumptions can't both be right.

Why Budgeting Stays Broken

Here's what most executives miss: budgeting was built for control, not competition. DuPont and GM created annual budgeting in the 1920s to manage massive hierarchies. The assumptions were simple – stable markets, predictable competition, clear boundaries.[1]

Those assumptions died decades ago. But the budgeting process lives on, consuming months of executive time while adding zero strategic value.

Think about the absurdity. You spend six months analyzing markets, making strategic choices, aligning on priorities. Then budget season arrives and you throw all that thinking away to argue about travel expenses and headcount ratios.

Why do smart companies keep doing this? Five uncomfortable truths:

It Shifts Power. Strategy-driven budgeting empowers people close to customers. Traditional budgeting keeps power at corporate. Guess which one executives prefer?

DOI: 10.4324/9781003682455-20

It Exposes Weak Strategy. If you have no clear Product-Market priorities, you have nothing to base a budget on. Traditional budgeting hides this. Strategic budgeting reveals it.
It Requires Real Dialogue. You can't do this by email and spreadsheet. You need actual conversation between strategy, finance, and operations. Many organizations have forgotten how.
It Breaks Comfortable Ritual. Everyone knows their role in budget negotiations. Even if it doesn't work, it's familiar. Change requires courage most companies lack.
It Demands Trust. Leaders must believe their teams will make smart decisions if given real ownership. Many don't.

Here's what I've learned: The people closest to customers and competition – the ones who own a P&L or even part of one – should be building the first version of their budget. If you've never asked them to, you're missing huge opportunity.[2]

Think about it. Your regional VPs, your product line leaders, your country managers – they collectively know more about their markets than corporate ever will. And they should. But most companies never tap this knowledge. Instead, corporate builds assumptions in spreadsheets while the real insights sit unused in the field.

When you let P&L owners build their initial budgets, something powerful happens. You install accountability because it's their thinking, their commitments, their ownership. Not targets imposed from above, but plans built from market reality.

Daniel's Different Approach

"What does it take to win in our top product-market segments, and how do we fund that first?"

Daniel brought the leadership team together. No PowerPoints. Just one heat-mapped Product-Market Matrix on the wall. Each cell showed where Farella was betting – Core, Growth, or Explore – and which capabilities needed strengthening.

Then they did something radical. They allocated dollars based on where they were playing to win:

- Core frozen meals markets got disproportionate funding to protect margin and share
- Growth snack segments received investment only where Farella had a clear edge
- Explore healthy bowls got seed funding with tight learning milestones

Instead of sending templates to every department, they started with strategy and only funded activities that advanced it.

"This isn't about cutting costs," Daniel told the team. "It's about aligning capital with conviction."

The process took three weeks instead of three months. Every line item tied back to a Product-Market cell or strategic initiative. They didn't need 14 versions of the same workbook. They needed one version of the truth – and that truth was the strategy they had already agreed to.

How Strategic Budgeting Works

Here's the fundamental shift: stop budgeting by department and start budgeting by strategic choice. Your PMM becomes your budget architecture.

Start with Competitive Reality

Look at each cell in your PMM. Ask three questions:

- What would it take to win here?
- What capabilities do we need?
- What's the minimum investment to succeed?

Be more specific. "Innovation" isn't a capability. "AI-powered demand sensing" is. "Growth" isn't a strategy. "Take 5 points of share from Bravora in frozen dinners" is.

Add Resource Logic to Each Cell

GREEN cells (Growth plays): These get expansion funding. New capabilities, new coverage, new capacity. If you're serious about growth, fund it seriously.

YELLOW cells (Explore plays): These get innovation funding. Experiments, pilots, learning loops. Small bets with clear milestones.

RED cells (Core/Milk plays): These get efficiency funding. Protect position, improve margins, generate cash for GREEN cells.

EXIT cells: These get transition funding. Either find a buyer or manage the decline. Stop pretending they'll turn around.

Make Trade-offs Visible

You'll identify more opportunities than you can fund. That's healthy. Now comes the strategic choice:

- Which two to three cells get full funding?
- Which get experiments only?
- Which get maintenance?
- Which get nothing?

The key: these are strategic choices based on market reality, not political negotiations based on who argues loudest.

Real Companies, Real Results

Let me show you what this looks like in practice.

U.S Medical Device Company

A U.S. medical device company with three product lines and four regions was struggling with budget allocation. Every regional VP wanted 20% more. Corporate finance cut everyone to 8%. Nobody was happy, nothing was strategic.[3]

They implemented Product-Market based budgeting in one quarter:

- Core diagnostics for hospitals (RED cell): Flat revenue target, invest $1.2M in service automation to protect margins
- New imaging for outpatient (GREEN cell): 25% growth target, invest $2.8M in sales specialists
- Legacy monitors for clinics (EXIT cell): Sunset over 18 months, redeploy team

Result: Overall growth exceeded targets because resources concentrated where they could win. More importantly, everyone understood why.

Regional Strategy That Made Sense

The same medical company faced the usual corporate mandate: 8% growth across all regions. The Asia-Pacific regional VP used Product-Market budgeting to show why that made no sense:

- Japan (GREEN): Aging population, regulatory tailwinds = 14% growth opportunity
- China (YELLOW): Policy uncertainty = Hold flat, watch closely

- India (RED): Price pressure = Focus on margins not growth
- Southeast Asia (EXIT): Subscale = Find local partner

Instead of spreading resources evenly, they concentrated investment in Japan, maintained position in China, improved margins in India, and found a buyer for Southeast Asia operations.

The CEO's response: "This is the clearest regional strategy I've ever seen. Every region should do this."

The real power comes from tapping the intelligence that already exists in your organization. Your P&L owners – whether they run regions, products, or segments – see patterns corporate misses. They know which assumptions are fantasy and which reflect reality. But traditional budgeting never asks them to share this intelligence systematically.

When you flip the process – when P&L owners build first drafts based on their Product-Market reality – you transform budgeting from compliance to strategy. The focus shifts from defending allocations to building plans that can win.

Making It Work in Your Company

Start Small: Pick one division with a clear leader and solid Product-Market Matrix. Let them prove the model while you learn what works in your culture. Success sells better than mandates.

Let P&L Owners Lead: Here's the key shift: Have your P&L owners build the first version of their budgets based on their PMM. Not finance. Not corporate strategy. The people who face customers and competitors every day.

Why? Because they know things corporate doesn't. They know which competitors are gaining share. They know which customers are shifting behavior. They know which products are commoditizing. They live it daily.

When P&L owners build their own budgets, you get three things:

1. **Better assumptions**: based on market reality, not spreadsheet formulas
2. **Real ownership**: it's their plan, their commitment, their accountability
3. **Faster execution**: no translation needed between corporate intent and field action

Run Parallel First Year: Yes, it's extra work to run both traditional and strategic budgeting. Do it anyway. When executives see strategic budgeting produces better answers, they'll abandon the old way naturally.

Make Your CFO Your Partner: This fails if finance fights it. Show your CFO this isn't about reducing their role – it's about elevating it from spreadsheet management to strategic partnership. The best CFOs love this because they finally get to influence strategy, not just track spending.

Track What Matters: When P&L owners build budgets, they make assumptions visible. Track these assumptions monthly. When they're wrong, learn why. When they're right, understand how they knew. This builds organizational intelligence that corporate planning never could.

Here's what I've learned: CFOs who resist this are usually protecting process, not adding value. CFOs who embrace it become true strategic partners. Which kind do you have?

The AI Advantage

Strategic budgeting becomes even more powerful with AI assistance. Not to make decisions, but to make trade-offs visible.

Use AI to analyze historical performance by Product-Market cell. Which cells consistently outperform? Which destroy value? AI can run these analyses in minutes, not weeks.

Model multiple allocation scenarios. What happens if you fully fund the top three GREEN cells versus spreading resources? AI can show value creation differences instantly.

But remember: AI doesn't make choices. It makes choices visible. Your judgment about competitive dynamics still matters. AI just ensures you're making informed bets, not hopeful guesses.

Enhanced AI Prompts for Strategic Budgeting

For Scenario Testing

ASK: "Using our Product-Market Matrix with [X] GREEN cells and [Y] RED cells, model 20 scenarios varying: growth rates (5–25%), competition response (aggressive/neutral/weak), and resource constraints. Show which scenarios produce highest ROIC and their early warning indicators." NOT: "What's a good growth target?"

For Assumption Validation

ASK: "Compare our budget assumptions for [specific market] against: actual performance last 3 years, competitor actions, and market growth rates. Flag assumptions that deviate >20% from historical patterns. What external factors could justify these deviations?" NOT: "Are these numbers reasonable?"

For Resource Optimization

ASK: "Given $[X]M total budget and these Product-Market priorities, show 5 allocation options that maximize: (1) GREEN cell funding, (2) capability building, (3) ROIC within 18 months. Include trade-offs for each." NOT: "How should we allocate the budget?"

For Monthly Tracking

ASK: "Create early warning dashboard: which budget assumptions are breaking? Which Product-Market cells are underperforming? What resource reallocations would improve trajectory? Use actual vs. budget data from [system]." NOT: "How are we doing against budget?"

Remember: Keep competitive data out of prompts. Focus on patterns and scenarios, not specifics about your strategic moves.

The Board Conversation

Here's what works with boards: "Our current budgeting process takes six months and produces departmental wish lists. We want to pilot strategic budgeting that links directly to our Product-Market strategy. We'll run both processes this year so you can see the difference."

Show them one clear example. Maybe it's that EXIT cell consuming 20% of resources. Maybe it's the GREEN cell starved of funding. Make the misalignment visible.

Boards care about three things:

1 Where are you placing bets?
2 Why do you expect to win?
3 Is capital following strategy?

Traditional budgeting can't answer these. Strategic budgeting makes it crystal clear.

Your Next Move

If you're still budgeting by department instead of strategic choice, you're funding yesterday's organization chart, not tomorrow's competitive advantage.

Pull out your PMM. For each cell, ask: What would it take to win here? What capabilities do we need? What investment is required?

Add it up. Compare to your current budget. The gaps will shock you.

Most companies discover they're overinvesting in dying cells and underinvesting in growth opportunities. They're spreading resources like peanut butter when they should be making focused bets.

Here's what you can do next week: Pull your P&L owners together. Give them their PMM. Ask them to build their budget based on what it takes to win in each cell. Watch what happens. You'll get better thinking in one session than three months of traditional budgeting.

Let's be honest – some P&L owners will test boundaries the first time. They'll ask for everything. But they quickly learn that visibility works both ways. When they own the assumptions, they own the results. Both the upside and the misses. That changes behavior fast.

If your CFO says "we can't change our process," here's what they really mean: "I don't want to lose control." Show them they gain strategic influence by letting go of spreadsheet control. The best CFOs get this immediately. They become strategic partners instead of process police.

Think about the time savings alone. Three weeks instead of three months. That's nine weeks your team can spend executing strategy instead of negotiating budgets. Nine weeks of competitive advantage while others are still arguing about travel policies.

The fix is straightforward but not easy. It requires admitting your budgeting process is broken. It requires trusting teams with real ownership. It requires making visible trade-offs.

But here's what you get: A budget that advances strategy instead of impeding it. Resource allocation that matches competitive reality. An organization aligned around where to win, not just how to save.

The companies that master this gain huge advantage. While competitors waste six months on budget negotiations, they're executing strategic moves. While others debate departmental allocations, they're funding competitive advantage.

You don't win by budgeting for the average. You win by concentrating resources where you can dominate.

The people closest to customers and competition should own their budgets. When they do, you get better assumptions, real accountability, and strategies that actually work in market.

Your budget reveals your real strategy. What does yours say?

Notes

1 H. Thomas Johnson and Robert S. Kaplan, *Relevance Lost: The Rise and Fall of Management Accounting* (Boston: Harvard Business School Press, 1987).
2 Based on the author's 25+ years of consulting and client experience.
3 Based on the author's 25+ years of consulting and client experience.

Chapter 16

BOARD READY

In Your First 100 Days, Move Up

Day 1 as CEO: You have 100 days to prove you get it, or spend the next 1,000 days fighting for credibility. Which do you choose?

Sarah had just been named CEO of GlobalRetail, a $4B company struggling with digital transformation and margin pressure. The board was clear: "We need strategic clarity fast. The last CEO spent two years studying the problem."[1]

Traditional wisdom said: Take six months. Listen to everyone. Don't make big moves. Build consensus slowly.

But Sarah knew better. Her competitors weren't waiting. Activist investors were circling. Key talent was getting nervous. She needed to build strategic clarity – and credibility – fast.

The Reality of CEO Transitions

From what I've seen, new CEOs often get caught in the same trap. They arrive with energy and good intentions. The board expects big things. The organization waits for direction. But months go by and not much changes.

Here's a pattern I've noticed:

- Days 1–30: Lots of meetings, listening sessions, trying to absorb everything
- Days 31–60: Bringing in outside help, commissioning studies, analysis mode
- Days 61–90: Forming committees, working on alignment, building buy-in
- Day 100: Rolling out a vision that could fit most companies

Six months in, they're still studying. Nine months in, still planning. Twelve months in, the board's getting nervous. Eighteen months in, they're looking for the next CEO.[2]

I've seen this happen with smart executives who had great track records. They somehow lose their edge when they step into the top job. Not because they lack capability – because they lack a system for building clarity fast.

In my experience, CEOs who drift through listening tours often find their boards getting restless.

Here's what often separates the CEOs who succeed from those who struggle: systematic thinking that builds strategic clarity fast. The same approach that's helped generate over $2B in incremental EBITDA across hundreds of companies. Not magic – just disciplined use of the right tools in the right sequence.[3]

When Traditional Approaches Struggle

New CEOs often face conflicting expectations. Boards want transformation but fear disruption. Teams want change but protect their turf. Investors want growth but punish any miss. Many want clarity but hesitate to commit.

DOI: 10.4324/9781003682455-21

So some CEOs default to process over progress. They manage perceptions instead of making moves. They build political capital instead of strategic advantage.

Consider what this means: while you're on your listening tour, competitors might be taking your customers. While you're building consensus, markets are shifting. While you're studying problems, opportunities can vanish.

The board faces their own dilemma. They hired you to drive change. But how do they evaluate progress without micromanaging? When should they worry versus wait?

Most boards default to checking activity: How many people have you met? How many customers visited? How many initiatives launched? But activity doesn't always equal progress.

From what I've observed, boards say they want transformation, but what they usually want is predictable improvement. Show them systematic thinking and they tend to relax. Show them random moves and they often panic.

What boards really need: A framework to evaluate strategic thinking, not just stakeholder management. They need to see that you can build clarity from complexity. That's what systematic use of MOVE provides.

A Different First 100 Days

"I don't have six months to figure out where we're going," Sarah told her leadership team on day one. "I have 100 days to show we know how to win."

She didn't announce she was using MOVE tools. She didn't pitch a new framework. She just started making the thinking visible by asking different questions. By day 30, her team noticed: "These aren't random questions. There's a method here."

But here's what made the difference: Sarah wasn't trying to have all the answers. She was creating a way for the team to find the answers together. Each session surfaced breadcrumbs – pieces of insight that others could build on.

"I'm not here to be right," she told them. "I'm here to help us be effective. The faster we can see our thinking, the faster we can improve it."

The Power of Building Step by Step

The value isn't in individual tools – it's in how they build on each other:

- SA give you external reality → Which enables better Vision choices
- VDF give you direction → Which focuses your Product-Market analysis
- PMM shows portfolio choices → Which MRC validates with customer data
- Advantage mapping identifies capability gaps → Which shapes your initiatives
- Initiatives make strategy real → Which strategic numbers track through leading indicators

Think about what this means: instead of random listening tours, you're building strategic clarity one piece at a time. Each conversation adds to the picture. Each session deepens understanding. By day 100, you have integrated strategy, not just good intentions.

After watching many successful CEO transitions, here's a pattern that often separates winners from those who struggle: they build clarity systematically, not randomly. They make thinking visible, not hidden. They align teams through logic, not just charisma.

Here's what many CEOs miss: boards don't need you to have all the answers on day 100. They need to see that you have a systematic way of finding answers. When they see these tools in action – even if you don't name them – they see disciplined thinking, not just charismatic leadership.

Here's where AI becomes your accelerator. You can analyze patterns from hundreds of industry transitions, spot weak signals your team missed, and pressure-test assumptions against global data. What used to take months of discovery happens in days. But only if you ask the right questions.

Days 1–30: Strategic Assumptions: See What's Really Happening

First month isn't about your vision – it's about understanding reality. Use SA to identify external Trends (what's changing), Constants (what's not changing), and Implications (what it means for your business).

Week 1: Executive Team Discovery. Run a session with your top team. The driving question: "What external forces are reshaping our industry?" Document their view of what's changing, what's staying the same, and what it means.

Sarah discovered her team saw different realities. The CMO tracked consumer behavior shifts. The CFO worried about input cost inflation. The digital lead saw technology disruption. No alignment on which trends mattered most.

But instead of declaring which view was "right," Sarah made all perspectives visible. Put them on the wall. Let the team see the pattern of their collective thinking. The breadcrumbs started appearing – connections between consumer shifts and cost pressures, links between digital disruption and channel evolution.

Think about the math: 5 executives making 20 decisions a month based on different assumptions = 100 decisions pulling in different directions. Make those assumptions visible and the team naturally starts aligning. Not because you told them to, but because they can see the disconnects.

Week 2: Functional Deep Dives. Same SA process with each function. Gather breadcrumbs: Sales sees channel shifts. Operations sees supply chain risks. IT sees technology gaps. Map the differences – they reveal blind spots.

Week 3: External Validation. Test internal assumptions with customers, suppliers, analysts. Not random conversations – structured SA validation: "We see these trends. What are we missing?"

Week 4: Synthesize SA Output. Consolidate into one-page SA. Maximum five Trends, three Constants, clear Implications. This becomes foundation for every subsequent decision.

Sarah's insight: "By day 30, we had shared view of external reality. First time in company history everyone agreed on what's actually changing."

Days 31–45: Vision and Driving Force: Define Where You're Going

With external reality clear, define internal direction. VDF push you beyond incremental thinking.

Week 5: Vision Options. Based on Implications from your assumptions work, develop three to five vision options. Not wordsmithing – genuinely different futures. Sarah's team generated five, from "Digital-First Retailer" to "Ecosystem Orchestrator."

Week 6: Driving Force Selection. What single capability gets you there? This is harder. Most teams want multiple driving forces. Force the choice. Sarah's team debated between "Digital Excellence" and "Channel Integration" before landing on "Omnichannel Convenience at Scale."

One vision. One driving force. Clarity achieved by day 45.

Days 46–65: Product-Market Matrix (PMM): Make Bets Visible

Now the hard work: where will you actually compete and win?

Week 7: Current State PMM. Map today's reality. Every product, every market, scored by profit and growth. Sarah discovered 40% of resources trapped in red cells – profitable but declining categories they couldn't let go.

Week 8: Future State PMM. Based on SA and VDF, design where you need to be. Which cells turn green? Which stay red? Which need testing? Visual clarity forces hard choices.

Week 9: MRC. Validate PMM choices against external data. What do customers actually value? Where are competitors investing? Sarah discovered two "strategic" bets had no customer pull – killed them immediately.

By day 65: Clear portfolio choices backed by market reality.

Days 66–80: Advantage + Future Capabilities: Build What Matters

With portfolio clear, identify capabilities that create competitive advantage.

Week 10: Current Advantage Assessment. What truly differentiates you today? Not aspirations – actual advantages. Sarah's team claimed five advantages. Honest assessment revealed two: store network and private-label capability.

Week 11: Future Capability Requirements. Based on PMM choices, what capabilities must you build? Sarah identified three: real-time inventory visibility, personalization engine, rapid fulfillment. Without these, the strategy fails.

Resource allocation becomes obvious: fund future capabilities, maintain current advantages, stop everything else.

Days 81–95: Strategic Project Portfolio and Numbers: Turn Strategy into Action

Convert strategic choices into focused initiatives with clear metrics.

Week 12: Initiative Design. Maximum three strategic initiatives that:

- Attack green Product-Market cells
- Build critical future capabilities
- Signal strategic intent clearly

Sarah chose:

1. Digital Foundation (table stakes for all future capabilities)
2. Channel Integration (driving force in action)
3. Strategic Exits (fund the transformation)

Week 13: Resource Allocation and Metrics. Move money and talent to match strategy. Sarah shifted $200M and her best operators to the three initiatives. Few things demonstrate strategy as clearly as resource moves.

Define your strategic numbers – the leading indicators that tell you if strategy is working before it shows up in financial results. Not lagging metrics like revenue, but leading indicators like customer acquisition cost in new channels, time to market for new products, or digital engagement rates.

Days 96–100: Board Presentation: Show Integrated Strategy

Pull it all together into a compelling narrative:

The Flow

1. "Here's how our world is changing" (SA)
2. "Here's where we're going and how we'll win" (Vision, Driving Force, and Product-Market choices)

3 "Here's what we're building to succeed" (Capabilities and Strategic Initiatives)
4 "Here's how we'll track progress" (strategic numbers – leading indicators)

60 minutes. No fluff. Just strategic clarity built systematically over 100 days.

Strategic Thinking Process, Not Just Outcomes: Show how you think, not just what you concluded. When boards see structured thinking (MOVE tools), they gain confidence in future decisions, not just current ones.

Choices Made Visible: Boards can't evaluate strategies they can't see. PMM makes portfolio choices visual. Resource allocation shows commitment. Clear initiatives demonstrate focus.

Leading Indicators of Success: Don't wait for financial results. Show strategic progress: assumptions validated, initiatives advancing, capabilities building. Boards need to see momentum before it hits the P&L.

Confidence Without Arrogance "Here's what we know, here's what we're testing, here's what we'll adjust." Boards trust CEOs who show structured confidence, not false certainty.

The Compound Effect

Sarah's first 100 days set a pattern that accelerated:

Year 1: Digital foundation fixed. Channels integrating. Margins improving. Board confident.
Year 2: Omnichannel advantage clear. Share gains accelerating. Talent wanting in, not out.
Year 3: Industry leadership acknowledged. Acquisition opportunities emerging. Board asking: "How can we support bigger moves?"

The pattern I've observed: CEOs who build strategic clarity fast tend to outperform those who drift through listening tours. Not because they're smarter or more experienced. Because they have a system for making strategy visible and actionable.[4]

The same systematic approach that's helped drive billions in EBITDA improvement works in the first 100 days. It's not about having all the answers – it's about having a proven way to find them.

For New CEOs: Your 100-Day Choice

You can follow traditional wisdom. Take six months to listen. Build consensus slowly. Hope the board stays patient. Hope competitors stay slow. Hope markets stay stable.

Or you can move differently.

Use your first 30 days to make collective thinking visible through structured questions. Use days 31–60 to explore strategic choices together. Use days 61–90 to focus resources based on what you've discovered. Present integrated clarity by day 100.

You're not trying to be the genius with all the answers. You're creating a process where answers emerge from the collective intelligence of your team. The tools make thinking visible. Visible thinking enables better decisions. Better decisions create value.

Don't announce "I'm using MOVE." Just use it. Let the quality of thinking speak for itself.

For Boards: What to Look For

Stop counting meetings attended. Start evaluating strategic thinking:

- Do assumptions about the future make sense?
- Are strategic choices clear and logical?
- Are resources following strategy?
- Are leading indicators improving?

Give new CEOs room to lead. But expect structured thinking, visible choices, and focused action. Those who deliver this in 100 days usually deliver results in 1,000.

The Bottom Line

First impressions matter. Build strategic clarity fast and you earn permission to lead. Drift through listening tours and you're playing catch-up for a while.

Here's what I've seen: Miss the first 100 days and you're not just 100 days behind. You're dealing with organizational drift, competitive moves, and lost momentum. While you studied, competitors acted. While you built consensus, customers may have defected. While you planned, talent might have left. Recovery takes much longer than the time you lost.

Markets rarely pause for new leadership. Competitors don't wait for your consensus. Investors focus on results more than process.

They care about your moves.

The first 100 days often set the pattern for the next 1,000. Build strategic clarity systematically and you earn the right to lead. Make thinking visible and teams tend to align naturally. Create conditions for answers to emerge and the organization moves with you.

The tools have proven helpful. The sequence tends to work. The choice is yours.

The first 100 days are your chance to build clarity and credibility. What approach makes sense for you?

Notes

1 Based on the author's 25+ years of consulting and client experience.
2 Michael E. Porter, Jay W. Lorsch, and Nitin Nohria, "Seven Surprises for New CEOs." *Harvard Business Review* 82, no. 10 (October 2004): 62–72.
3 Based on the author's 25+ years of consulting and client experience.
4 Based on the author's 25+ years of consulting and client experience.

Chapter 17

MOVE What Matters

One System, Everywhere You Go

Strategy isn't what you plan. It's what you do. And what separates those who win from those who don't is the willingness to move.

Twenty-five years. Thousands of executives. Four continents. Every industry you can name.

The pattern never changes: Companies don't fail because they lack smart people or good intentions. They fail because they don't move. They analyze, they plan, they discuss – but they don't act with strategic coherence.

Let's be honest about where you are right now. You've read this book. You understand the tools. You see how traditional strategy is failing. You know AI is changing the game. The question is: what are you going to do about it?

Here's what I've learned after 25 years and helping clients realize over $2B in incremental EBITDA: the executives who create extraordinary value aren't necessarily the smartest or best resourced. They're simply the ones willing to move.[1]

The Choice Every Executive Faces

You're about to close this book and face the same choice every reader faces:

Go back to business as usual. Run the same planning processes. Build the same PowerPoints. Hope for different results. Your bookshelf will be fuller. Your strategies will look the same.

Or use what you've learned to build something different. A strategic capability that travels with you. Tools that work in any company, any industry, any situation. Not because they're magic – because they force the behaviors that matter.

Most executives learn new planning processes at each company, mastering none. Those who bring their own proven system create value from day one. Which executive do you want to be?

I know what you're thinking – "Another framework to add to the pile." But frameworks fail when they stay theoretical.

What Makes a MOVE Master

The difference isn't knowledge. It's application. Here's what separates those who deliver from those who don't:

They Make Thinking Visible

Walk into their strategy sessions. Ideas on walls, not in heads. Assumptions written out, not hidden. Disagreements surfaced, not buried. When thinking is visible, politics die and progress accelerates.

DOI: 10.4324/9781003682455-22

One CEO put it simply: "If it's not on the wall, it's not in the room." That single rule transformed her company's culture. The quiet engineer's insight suddenly carried as much weight as the charismatic sales leader's opinion. Strategic breakthroughs came from unexpected places.[2]

You know it's working when you find yourself asking for a flipchart or dry-erase pen in every meeting. When your first instinct becomes "let's map this out" instead of "let's talk about it." When you walk into conference rooms and immediately scan for writing surfaces. That's when visible thinking has become your default mode.

Show me a company where strategy lives only in PowerPoints, and I'll show you a company where everyone's guessing what the strategy really is. It's like reading a comic strip without captions – the best you can do is guess what's happening.

Think about the math: if you can get everyone to make one better, more strategically aligned decision each month, you've got yourself a winner. One hundred people making twelve better decisions a year – that's 1,200 decisions moving in the same direction instead of canceling each other out.

They Stay Ruthlessly Focused

In a world of infinite opportunities, they choose. Not everything possible, but the few things that matter. They'd rather execute three initiatives excellently than manage thirty adequately.

A division president told me: "I used to pride myself on juggling twenty initiatives. Now I pride myself on saying no to seventeen." His division's performance tripled when resources concentrated where they'd actually move the needle.[3]

You know it's working when you realize some areas in your company are just at competitive parity – and that's okay. When you stop believing you have competitive advantage everywhere and start building real advantage where it matters. When the P&L finally reflects the advantages you actually have, not the ones you wish you had. Now you have a real starting point.

Be more specific: What are your three biggest bets right now? If you named more than three, you don't have a strategy. You have a wish list.

They Commit Resources Visibly

No hedging. No spreading bets thin. When they choose, they fund. Resources follow strategy, not organizational politics. If it's strategic, it's funded. If it's not funded, it's not strategic.

You know it's working when you say no to bet numbers 4 and 5 to properly fund bets 1 through 3. When you stop the "just in case" investments that dilute your real bets. When your CFO stops asking "can we hedge this?" and starts asking "are we investing enough to win?"

Watch their allocation meetings. Strategic initiatives get the best people, real budget, CEO attention. Everything else gets managed efficiently. Strategic bets get led passionately.

They Execute in Rhythm

Not annual planning in monthly markets. They sense, decide, execute, learn – then do it again. Faster each time. Planning cycles replaced by learning cycles.

One retail CEO shared her rhythm: Strategic assumption review monthly. Product-Market Matrix check quarterly. Initiative progress weekly. Major pivots when needed, not when scheduled. "We move at market speed, not calendar speed."[4]

You know it's working when your team starts shortening presentations and getting quickly to the "why" and "what to do about it" – which you've probably been asking them anyway. When meetings shift from information download to decision and action. When "let's take this offline to analyze" becomes "let's decide now and adjust later."

Your Strategic Decision-Making System

MOVE isn't something you implement once. It's something you own forever. A complete system for strategic thinking and action that works anywhere:

New company? Use the tools quietly. Never walk in announcing "here's our new strategic approach." Instead, ask the SA questions in regular meetings. "What do we think is changing in our market?" "How might technology shift our customer needs?" Get people to write their thoughts on a whiteboard. They'll start seeing the contradictions themselves. Within a week, you'll understand the business deeply – and more importantly, your team will see you as someone with a logical approach to problems. Slowly introduce the tools as "ways to structure our thinking." Change happens through questions, not proclamations.

Crisis hits? Deploy the right tool immediately. While others convene committees, you'll have strategic options ready quickly. Pull out your PMM and see which cells are under attack. Use SA to understand if this is a one-time event or part of a larger shift. Check your Advantage-Capabilities to see if you're equipped to respond. The tools force clarity when emotions run high.

Opportunity emerges? Test it fast with focused PMM analysis. Know which cells to attack, which to defend, which to ignore. When acquisition targets come available with short decision windows, PMM shows exactly where there's strategic fit and where there's dangerous overlap. You can see synergies and conflicts in hours, not weeks. Move while others debate whether the opportunity is real.

Team stuck? Make their thinking visible with any MOVE tool. Usually it's SA – everyone thinks they agree on market direction but they don't. Sometimes it's VDF – the vision is fuzzy so every decision becomes a debate. Occasionally it's AFC – they're trying to build 12 capabilities with resources for 3. Problems that seemed personal become solvable when you can see the conflicting assumptions.

Board needs answers? Show them your SPP, not PowerPoint promises. When board members see initiatives mapped against strategic priorities with clear scoring, they get it. When they see your quarterly rhythm of reviewing and adjusting, they relax. When they see strategic bets clearly connected to capability builds with milestone tracking, they shift from questioning to supporting.

Traditional strategy ties you to specific contexts. MOVE gives you capability for any context. It's yours now. Nobody can take it away. Owning tools is one thing. Using them is another.

The Speed Imperative

This probably sounds logical. So why do so few companies actually work this way? Because speed changes the game.

In fast markets, perfect strategy delivered slowly loses to good strategy delivered quickly. Every time.

The gap between companies using these tools and those using traditional planning widens daily. While planners schedule quarterly reviews, AI-enhanced competitors adjust strategy continuously. While consultants build analyses, entrepreneurs test and pivot.

But here's what most people miss: speed isn't recklessness. It's discipline.

Think about what this means. With AI as your thinking partner, you can pressure-test assumptions in minutes that used to take weeks. You can spot patterns across industries you've never worked in. You can generate strategic options while your competitors are still scheduling meetings.

The pattern is consistent: You see changes before they're obvious – because you're looking systematically, not sporadically. You decide while others debate – because your tools create clarity, not confusion. You execute while others plan – because you've aligned on what matters. You learn while others defend – because you treat strategies as hypotheses, not doctrines.

Speed without structure creates chaos. Structure without speed creates irrelevance. You need both.

Real Results, Not Reports

"Does This Actually Work?" Here Are Some Numbers

These aren't theories. They're battle-tested tools that deliver measurable EBITDA impact:

Strategic Assumptions saved a tech company from a $2B acquisition when hidden assumptions revealed the target's market was about to shift. What would have taken weeks of traditional analysis happened in 72 hours – with AI surfacing precedent patterns from failed acquisitions in adjacent industries.[5]

The full MOVE system helped a mid-market company grow from $400M to $2B in five years. Not through one brilliant strategy, but through consistent application of MOVE tools every quarter. Their EBITDA margin expanded 800 basis points. Real money from better decisions.[6]

Product-Market Matrix revealed $150M in trapped value at a consumer goods company. They were investing in dying cells while starving for growth opportunities. One tool, one session, clear path to value.[7]

But let's be clear: the tools don't make strategy. You do. The tools just make you better at it. Faster at seeing opportunities. Clearer about choices. More focused in execution. They're amplifiers of strategic thinking, not substitutes for it.

Your Next Move

We've covered systems, tools, behaviors, results. None of it matters unless you do something different tomorrow.

You face a choice. Not someday. Now.

Take one thing from this book. One tool that resonated. One insight that challenged you. One question that made you uncomfortable.

Apply it this week.

Not next quarter when things calm down – things never calm down. Not after you've studied all the options – you'll never have all the options. Not when conditions are perfect – conditions are never perfect.

This week.

Pick the tool that matches your biggest current challenge:

- Running SA to see your market differently
- Using PMM to find your next growth cell
- Launching one focused initiative instead of ten scattered projects
- Making your team's thinking visible instead of guessing what they believe

The specific tool doesn't matter. The movement does.

The Compound Effect

Here's what happens to those who start:

Week 1: First tool creates clarity where there was confusion. Your team says, "Why haven't we always worked this way?"

Month 1: Team starts speaking the same strategic language. Meetings become productive. Politics decrease. Progress accelerates.

Quarter 1: Visible progress on what actually matters. Board sees the difference. Team feels the momentum. Competitors notice you're moving differently.

Year 1: Competitive advantage shows in results. Not because you had better strategies, but because you executed better moves. The compound effect of clarity, focus, and speed.

Your career: Strategic thinking becomes your edge everywhere. Every company, every role, every challenge. You become known as the executive who doesn't just plan – you deliver.

But it only compounds if you start. If you move. Starting is always the hardest part.

The Final Question

Twenty-five years of watching success and failure taught me something about strategic leadership:

Strategy represents the fastest way to impact the greatest number of people. A 1,000-person workforce represents 4,000 lives when you count families. The strategy you build and execute touches all of them. That's both the privilege and responsibility of leadership.

Over 25 years, working with thousands of executives taught me this: The ones who created extraordinary value – who delivered the $2B in incremental EBITDA I mentioned – weren't necessarily the smartest or best resourced. They were simply the ones willing to move. To try. To learn. To adjust. To move again.

You're now equipped to be one of them. The question isn't whether you can – you can. The question is whether you will.

While you're deciding, someone else is moving. And in a fast world, the movers win.

Your Strategic Commitment

End of the book. Beginning of your choice.

Whatever you've been thinking about, analyzing, debating – stop preparing and start moving.

Make your thinking visible. Choose your bets. Commit your resources. Execute in rhythm.

Do it imperfectly – imperfect action beats perfect analysis. Do it incrementally – small moves compound into big advantages. But do it now – time is the only resource you can't recover.

You now own a system for making strategic decisions that create value. Not just knowledge – capability. Not just ideas – tools. Not just theory – a practical system that works wherever you work.

The tools are proven. The need is clear. The choice is yours.

Strategy is the sum of your moves. Make them count.

Move what matters.

Start today.

Notes

1 Based on the author's 25+ years of consulting and client experience.
2 Based on the author's 25+ years of consulting and client experience.
3 Based on the author's 25+ years of consulting and client experience.
4 Based on the author's 25+ years of consulting and client experience.
5 Based on the author's 25+ years of consulting and client experience.
6 Based on the author's 25+ years of consulting and client experience.
7 Based on the author's 25+ years of consulting and client experience.

Glossary of MOVE Terms

MOVE Framework Tools

AFC Advantage + Future Capabilities. MOVE Tool #4 that identifies current competitive advantages and maps future capabilities needed to win in validated market opportunities.

MRC Market Reality Check. MOVE Tool #3B that validates PMM choices against external market data, competitive dynamics, and customer reality.

MOVE The complete strategic decision-making system consisting of eight integrated tools that transform strategy from planning into action. The acronym represents the four essential behaviors that separate companies that win from those that don't:

- **M**ake thinking visible
- **O**rient around advantage
- **V**isibly choose bets
- **E**xecute in rhythm

MOVE +1 The approach for enhancing strategy post-acquisition by combining strategic intelligence from both companies using MOVE tools.

NQA Next Quarter Actions. Part of the Two-Page QBR (Tool #7B) that defines specific corrective actions with owners, timing, and success probability.

PMM Product-Market Matrix. MOVE Tool #3A that maps all product-market combinations, scores them using consistent criteria, and guides resource allocation.

RCA Root Cause Analysis. Part of the Two-Page QBR (Tool #7A) that identifies why performance gaps occurred using Revenue-Cost=Profit framework.

SA Strategic Assumptions. MOVE Tool #1 that surfaces external trends, constants, and their implications for strategic choices.

SN Strategic Numbers. MOVE Tool #5 that tracks six to eight leading indicators predicting strategic success.

SPP Strategic Project Portfolio. MOVE Tool #6 that consolidates initiatives into two to three signature programs aligned with strategic priorities.

VDF Vision + Driving Force. MOVE Tool #2 that defines strategic direction through ten integrated parameters, including mission, products, markets, and competitive advantage.

Color Coding System

BLUE cells Low strategic priority cells in the PMM. Minimize resources or consider exit.

EXIT cells Product-market combinations targeted for divestment or elimination.

GREEN cells Highest strategic priority cells in the PMM. Concentrate resources and management attention here.

RED cells In some contexts, core/mature cells managed for cash generation (note: book primarily uses GREEN/YELLOW/BLUE system).

YELLOW cells Medium strategic priority cells in the PMM. Maintain position and invest selectively.

Key Concepts

Breadcrumbs Clues or insights that emerge during strategic discussions, pointing toward larger patterns or opportunities.

Driving Force The single dominant capability that propels an organization toward its vision.

Exception-based reporting Dashboard approach focusing only on RED or YELLOW indicators requiring attention, not GREEN successes.

In the room Being present where strategic decisions are made; having access to real strategic discussions.

Leading indicators Metrics that predict future performance, contrasted with lagging indicators that report past results.

Root cause The fundamental reason for performance gaps, not surface symptoms.

Signature initiatives The two to three major strategic programs that consolidate multiple projects and command disproportionate resources.

T-shirt test If employees wouldn't proudly wear your initiative name on a t-shirt, it's not clear or compelling enough.

Two-Page QBR Quarterly Business Review format using only two pages: RCA and NQAs.

Visible thinking Making strategic logic, assumptions, and choices explicit on walls or boards where everyone can see and challenge them.

Common Acronyms Used

B2B Business to Business

CEO/CFO/COO/CMO Chief Executive/Financial/Operating/Marketing Officer

EBITDA Earnings Before Interest, Taxes, Depreciation, and Amortization

GenAI Generative Artificial Intelligence

KPI Key Performance Indicator

M&A Mergers and Acquisitions

P&L Profit and Loss statement

QBR Quarterly Business Review

R&D Research and Development

ROIC Return on Invested Capital

ROI Return on Investment

Index

For Product Safety Concerns and Information please contact our EU representative GPSR@taylorandfrancis.com Taylor & Francis Verlag GmbH, Kaufingerstraße 24, 80331 München, Germany